11-20-73

# CHILTON'S Repair and Tune-Up Guide

# Volkswagen 2

ILLUSTRATED

Prepared by the

**Automotive Editorial Department**

Chilton Book Company

Chilton Way
Radnor, Pa. 19089
215—687-8200

editor-in-chief **JOHN D. KELLY;** managing editor **JOHN H. WEISE, S.A.E.;** assistant managing editor **PETER J. MEYER;** senior editor **STEPHEN J. DAVIS;** editor **IVER T. ROSENLUND, JR.;** technical editors **David P. Galluccio, William J. Jones, John M. McGuigan, Ronald L. Sessions, N Banks Spence Jr**

**CHILTON BOOK COMPANY**                    RADNOR, PENNSYLVANIA

Library of Congress Cataloging in Publication Data

Chilton Book Company. Automotive Editorial Dept.
  Chilton's repair and tune-up guide: Volkswagen 2.

  Continues Chilton's repair and tune-up guide for
Volkswagen, prepared by the Automotive Book Dept.
of the Chilton Book Company, 1971.
  1. Volkswagen automobile.   I. Chilton Book
Company.  Automotive Book Dept.  Chilton's repair
and tune-up guide for the Volkswagen.   II. Title.
TL215.V6C5   1974          629.28'7'22          74-3160
ISBN   0-8019-5865-2
ISBN   0-8019-5911-X (pbk.)

## ACKNOWLEDGMENTS

Chilton Book Company expresses gratitude to Volkswagen of America, Inc. for technical information and illustrations.

Although information in this guide is based on industry sources and is as complete as possible at the time of publication, the possibility exists that the manufacturer made changes which could not be included here. While striving for total accuracy, Chilton Book Company cannot assume responsibility for any errors, changes, or omissions that may occur in the compilation of this data.

# Contents

## 1816762

# Chapter One

# General Information and Maintenance

## Introduction

In 1932, Ferdinand Porsche produced prototypes for the NSU company of Germany which eventually led to the design of the Volkswagen. The prototypes had a rear mounted, air-cooled engine, torsion bar suspension, and the spare tire mounted at an angle in the front luggage compartment. In 1936, Porsche produced three Volkswagen prototypes, one of which was a 995 cc, horizontally opposed, four cylinder automobile. Passenger car development was sidetracked during World War II, when all attention was on military vehicles. In 1945, Volkswagen production began and 1,785 Beetles were built. The Volkswagen convertible was introduced in 1949, the same year that only two Volkswagens were sold in the United States. 1950 marked the beginning of the sunroof models and the transporter series. The Karmann Ghia was introduced in 1956, and still remains in the same basic styling format. The 1500 Squareback was introduced in the United States in 1966 to start the Type 3 series. The Type 4 was imported to the U.S.A. beginning with the 1971 model.

Type numbers are the way Volkswagen designates its various groups of models. The Type 1 group contains the Beetle, Super Beetle, and the Karmann Ghia. Type 2 vehicles are the Delivery Van, the Micro Bus, and the Kombi. The Type 3 designation is for the Fastback and the Squareback sedans. The Type 4 is for the 411 and 412 sedans and wagon. These type numbers will be used throughout the book when it is necessary to refer to models.

An explanation of the terms suitcase engine and upright fan engine is, perhaps, necessary. The upright fan engine refers to the engine used in the Type 1 and 2 vehicles. This engine has the engine cooling fan mounted on the top of the engine and is driven by the generator. The fan is mounted vertically in contrast to a horizontally mounted fan as found on the Corvair engine. The suitcase engine is a comparatively new engine and was designed as a more compact unit to fit in the Type 3 and 4 and some Type 2 engine compartments. On this engine, the cooling fan is mounted on the crankshaft giving the engine a rectangular shape similar to that of a suitcase.

Type 1 Convertible

Type 1 Sedan

Type 1 Karmann Ghia

Type 2 Micro Bus

Type 3 Squareback Sedan

Type 3 Fastback Sedan

Type 4 4 Door Sedan

Type 4 3 Door Sedan

## Serial Number Identification

### VEHICLE

The first two numbers are the first two digits of the car's model number and the third digit stands for the car's model year. For example a 0 as the third digit means that the car was produced during the 1970 model year, a 1 would signify 1971, and so forth.

The chassis number is on the frame tunnel under the back seat in the Type 1, 3, and 4. In the Type 2, the chassis number is on the right engine cover plate in the engine compartment. All models also have an identification plate bearing the chassis number on the top of the instrument panel at the driver's side. This plate is easily visible through the windshield and aids in rapid identification.

Another identification plate bearing the vehicle's serial number and paint, body, and assembly codes, is found in the luggage compartment of each vehicle.

Chassis number location on dash board

Chassis number location under rear seat

Identification plate in luggage compartment

## Vehicle Identification Chart

| Vehicle Type | Model | Body Type |
|---|---|---|
| 1 | 111 | Standard Beetle |
| 1 | 14 | Karmann Ghia |
| 1 | 113 | Super Beetle |
| 2 | 211 | Panel Delivery Truck |
| 2 | 221 | 7 Passenger Hardtop Bus |

## Vehicle Identification Chart

| Vehicle Type | Model | Body Type |
|---|---|---|
| 2 | 222 | 7 Passenger Bus |
| 2 | 223 | 9 Passenger Bus |
| 2 | 225 | 7 Passenger Sunroof Bus |
| 2 | 232 | 8 Passenger Kombi |
| 2 | 233 | 5 Passenger Kombi |
| 2 | 236 | 5 Passenger Kombi |
| 2 | 239 | Camper bus |
| 3 | 310 | Basic Compact |
| 3 | 311 | Sedan |
| 3 | 313 | Sedan Sunroof |
| 3 | 361 | Squareback |
| 3 | 363 | Squareback Sunroof |
| 4 | 411 | 2 Door Sedan |
| 4 | 421 | 4 Door Sedan |
| 4 | 461 | 3 Door Wagon |
| 4 | 412 | Sedan |

### ENGINE

On Type 1 and 2 vehicles, which have the upright engine cooling fan housing, the engine number is on the crankcase flange for the generator support.

## Engine Identification Chart

| Engine Code Letter | Type Vehicle | First Production Year | Last Production Year [1] | Engine Type | Common Designation |
|---|---|---|---|---|---|
| B | 1, 2 | 1967 | 1970 | Upright Fan | 1600 |
| AD | 1, 2 | 1970 | In Production | Upright Fan | 1600 |
| AE | 1, 2 | 1971 | 1972 | Upright Fan | 1600 |
| AH | 1 | 1972 | In Production | Upright Fan | 1600 |
| CB | 2 | 1971 | In Production | Suitcase | 1700 |
| CD | 2 | 1972 | In Production | Suitcase | 1700 |
| U | 3 | 1968 | In Production | Suitcase | 1600 |
| X | 3 | 1972 | In Production | Suitcase | 1600 |
| W | 4 | 1971 | 1972 | Suitcase | 1700 |
| EA | 4 | 1972 | In Production | Suitcase | 1700 |
| EB | 4 | 1973 | In Production | Suitcase | 1700 |
|  | Calif. Only |  |  |  |  |

[1] In production means as of publication of this book.

Engine number location on the upright fan engine

Engine number location on the "suitcase" engine

The number can readily be seen by looking through the center of the fan belt. On Type 3 and 4 suitcase engines, the number is along the crankcase joint between the oil cooler and the air cleaner. The engine can be identified by the letter or pair of letters preceding the serial number. Engine specifications are listed according to the letters and model year.

## Transmission Identification Chart

| Code Letter | Type Transmission | Vehicle Type | Engine |
|---|---|---|---|
| AH | Manual | 1 | 1600 |
| AT | Manual | 1 | 1600 |
| BA | Automatic Stick Shift | 1 | 1600 |
| CA | Manual | 2 | 1600 |
| CE | Manual | 2 | 1700 |
| NA | Automatic | 2 | 1700 |
| DC | Manual | 3 | 1600 |
| EB | Automatic | 3 | 1600 |
| FC | Manual | 4 | 1700 |
| EG | Automatic | 4 | 1700 |
| EH | Automatic | 4 | 1700 |

## TRANSMISSION

Transmission identification marks are stamped into the bellhousing or on the final drive housing.

## Routine Maintenance

### AIR CLEANER

#### Oil Bath Type

##### TYPE 1 AND 2

This type cleaner should be cleaned after there is $5/16$ in. of oil above the layer of sludge in the bottom of the air cleaner.

1. To clean the air cleaner, remove the hoses attached to the air cleaner.

CAUTION: *Be careful to note the places where the hoses are attached. Interchanging the hoses will affect the operation of the engine.*

2. Next, loosen the air cleaner support bracket screw and the air cleaner clamp screw.

3. Disconnect the warm air flap cable. Lift the air cleaner off the engine. Keep the carburetor hole down to prevent spilling the oil out of the air cleaner.

4. Loosen the spring clips which secure the top of the air cleaner to the bottom and then separate the halves.

5. Put the upper half of the air cleaner down with the filter element facing downward. Thoroughly clean the bottom half.

6. Fill the air cleaner with 0.9 pints of oil or, if present, to the oil level mark stamped into the side of the air cleaner.

7. Reassemble the air cleaner and install it on the engine.

##### TYPE 3

1. To remove the air cleaner, it is first necessary to remove the connecting rod for the right hand carburetor which runs between the bell crank and the carburetor.

2. Remove the crankcase ventilation hose. Unscrew the three wing nuts and leave the two outer nuts attached to their carburetors.

NOTE: *Leave the rubber sealing rings on the carburetors.*

3. Remove the air cleaner assembly from the engine, but do not separate the halves yet.

Carbureted Type 3 air cleaner and related components

1. Connecting rod to right hand carburetor
2. Crankcase ventilation hose
3. Air cleaner air intake hose

4. Outer wing nuts
4. (Center) Middle wing nuts

4. Disassemble the air cleaner halves, clean the lower half, and fill it with oil to the level mark.

5. Reinstall the air cleaner on the engine.

CAUTION: *Tighten the two outer wing nuts before tightening the middle wing nut. Make sure the top half is properly aligned with the lower half. There are alignment arrows for this purpose.*

6. After the two outer wing nuts are tightened, it may be necessary to adjust the height to the middle wing nut stud. It should just touch the air cleaner. If it is higher or lower when the middle wing nut is tightened, the air cleaner will be bowed and will not seal the carburetor properly.

### Fuel Injected Type 3, Type 4

1. Disconnect the activated charcoal filter hose, the rubber elbow, and the crankcase ventilation hose. Remove the wing nut in the center of the air cleaner and lift the air cleaner assembly off of the engine.

2. Release the spring clips which keep the air cleaner halves together and take the cleaner apart.

3. Clean the lower half and refill it with oil to the level mark. When reassembling

the air cleaner, align the marks for the upper and lower halves.

4. Reinstall the air cleaner on the engine. Make sure it is properly seated.

### Paper Element Type

#### Type 1

1. Disconnect the hoses from the air cleaner.

CAUTION: *Do not interchange the position of the hoses.*

2. Loosen the air cleaner clamp and remove the air cleaner from the engine. Release spring clamps which keep the halves of the cleaner together and separate the halves.

3. Clean the inside of the air cleaner housing.

4. The paper element should be replaced every 18,000 miles under normal service. It should be replaced more often under severe operating conditions. A paper element may be cleaned by blowing through the element from the inside with compressed air. Never use a liquid solvent to clean a paper element.

5. Install the air cleaner element in the air cleaner housing and install the spring

clips, making sure the halves are properly aligned. Install the cleaner on the engine.

TYPE 2, 1700 ENGINE

1. Disconnect the hoses from the air cleaner.

CAUTION: *Do not interchange the position of the hoses.*

2. Release the two clamps which secure the air cleaner to the carburetors. Release the clips which secure the air ducts to each carburetor.

3. Remove the air ducts separately. Remove the air cleaner housing.

4. Release the four spring clips which secure the cleaner halves together and then separate the halves.

5. Clean the inside of the housing. The paper element should be replaced every 18,000 miles under normal service. It should be replaced more often under severe operating conditions. A paper element may be cleaned by blowing through the element from the inside with compressed air. Never use a liquid solvent.

6. Assemble the air cleaner halves, making sure that they are properly aligned. Install the air cleaner by reversing the above. Make sure that the rubber sleeves on the air ducts and the rubber seals on the carburetors are seated properly.

## CRANKCASE VENTILATION

The crankcase is vented by a hose running from the crankcase to the bottom of the air cleaner. In some cases the hose is attached to the air inlet for the air cleaner.

The air cleaner end of the crankcase ventilation hose has a weighted flap mounted above it. This flap closes at idle and low engine speeds to insure adequate vacuum to draw fumes from the crankcase into the air cleaner. 1971 models are equipped with a thermostat to control the flap; 1972–73 models have a temperature sensing valve.

This system needs no maintenance other than keeping the hose clear and making sure the flap moves freely.

## FUEL TANK EVAPORATION SYSTEM

This system consists of an expansion chamber, an activated charcoal filter, and a hose which connects the parts into a closed system.

When fuel in the gas tank expands due to heat, the fuel travels to the expansion chamber. Any fumes generated either in the gas tank or the expansion chamber are trapped in the activated charcoal filter found in a line connecting the tank and chamber. The fumes are purged from the filter when the engine is started. Air from the engine cooling fan is forced through the filter. From the filter, this air/fuel vapor mixture is routed to the inside of the air cleaner where it is sent to the engine to be burned.

Because the charcoal filter is constantly purged by operating the engine and no other components of this system require attention, there is no routine maintenance for this system.

## FLUID LEVEL CHECKS

### Engine Oil

To check the engine oil level, park the car on level ground and wait 5 minutes to allow all the oil in the engine to drain into the crankcase.

Check the oil level by withdrawing the dipstick and wiping it clean. Insert the dipstick into its hole and note the position of the oil level on the bottom of the stick. The level should be between the two marks on the bottom of the stick. The distance between the two marks represents one quart of oil.

On upright fan engines, the dipstick is located directly beneath the generator; oil is added at the cap on the passenger side of the generator. On Type 2 suitcase engines, the dipstick is located next to the alternator. On Type 3 vehicles, it is neces-

Oil filter and dipstick on suitcase engine

Station wagon dipstick location

sary to raise the back door and locate the dipstick in the lower door jamb. On Type 4 two door and four models, the dipstick is located at the center of the engine next to the oil filler cap; on wagon models, it is under the rear door jamb.

## Transmission

### MANUAL TRANSMISSION

The oil level is checked by removing the 17 mm socket head plug located on the driver's side of the transaxle. The oil level should be even with the hole.

CAUTION: *Do not fill the transaxle too fast because it may overflow from the filler hole and give the impression that the unit has been filled when it has not.*

### AUTOMATIC AND AUTOMATIC STICK SHIFT TRANSMISSION

The Automatic Stick Shift transmission is checked by means of a dipstick. The oil level should be between the two marks at the bottom of the stick. The engine should be warm when the transmission oil level is checked.

NOTE: *The engine must be turned off when checking the transmission oil level.*

Automatic transmissions are checked in the same manner as Automatic Stick Shift transmissions, except that the engine should be running at an idle.

### Brake Fluid Reservoir

The brake fluid reservoir is located under the driver's seat in Type 2 vehicles and in the luggage compartment on all other vehicles. The fluid level in all vehicles should be at the top of the reservoir. Fill the reservoir only with new, clean heavy-duty brake fluid. If the vehicle is equipped with disc brakes, make sure the fluid is marked for use with disc brakes.

### Steering Gear

Types 1 and 3, except the Super Beetle, are filled with 5.4 ozs of gear oil which is added to a plug at the top of the gear box. The Super Beetle holds 5.9 ozs of steering gear oil. The Type 2 holds 9.4 ozs of gear

## Capacities Chart

| Year | Type and Model | Engine Displacement (cc) | Engine Crankcase (qts) With Filter | Engine Crankcase (qts) Without Filter | Transaxle (pts) Manual | Transaxle (pts) Automatic Conv. | Transaxle (pts) Automatic Final Drive | Gasoline Tank (gals) |
|---|---|---|---|---|---|---|---|---|
| 1970–73 | 1, 111, 114 | 1600 | —— | 2.5 | 6.3 | 7.6 | 6.3① | 10.6 |
| 1970–73 | 1, 113 | 1600 | —— | 2.5 | 6.3 | 7.6 | 6.3① | 11.1 |
| 1970–73 | 2, All | 1600 | —— | 2.5 | 7.4 | 12.6② | 3.0 | 15.8 |
| 1970–73 | 2, All | 1700 | 4.4 | 3.7 | 7.4 | 12.6② | 3.0 | 15.8 |
| 1970–73 | 3, All | 1600 | —— | 2.5 | 6.3 | 12.6② | 2.1 | 10.6 |
| 1970–73 | 4, All | 1700 | 4.4 | 3.7 | 5.3 | 12.6② | 2.1 | 13.2 |

Conv—Torque Converter      ①—5.3 when changed      ②—6.3 when changed oil in the steering gear box. The Type 4 holds 9 ozs.

Unless the steering gear box has been rebuilt or is leaking severely, there is no reason to add or change gear box oil.

### Battery

The battery is located in the engine compartment on all Type 2 vehicles. On all Type 1 and 3 vehicles, the battery is located under the back seat. On Type 4 vehicles, it is located under the driver's seat.

Make it a habit to check the electrolyte level frequently. Use only distilled water to top up the battery. Tap water contains minerals that will shorten battery life. Keep the top of the battery clean and dry to prevent current leakage which can completely discharge the battery. Wire brush the battery posts and cable clamps occasionally and coat the posts (with the clamps installed) with grease.

To properly clean dirty battery posts, the clamp must be removed from the posts and the contacting surfaces cleaned to shiny metal.

### TIRES AND WHEELS

#### Tire Pressure

Tire pressures vary greatly from vehicle to vehicle. Each vehicle has a sticker bearing the proper tire inflation pressures on the back of the glove compartment lid. Follow these pressure recommendations.

Tire inflation should be checked every three or four weeks.

Improper tire pressures can cause excessive tire wear. An over-inflated tire will wear out the center of the tire and an under-inflated tire will wear out both edges.

#### TIRE BALANCING

A tire should be balanced before it is put on the car. However, during use the tire can become unbalanced and it is a good idea to have the tires balanced from time to time.

If the tire has been repaired or loses a weight, the tire should be rebalanced. Cupping of the tire tread is caused by incorrect balance.

#### TIRE ROTATION

The tires should be rotated, as illustrated, several times a year. Tire rotation promotes even tire wear and will help extend tire life.

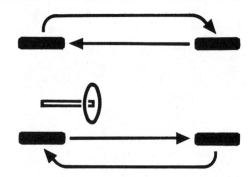
Tire rotation pattern

#### TREAD-WEAR INDICATORS

Standard equipment tires have built-in tire tread-wear indicators. These indicators are molded into the bottom of the tire tread grooves and will appear as $\frac{1}{2}$ in. bands when the depth of the tire tread reaches $\frac{1}{16}$ in. When two or more bands appear, or if a band extends over three or more tread grooves, it is time to replace the tire.

#### FUEL FILTER

On carbureted models, the fuel filter is located in the fuel pump. There are two types of fuel pumps. One type has a single screw holding a cover on the top of the pump. To remove the filter screen, undo the screw and carefully lift the cover off the pump. Remove the cover gasket and filter screen taking careful note of the position of the screen. Blow the screen out with air and replace the screen and cover using a new gasket if necessary.

Fuel injection in-line fuel filter (arrow towards pump)

Fuel injection in-line fuel filter mounted to the fuel pump by cotter pin and bracket

## Oil Selection Chart

| SAE<br>Viscosity | Outside Temperature |
|---|---|
| SAE 40 | In warm seasons and all hot climates. Do not use when the average seasonal temperature is below 45° |
| SAE 30 | Same as above. Temperature range is from 80° to 30° |
| SAE 20 | In winter seasons. Temperature range is from 40° to 0° |
| SAE 10 | In areas where the average temperature is below 0°; no long distance high speed driving if temperature is above 10° |

The second type of fuel pump has four screws securing the top cover to the pump. This type of pump has a large plug with a hexagonal head. Remove this plug to gain access to the cylindrical filter screen located beneath the plug. Blow the screen out with air and replace it in its bore with the open end facing into the pump. Do not overtighten the plug.

Fuel injected engines have an electric fuel pump located near the front axle. This type of engine has an in-line fuel filter located near the fuel pump in the suction line for the fuel pump. The suction line is the line running from the gas tank to the "S" connection at the fuel pump. To change the fuel filter, disconnect the gas lines from either end of the filter and insert a new filter. This type of filter cannot be cleaned.

## Lubrication

### OIL AND FUEL RECOMMENDATIONS

Only oils which are high detergent and are graded MS or SE should be used in the engine. Oils should be selected for the SAE viscosity which will perform satisfactorily in the temperatures expected before the next oil change.

Factory recommendations for fuel are regular gasoline with an octane rating of 91 RON or higher for Type 1, 2, 3, and 1973 Type 4. The 1971–72 Type 4 requires premium gasoline with an octane rating of 98 RON or better.

If the vehicle is used for towing, it may be necessary to buy a higher grade of gasoline. The extra load caused by the trailer may be sufficient to cause elevated engine operating temperatures which promote engine knock or ping. This condition, when allowed to continue over a period of time, will cause extreme damage to the engine. Furthermore, ping or knock has several causes beside low octane. An engine in need of a tune-up will ping. If there is an excessive carbon build-up and lead deposits in the combustion chamber, ping will also result.

### OIL CHANGES

#### Engine

The engine oil should be changed only after the engine has been warmed up to operating temperatures. In this way, the oil holds in suspension many of the contaminants that would otherwise remain in the engine. As the oil drains, it carries dirt and sludge from the engine. After the initial oil change at 600 miles, the oil should be changed regularly at a period not to exceed 3,000 miles or three months. If the car is being operated mainly for short slow speed trips, it may be advisable to change the oil at 2,000 mile intervals.

When changing the oil in Type 1, 2/1600, and 3 vehicles, first unscrew the drain plug in the crankcase and allow dirty oil to drain. The oil strainer should also be cleaned. This wire mesh strainer is held in

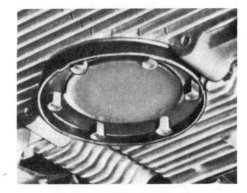

Type 1 and 2/1600 oil screen

place by six cap nuts, and should be cleaned thoroughly with a solvent. The strainer plate should also be cleaned. This lowest part of the crankcase collects a great deal of sludge in the course of 3,000 miles. Replace the assembly, using new gaskets. Refill the crankcase with 2.5 quarts of oil.

Type 2/1700, 3, and 4 oil screen and oil drain plug

Types 2/1700, and 4 require a different oil changing procedure. The crankcase drain plug is to one side of the oil strainer. The oil should be drained before removing the strainer. The strainer is located in the center of the crankcase and is held in position by a plug. Remove the plug and remove the strainer assembly from the crankcase. Clean the strainer in solvent and reinstall it in the crankcase with new gaskets.

The Type 2/1700 and Type 4 also have a spin-on oil filter located near the engine cooling fan. This filter is removed by unscrewing it from its fitting. When reinstalling the new filter, lubricate the filter gasket with oil. Refill the crankcase and start the engine. Run the engine until it picks up oil pressure and then stop the engine. Recheck the engine oil level.

Removing Type 2/1700 and 4 oil filter

**Transmission**

The automatic transmission fluid (ATF) should be changed every 30,000 miles, or every 18,000 miles under heavy duty operating conditions.

Drain the ATF by removing the drain plug from the pan. Remove the pan and clean the ATF strainer. Install the pan using a new gasket and tighten the pan screws in a criss-cross pattern to 7 ft lbs. Retighten the screws two or three times at five minute intervals to compensate for settling of the gasket. Refill the transmission with the proper type transmission fluid using a funnel with a 20 in. long neck. Use Type b or Dexron ATF.

The manual transmission is drained by removing the 17 mm plug in the bottom of the transmission case. It is refilled through another 17 mm plug in the side of the transmission case. The plug in the side of the case also functions as the fluid level hole.

NOTE: *When refilling the transmission, do not fill it too fast because it may overflow from the filler hole and give the impression that the unit has been filled when it has not.*

After the transmission oil is changed at 600 miles, it is generally not necessary to change the oil. However, the factory does recommend the fluid level be checked every 6,000 miles and topped up if necessary. Refill the transmission with SAE 90 hypoid gear oil.

The Automatic Stick Shift transmission uses hypoid gear oil in the rear section of the transmission and is drained and refilled using the same method as the manual transmission. The front section of the transmission uses ATF, however it does not have to be changed. The level should be checked every 6,000 miles.

NOTE: *The engine should be off when the level is checked.*

Use Type b or Dexron ATF.

### CHASSIS GREASING

There are four grease fittings. They are located at the end of each front torsion bar housing. There is a fifth fitting at the center of the front torsion bar housings for the steering linkage on Type 2 vehicles. Wipe off each fitting before greasing. Super Beetles and Type 4 require no greasing. The vehicle should be greased every 6,000 miles.

### WHEEL BEARINGS

See Chapter Nine.

## Pushing, Towing, and Jump Starting

A vehicle equipped with an automatic or Automatic Stick Shift cannot be pushed or tow started. To push start a vehicle with a manual transmission, switch on the ignition, select the highest forward gear, and keep the clutch pedal depressed until suitable speed has been provided by pushing the vehicle. When the vehicle is going about 15 mph, slowly release the clutch to start the engine.

There are two towing eyes on all models except Type 4. The front eye is located on the lower right front and the rear eye is located under the right rear bumper bracket. Tow the vehicle with the transmission in Neutral and the brakes off. Tow the Type 4 by its bumper bracket.

When jump starting the car, be sure that the booster cables are properly connected. Connect the positive pole of the jumper battery to the positive pole of the car battery. Be careful to avoid causing sparks.

## Jacking and Hoisting

Whenever the car is jacked up, always place a jackstand under the axle.

The vehicle may be hoisted under the axles or the jacking points.

Type 1 and 3 front end grease fittings

# Chapter Two

# Tune-Up and Troubleshooting

## Tune-Up Procedures

The following procedures are specific tune-up procedures applicable to Volkswagens. There is a general tune-up section at the end of this chapter.

### SPARK PLUGS

Before attempting any work on the cylinder head, it is very important to note that the cylinder head is aluminum. This means that it is extremely easy to damage threads in the cylinder head. Care must be taken not to cross-thread the spark plugs or any bolts or studs. Never overtighten the spark plugs, bolts, or studs.

    CAUTION: *To prevent seizure, always lubricate the spark plug threads with liquid silicon or Never-Seez®.*

To avoid cross-threading the spark plugs, always start the plugs in their threads with your fingers. Never force the plugs into the cylinder head. Do not use a wrench until you are certain that the plug is correctly threaded.

VW spark plugs should be cleaned and regapped every 6,000 miles and replaced every 12,000 miles.

### Removing and Installing Spark Plugs

To install the spark plugs, remove the spark plug wire from the plug. Grasp the plug connector and, while removing, do not pull on the wire. Using a $1^{13}/_{16}$ in. spark plug socket, remove the old spark plugs. Examine the threads of the old plugs; if one or more of the plugs have aluminum clogged threads, it will be necessary to re-thread the spark plug hole. See the following section for the necessary information.

Obtain the proper heat range and type of new plug. Set the gap by bending the side electrode only. Do not bend the center electrode to adjust the gap. The proper gap is listed in the "Tune-Up Specifications" chart.

Start each new plug in its hole using your fingers. Tighten the plug several turns by hand to assure that the plug is not cross-threaded. Using a wrench, tighten the plug just enough to compress the gasket. Do not overtighten the plug.

### Rethreading Spark Plug Hole

It is possible to repair light damage to spark plug hole threads by using a spark plug hole tap of the proper diameter and thread. Plenty of grease should be used on the tap to catch any metal chips. Exercise

## Tune-Up Specifications

| Year | Code | Type | Common Designation | Spark Plugs Type | Gap (in.) | Distributor Point Dwell (deg) | Point Gap (in.) | Ignition Timing (deg) MT | AT | Fuel Pump Pressure (psi) | Compression Pressure (psi) | Idle Speed (rpm) MT | AT | Valve Clearance (in.) Cold In | Ex |
|---|---|---|---|---|---|---|---|---|---|---|---|---|---|---|---|
| 1970 | B | 1, 2 | 1600 | Bosch W 145 T1 | 0.026 | 47°–53° | 0.016 | TDC | TDC | — | 114–142 | 800–900 | 800–900 | 0.006 | 0.006 |
| 1970–71 | AD | 1, 2 | 1600 | Bosch W 145 T1 | 0.028 | 44°–50° | 0.016 | 5° ATDC | 5° ATDC | — | 114–142 | 800–900 | 800–900 | 0.006 | 0.006 |
| 1971–72 | AE | 1, 2 | 1600 | Champion L 88 A | 0.028 | 44°–50° | 0.016 | 5° ATDC① | 5° ATDC① | 3–5 | 114–142 | 800–900 | 800–900 | 0.006 | 0.006 |
| 1973 | AK | 1 | 1600 | Champion L 88 A | 0.028 | 44°–50° | 0.016 | 5° ATDC① | 5° ATDC① | 3–5 | 114–142 | 800–900 | 800–900 | 0.006 | 0.006 |
| 1971–73 | AH | 1 | 1600 | Champion L 88 A | 0.028 | 44°–50° | 0.016 | 5° ATDC① | 5° ATDC① | 3–5 | 107–135 | 800–900 | 800–900 | 0.006 | 0.006 |
| 1971–73 | CB | 2 | 1700 | Bosch W 175 T2 | 0.028 | 44°–50° | 0.016 | 5° ATDC② | 5° ATDC② | 5 | 100–135 | 800–900 | 800–900 | 0.006 | 0.008 |
| 1972–73 | CD | 2 | 1700 | Bosch W 175 T2 | 0.028 | 44°–50° | 0.016 | ⑤ | 5° ATDC② | 5 | 100–135 | ⑤ | 900–1000 | 0.006 | 0.008 |
| 1970–73 | U | 3 | 1600 | Champion L 88 A | 0.028 | 44°–50° | 0.016 | 5° BTDC③ | 5° BTDC③ | — | 114–142 | 800–900 | 800–900 | 0.006 | 0.006 |
| 1972–73 | X | 3 | 1600 | Champion L 88 A | 0.028 | 44°–50° | 0.016 | 5° BTDC③ | 5° BTDC③ | — | 107–135 | 800–900 | 800–900 | 0.006 | 0.006 |
| 1971–72 | W | 4 | 1700 | Bosch W 175 T2 | 0.028 | 44°–50° | 0.016 | 27° BTDC④ | 27° BTDC④ | — | 128–156 | 800–900 | 800–900 | 0.006 | 0.008 |
| 1972–73 | EA | 4 | 1700 | Bosch W 175 T2 | 0.028 | 44°–50° | 0.016 | 27° BTDC④ | 27° BTDC④ | — | 128–156 | 800–900 | 800–900 | 0.006 | 0.008 |
| 1973 | EB Calif. Only | 4 | 1700 | Bosch W 175 T2 | 0.028 | 44°–50° | 0.016 | 27° BTDC④ | 27° BTDC④ | — | 128–156 | 800–900 | 800–900 | 0.006 | 0.008 |

① At idle, vacuum hoses on
② 1973 10 ATDC
③ At idle, throttle valve closed, vacuum hoses off. 1972–73 5° BTDC
④ 3500 rpm, vacuum hoses off
⑤ This engine used with automatic transmission only

MT—Manual Transmission
AT—Automatic Transmission
ATDC—After top dead center
BTDC—Before top dead center

caution when using the tap as it is possible to cut a second set of threads instead of straightening the old ones.

If the old threads are beyond repair, then the hole must be drilled and tapped to accept a steel bushing or Heli-Coil®. It is necessary to remove the cylinder head to rethread the spark plug holes. Bushing kits, Heli-Coil® kits, and spark plug hole taps are available at most auto parts stores. Heli-Coil® information is contained in the "Engine Rebuilding" section of Chapter Three.

## BREAKER POINTS AND CONDENSER

### Removal and Installation

1. Release the spring clips which secure the distributor cap and lift the cap from the distributor. Pull the rotor from the distributor shaft.

2. Disconnect the points wire from the condenser connection at the side of the distributor.

3. Remove the locking screw from the stationary breaker point.

4. To remove the condenser which is located on the outside of the distributor, remove the screw which secures the condenser bracket and condenser connection to the distributor.

5. Disconnect the condenser wire from the coil.

6. With a clean rag, wipe the excess oil from the breaker plate.
NOTE: *Make sure that the new point contacts are clean and oil free.*

7. Installation of the point set and condenser is the reverse of the above; however, it will be necessary to adjust the point gap, also known as the dwell, and check the timing. Lubricate the point cam with a small amount of lithum or white grease. Set the dwell, or gap, before the ignition timing.

### Adjusting Point Gap

1. Remove the distributor cap and rotor.
2. Turn the engine by hand until the fiber rubbing block on the movable breaker point rests on a high point of the cam lobe. The point gap is the maximum distance between the points and must be set at the top of a cam lobe.
3. Using a screwdriver, loosen the locking screw of the stationary breaker point.

Fiber rubbing block on the high point of the distributor cam lobe

| | |
|---|---|
| 1. Condenser | 3. Cable |
| 2. Cable entry | 4. Insulation on breaker arm spring |

4. Move the stationary point plate so that the gap is set as specified and then tighten the screw. Make sure that the feeler gauge is clean. After tightening the screw, recheck the gap.

5. It is important to set the point gap before setting the timing.

## DWELL ANGLE

Setting the dwell angle with a dwell meter achieves the same effect as setting the point gap but offers better accuracy.
NOTE: *The dwell must be set before setting the timing. Setting the dwell will alter the timing, but when the timing is set, the dwell will not change.*

Attach the positive lead of the dwell meter to that coil terminal which has a wire leading to the distributor. The negative lead should be attached to a good ground.

Remove the distributor cap and rotor. Turn the ignition ON and turn the engine over using the starter or a starter button. Read the dwell from the meter and open or close the points to adjust the dwell.
NOTE: *Increasing the gap decreases the dwell and decreasing the gap increases the dwell.*
Dwell specifications are listed in the "Tune-Up Specifications" chart.

Reinstall the cap and rotor and start the engine. Check the dwell and reset it if necessary.

## IGNITION TIMING

Dwell or point gap must be set before the timing is set.

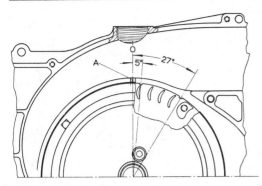

Type 4 timing marks

27° before TDC = red
5° before TDC = black
A = notch in fan housing

NOTE: *The engine must be hot before the timing is set.*

Remove the No. 1 spark plug wire from the distributor cap and attach the timing light lead. Disconnect the vacuum hose if so advised by the "Tune-Up Specifications" chart. Start the engine and run it at the specified rpm. Aim the timing light at the crankshaft pulley on upright fan engines and at the engine cooling fan on the suitcase engines. The rubber plug in the fan housing will have to be removed before the timing marks on the suitcase engine can be seen.

Read the timing and rotate the distributor accordingly.

NOTE: *Rotate the distributor in the opposite direction of normal rotor rotation to advance the timing. Retard the timing by turning the distributor in the normal direction of rotor rotation.*

It is necessary to loosen the clamp at the base of the distributor before the distributor can be rotated. It may also be necessary to put a small amount of white paint or chalk on the timing marks to make them more visible.

*VALVE LASH*

Preference should be given to the valve clearance specified on the engine fan housing sticker, if they differ from those in the "Tune-Up Specifications" chart.

NOTE: *The engine must be as cool as possible before adjusting the valves.*

Adjust the valves as follows:

1. Remove the distributor cap and turn the engine until the rotor points to the No. one spark plug wire post in the distributor

Distributor rotor pointing at No. 1 spark plug wire position

1. Terminal 1        3. No. 1 cylinder mark
2. Rotor arm

cap. To bring the piston to exactly top dead center (TDC) on the compression stroke, align the crankshaft timing marks on 0° TDC.

2. Remove the rocker arm cover of No. 1 and 2 cylinders.

3. With the proper feeler gauge, check the clearance beween the adjusting screw and the valve stem of both valves for the No. 1 cylinder. If the feeler gauge slides in snugly without being forced, the clearance is correct. It is better that the clearance is a little loose than a little tight.

Adjusting valve lash

4. If the clearance is incorrect, the lock nut must be loosened and the adjusting screw turned until the proper clearance is obtained. After tightening down the lock nut, it is then advisable to recheck the clearance. It is possible to alter the adjustment when tightening the lock nut.

5. The valves are adjusted in a 1–2–3–4 sequence. To adjust cylinders 2 through 4, the distributor rotor must be pointed at the appropriate distributor cap post. Align the crankshaft timing marks for each cylinder, remembering that the piston must be at TDC on the compression stroke when the valves are adjusted.

### CARBURETOR

See Chapter Four for additional adjustments.

### Idle Speed and Mixture

Before adjustment is begun, the engine should be at normal operating temperature and the idle adjusting screw must not be resting on the fast idle cam of the automatic choke.

#### SINGLE CARBURETOR ENGINES

1. With the engine warm and running, turn the idle speed adjusting screw in or out until the proper idling speed is obtained.

2. With the engine running at the proper idle speed, turn the idle mixture control screw slowly clockwise until the engine speed begins to drop, then slowly turn it

Carburetor adjusting screws

1. Idle speed    2. Mixture

in the counterclockwise direction until the engine is running smoothly again. Continue turning the mixture control screw another ¼ to ½ turn counterclockwise to complete the adjustment.

Dual carburetor throttle linkage

1. Accelerator cable            3. Connecting rod—left
2. Connecting rod—right    4. Pull rods for carburetor

3. It may be necessary to readjust the idle speed.

### DOUBLE CARBURETOR ENGINES
#### (EXCEPT 1972–73 TYPE 2 WITH AIR PUMP)

Adjusting the carburetors on the dual carb models requires the use of a special instrument to measure air-flow. A commonly used instrument is the Uni-Syn®, available from auto parts stores and auto parts mail order houses. This device measures the vacuum created inside the carburetor and gives a way of adjusting the carburetors equally. An adapter is necessary to use the Uni-Syn® on the VW carburetors. A small frozen juice can with both ends removed will do.

1. Remove the right-hand connecting rod of the carburetor linkage system. This is the rod which connects the center bell crank with the right-hand carburetor.

2. Remove the air cleaner.

3. With the engine running and the Uni-Syn® in place, balance the carburetors by turning the idle speed screws. Disregard the idle speed when balancing the carburetors.

NOTE: *It is easier to balance the carburetors first and adjust the idle speed later.*

4. Adjust the idle speed to specifications by turning both idle speed screws an equal amount until the proper speed is reached. Recheck the balance and idle speed in that order.

5. Next, adjust the volume control screw for each carburetor. Slowly turn the screw clockwise until the engine speed begins to drop, then turn the screw counterclockwise until the engine runs smoothly once again. Turn the screw ¼ turn farther in the counterclockwise direction.

6. Recheck the idle speed adjustment.

7. Reinstall the carburetor linkage and recheck the carburetor balance. If the balance is off, adjust the length of the linkage to restore balance. Lubricate the linkage pivot points with lithium grease.

### TYPE 2 WITH AIR PUMP

Idle speed is set at the center adjusting screws. If a satisfactory idle cannot be obtained and all other conditions are correct (ignition timing, valve clearance, and choke fully open), use the following procedure to adjust the idle speed.

NOTE: *Since the idle mixture will be adjusted, it is mandatory that the CO level be checked with an exhaust analyzer as part of this procedure.*

1. Connect the tachometer and exhaust analyzer to the engine.

2. Disconnect the throttle rod from the right side carburetor.

3. Remove the vacuum *retard* hose from the distributor.

4. Unplug the cut-off valve wire at the center idle system. Disconnect and plug the air pump hose.

5. Turn the idle mixture screws on both carburetors all the way in.

CAUTION: *Do not force the screws or the tips will be distorted.*

Turn both screws out 2½ turns.

6. Start the engine and set the idle speed at 500–700 rpm (CO level 3–5%) by equally adjusting both mixture screws.

7. Disconnect the idle cut-off wire at one carburetor and note the decrease in idle speed. Repeat this operation on the other carburetor. The idle speed decrease should be the same for both sides. If not, readjust the mixture screws.

8. Connect the cut-off valve at the center idle system and install the air pump hose.

9. Race the engine for a moment and then adjust the idle speed with center idle system screws (CO level 1–3%).

### FUEL INJECTION IDLE SPEED ADJUSTMENT

The idle speed is adjusted by a screw located on the left side of the intake air distributor. To adjust the idle speed, loosen the lock nut and turn the screw with a

Adjusting the idle speed for a fuel injected engine

| a. Decrease | c. Tighten |
|---|---|
| b. Increase | locknut |

screwdriver until the idle speed is adjusted to specification.

### Throttle Regulator Adjustment

On 1970 and later Beetles the throttle regulator consists of two parts connected by a hose. The operating part is mounted at the carburetor and the control portion is located on the left sidewall of the engine compartment.

This device holds the throttle open slightly during deceleration to prevent an excessively rich mixture and to reduce exhaust emissions.

1. Warm the engine up and make sure the automatic choke is fully open.

2. While the engine is running, pull the throttle positioner lever back until it touches the stop screw on the mounting bracket. Engine speed should be 1700–1800 rpm.

3. Readjust the stop screw if engine speed is incorrect.

4. Loosen the seat screw at the end of the control section of the throttle positioner.

5. Increase engine speed to 3000 rpm and release the throttle valve lever. The engine should take 3–4 seconds to return to idle.

6. Tighten the set screw and check the rpm drop as in step 5.

Incorrect throttle regulator adjustment may cause erratic idle, excessively high idle speed, and backfiring on deceleration.

# Engine Tune-Up

Engine tune-up is a procedure performed to restore engine performance, deteriorated due to normal wear and loss of adjustment. The three major areas considered in a routine tune-up are compression, ignition, and carburetion, although valve adjustment may be included.

A tune-up is performed in three steps: *analysis*, in which it is determined whether normal wear is responsible for performance loss, and which parts require replacement or service; *parts replacement or service*; and *adjustment*, in which engine adjustments are returned to original specifications. Since the advent of emission control equipment, precision adjustment has become increasingly critical, in order to maintain pollutant emission levels.

## Analysis

The procedures below are used to indicate where adjustments, parts service or replacement are necessary within the realm of a normal tune-up. If, following these tests, all systems appear to be functioning properly, proceed to the Troubleshooting Section for further diagnosis.

—Remove all spark plugs, noting the cylinder in which they were installed. Remove the air cleaner, and position the throttle and choke in the full open position. Disconnect the coil high tension lead from the coil and the distributor cap. Insert a compression gauge into the spark plug port of each cylinder, in succession, and crank the engine with

| Maxi. Press. Lbs. Sq. In. | Min. Press. Lbs. Sq. In. | Max. Press. Lbs. Sq. In. | Min. Press. Lbs. Sq. In. |
|---|---|---|---|
| 134 | 101 | 188 | 141 |
| 136 | 102 | 190 | 142 |
| 138 | 104 | 192 | 144 |
| 140 | 105 | 194 | 145 |
| 142 | 107 | 196 | 147 |
| 146 | 110 | 198 | 148 |
| 148 | 111 | 200 | 150 |
| 150 | 113 | 202 | 151 |
| 152 | 114 | 204 | 153 |
| 154 | 115 | 206 | 154 |
| 156 | 117 | 208 | 156 |
| 158 | 118 | 210 | 157 |
| 160 | 120 | 212 | 158 |
| 162 | 121 | 214 | 160 |
| 164 | 123 | 216 | 162 |
| 166 | 124 | 218 | 163 |
| 168 | 126 | 220 | 165 |
| 170 | 127 | 222 | 166 |
| 172 | 129 | 224 | 168 |
| 174 | 131 | 226 | 169 |
| 176 | 132 | 228 | 171 |
| 178 | 133 | 230 | 172 |
| 180 | 135 | 232 | 174 |
| 182 | 136 | 234 | 175 |
| 184 | 138 | 236 | 177 |
| 186 | 140 | 238 | 178 |

**Compression pressure limits**
© Buick Div. G.M. Corp.)

the starter to obtain the highest possible reading. Record the readings, and compare the highest to the lowest on the compression pressure limit chart. If the difference exceeds the limits on the chart, or if all readings are excessively low, proceed to a wet compression check (see Troubleshooting Section).

—Evaluate the spark plugs according to the spark plug chart in the Troubleshooting Section, and proceed as indicated in the chart.

—Remove the distributor cap, and inspect it inside and out for cracks and/or carbon tracks, and inside for excessive wear or burning of the rotor contacts. If any of these faults are evident, the cap must be replaced.

—Check the breaker points for burning, pitting or wear, and the contact heel resting on the distributor cam for excessive wear. If defects are noted, replace the entire breaker point set.

—Remove and inspect the rotor. If the contacts are burned or worn, or if the rotor is excessively loose on the distributor shaft (where applicable), the rotor must be replaced.

—Inspect the spark plug leads and the coil high tension lead for cracks or brittleness. If any of the wires appear defective, the entire set should be replaced.

—Check the air filter to ensure that it is functioning properly.

## Parts Replacement and Service

The determination of whether to replace or service parts is at the mechanic's discretion; however, it is suggested that any parts in questionable condition be replaced rather than reused.

—Clean and regap, or replace, the spark plugs as needed. Lightly coat the threads with engine oil and install the plugs. CAUTION: *Do not over-torque taper-seat spark plugs, or plugs being installed in aluminum cylinder heads.*

## SPARK PLUG TORQUE

| Thread size | Cast-Iron Heads | Aluminum Heads |
|---|---|---|
| 10 mm. | 14 | 11 |
| 14 mm. | 30 | 27 |
| 18 mm. | 34* | 32 |
| 7/8 in.—18 | 37 | 35 |

* 17 ft. lbs. for tapered plugs using no gaskets.

—If the distributor cap is to be reused, clean the inside with a dry rag, and remove corrosion from the rotor contact points with fine emery cloth. Remove the spark plug wires one by one, and clean the wire ends and the inside of the towers. If the boots are loose, they should be replaced.

If the cap is to be replaced, transfer the wires one by one, cleaning the wire ends and replacing the boots if necessary.

—If the original points are to remain in service, clean them lightly with emery cloth, lubricate the contact heel with grease specifically designed for this purpose. Rotate the crankshaft until the heel rests on a high point of the distributor cam, and adjust the point gap to specifications.

When replacing the points, remove the original points and condenser, and wipe out the inside of the distributor housing with a clean, dry rag. Lightly lubricate the contact heel and pivot point, and install the points and condenser. Rotate the crankshaft until the heel rests on a high point of the distributor cam, and adjust the point gap to specifications. NOTE: *Always replace the condenser when changing the points.*

—If the rotor is to be reused, clean the contacts with solvent. Do not alter the spring tension of the rotor center contact. Install the rotor and the distributor cap.

—Replace the coil high tension lead and/or the spark plug leads as necessary.

—Clean the carburetor using a spray solvent (e.g., Gumout Spray). Remove the varnish from the throttle bores, and clean the linkage. Disconnect and plug the fuel line, and run the engine until it runs out of fuel. Partially fill the float chamber with solvent, and reconnect the fuel line. In extreme cases, the jets can be pressure flushed by inserting a rubber plug into the float vent, running the spray nozzle through it, and spraying the solvent until it squirts out of the venturi fuel dump.

—Clean and tighten all wiring connections in the primary electrical circuit.

### Additional Services

The following services *should* be performed in conjunction with a routine tune-up to ensure efficient performance.

—Inspect the battery and fill to the proper level with distilled water. Remove the cable clamps, clean clamps and posts thoroughly, coat the posts lightly with petroleum jelly, reinstall and tighten.

—Inspect all belts, replace and/or adjust as necessary.

—Test the PCV valve (if so equipped), and clean or replace as indicated. Clean all crankcase ventilation hoses, or replace if cracked or hardened.

—Adjust the valves (if necessary) to manufacturer's specifications.

## Adjustments

—Connect a dwell-tachometer between the distributor primary lead and ground. Remove the distributor cap and rotor (unless equipped with Delco externally adjustable distributor). With the ignition off, crank the engine with a remote starter switch and measure the point dwell angle. Adjust the dwell angle to specifications. NOTE: *Increasing the gap decreases the dwell angle and vice-versa.* Install the rotor and distributor cap.

—Connect a timing light according to the manufacturer's specifications. Identify the proper timing marks with chalk or paint. NOTE: *Luminescent (day-glo) paint is excellent for this purpose.* Start the engine, and run it until it reaches operating temperature. Disconnect and plug any distributor vacuum lines, and adjust idle to the speed required to adjust timing, according to specifications. Loosen the distributor clamp and adjust timing to specifications by rotating the distributor in the engine. NOTE: *To advance timing, rotate distributor opposite normal direction of rotor rotation, and vice-versa.*

—Synchronize the throttles and mixture of multiple carburetors (if so equipped) according to procedures given in the individual car sections.

—Adjust the idle speed, mixture, and idle quality, as specified in the car sections. Final idle adjustments should be made with the air cleaner installed. CAUTION: *Due to strict emission control requirements on 1969 and later models, special test equipment (CO meter, SUN Tester) may be necessary to properly adjust idle mixture to specifications.*

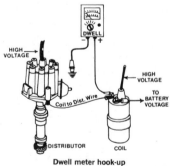

**Dwell meter hook-up**

# Trouble-shooting

The following section is designed to aid in the rapid diagnosis of engine problems. The systematic format is used to diagnose problems ranging from engine starting difficulties to the need for engine overhaul. It is assumed that the user is equipped with basic hand tools and test equipment (tach-dwell meter, timing light, voltmeter, and ohmmeter).

Troubleshooting is divided into two sections. The first, *General Diagnosis*, is used to locate the problem area. In the second, *Specific Diagnosis*, the problem is systematically evaluated.

## General Diagnosis

| PROBLEM: Symptom | Begin diagnosis at Section Two, Number ——— |
|---|---|
| *Engine won't start:* | |
| Starter doesn't turn | 1.1, 2.1 |
| Starter turns, engine doesn't | 2.1 |
| Starter turns engine very slowly | 1.1, 2.4 |
| Starter turns engine normally | 3.1, 4.1 |
| Starter turns engine very quickly | 6.1 |
| Engine fires intermittently | 4.1 |
| Engine fires consistently | 5.1, 6.1 |
| *Engine runs poorly:* | |
| Hard starting | 3.1, 4.1, 5.1, 8.1 |
| Rough idle | 4.1, 5.1, 8.1 |
| Stalling | 3.1, 4.1, 5.1, 8.1 |
| Engine dies at high speeds | 4.1, 5.1 |
| Hesitation (on acceleration from standing stop) | 5.1, 8.1 |
| Poor pickup | 4.1, 5.1, 8.1 |
| Lack of power | 3.1, 4.1, 5.1, 8.1 |
| Backfire through the carburetor | 4.1, 8.1, 9.1 |
| Backfire through the exhaust | 4.1, 8.1, 9.1 |
| Blue exhaust gases | 6.1, 7.1 |
| Black exhaust gases | 5.1 |
| Running on (after the ignition is shut off) | 3.1, 8.1 |
| Susceptible to moisture | 4.1 |
| Engine misfires under load | 4.1, 7.1, 8.4, 9.1 |
| Engine misfires at speed | 4.1, 8.4 |
| Engine misfires at idle | 3.1, 4.1, 5.1, 7.1, 8.4 |

| PROBLEM: Symptom | Probable Cause |
|---|---|
| *Engine noises:* ① | |
| Metallic grind while starting | Starter drive not engaging completely |
| Constant grind or rumble | *Starter drive not releasing, worn main bearings |
| Constant knock | Worn connecting rod bearings |
| Knock under load | Fuel octane too low, worn connecting rod bearings |
| Double knock | Loose piston pin |
| Metallic tap | *Collapsed or sticky valve lifter, excessive valve clearance, excessive end play in a rotating shaft |
| Scrape | *Fan belt contacting a stationary surface |
| Tick while starting | S.U. electric fuel pump (normal), starter brushes |
| Constant tick | *Generator brushes, shreaded fan belt |
| Squeal | *Improperly tensioned fan belt |
| Hiss or roar | *Steam escaping through a leak in the cooling system or the radiator overflow vent |
| Whistle | *Vacuum leak |
| Wheeze | Loose or cracked spark plug |

①—It is extremely difficult to evaluate vehicle noises. While the above are general definitions of engine noises, those starred (*) should be considered as possibly originating elsewhere in the car. To aid diagnosis, the following list considers other potential sources of these sounds.

Metallic grind:
Throwout bearing; transmission gears, bearings, or synchronizers; differential bearings, gears; something metallic in contact with brake drum or disc.

Metallic tap:
U-joints; fan-to-radiator (or shroud) contact.

Scrape:
Brake shoe or pad dragging; tire to body contact; suspension contacting undercarriage or exhaust; something non-metallic contacting brake shoe or drum.

Tick:
Transmission gears; differential gears; lack of radio suppression; resonant vibration of body panels; windshield wiper motor or transmission; heater motor and blower.

Squeal:
Brake shoe or pad not fully releasing; tires (excessive wear, uneven wear, improper inflation); front or rear wheel alignment (most commonly due to improper toe-in).

Hiss or whistle:
Wind leaks (body or window); heater motor and blower fan.

Roar:
Wheel bearings; wind leaks (body and window).

## Specific Diagnosis

This section is arranged so that following each test, instructions are given to proceed to another, until a problem is diagnosed.

### INDEX

| Group | | Topic |
|---|---|---|
| 1 | * | Battery |
| 2 | * | Cranking system |
| 3 | * | Primary electrical system |
| 4 | * | Secondary electrical system |
| 5 | * | Fuel system |
| 6 | * | Engine compression |
| 7 | ** | Engine vacuum |
| 8 | ** | Secondary electrical system |
| 9 | ** | Valve train |
| 10 | ** | Exhaust system |
| 11 | ** | Cooling system |
| 12 | ** | Engine lubrication |

*—The engine need not be running.
**—The engine must be running.

### SAMPLE SECTION

| Test and Procedure | Results and Indications | Proceed to |
|---|---|---|
| 4.1—Check for spark: Hold each spark plug wire approximately ¼″ from ground with gloves or a heavy, dry rag. Crank the engine and observe the spark. | If no spark is evident: | 4.2 |
| | If spark is good in some cases: | 4.3 |
| | If spark is good in all cases: | 4.6 |

### DIAGNOSIS

| | | |
|---|---|---|
| 1.1—Inspect the battery visually for case condition (corrosion, cracks) and water level. | If case is cracked, replace battery: | 1.4 |
| | If the case is intact, remove corrosion with a solution of baking soda and water (CAUTION: *do not get the solution into the battery*), and fill with water: | 1.2 |
| 1.2—Check the battery cable connections: Insert a screwdriver between the battery post and the cable clamp. Turn the headlights on high beam, and observe them as the screwdriver is gently twisted to ensure good metal to metal contact. | If the lights brighten, remove and clean the clamp and post; coat the post with petroleum jelly, install and tighten the clamp: | 1.4 |
| | If no improvement is noted: | 1.3 |

Testing battery cable connections using a screwdriver

| | | |
|---|---|---|
| 1.3—Test the state of charge of the battery using an individual cell tester or hydrometer. | If indicated, charge the battery. NOTE: *If no obvious reason exists for the low state of charge (i.e., battery age, prolonged storage), the charging system should be tested:* | 1.4 |

| Spec. Grav. Reading | Charged Condition |
|---|---|
| 1.260-1.280 | Fully Charged |
| 1.230-1.250 | Three Quarter Charged |
| 1.200-1.220 | One Half Charged |
| 1.170-1.190 | One Quarter Charged |
| 1.140-1.160 | Just About Flat |
| 1.110-1.130 | All The Way Down |

State of battery charge

Electrolyte temperature (°F) / Specific gravity correction

| +120 | +.016 |
| +100 | +.012 |
| | +.008 | ADD to reading |
| | +.004 |
| +80 | no correction |
| | −.004 |
| +60 | −.008 |
| | −.012 |
| +40 | −.016 |
| | −.020 |
| +20 | −.024 | SUBTRACT from reading |
| | −.028 |
| 0 | −.032 |
| | −.036 |
| −20 | −.040 |

The effect of temperature on the specific gravity of battery electrolyte

| *Test and Procedure* | *Results and Indications* | *Proceed to* |
|---|---|---|
| 1.4—Visually inspect battery cables for cracking, bad connection to ground, or bad connection to starter. | If necessary, tighten connections or replace the cables: | 2.1 |

**Tests in Group 2 are performed with coil high tension lead disconnected to prevent accidental starting.**

| | | |
|---|---|---|
| 2.1—Test the starter motor and solenoid: Connect a jumper from the battery post of the solenoid (or relay) to the starter post of the solenoid (or relay). | If starter turns the engine normally: | 2.2 |
| | If the starter buzzes, or turns the engine very slowly: | 2.4 |
| | If no response, replace the solenoid (or relay). | 3.1 |
| | If the starter turns, but the engine doesn't, ensure that the flywheel ring gear is intact. If the gear is undamaged, replace the starter drive. | 3.1 |
| 2.2—Determine whether ignition override switches are functioning properly (clutch start switch, neutral safety switch), by connecting a jumper across the switch(es), and turning the ignition switch to "start". | If starter operates, adjust or replace switch: | 3.1 |
| | If the starter doesn't operate: | 2.3 |
| 2.3—Check the ignition switch "start" position: Connect a 12V test lamp between the starter post of the solenoid (or relay) and ground. Turn the ignition switch to the "start" position, and jiggle the key. | If the lamp doesn't light when the switch is turned, check the ignition switch for loose connections, cracked insulation, or broken wires. Repair or replace as necessary: | 3.1 |
| | If the lamp flickers when the key is jiggled, replace the ignition switch. | 3.3 |

**Checking the ignition switch "start" position**

| | | |
|---|---|---|
| 2.4—Remove and bench test the starter, according to specifications in the car section. | If the starter does not meet specifications, repair or replace as needed: | 3.1 |
| | If the starter is operating properly: | 2.5 |
| 2.5—Determine whether the engine can turn freely: Remove the spark plugs, and check for water in the cylinders. Check for water on the dipstick, or oil in the radiator. Attempt to turn the engine using an 18″ flex drive and socket on the crankshaft pulley nut or bolt. | If the engine will turn freely only with the spark plugs out, and hydrostatic lock (water in the cylinders) is ruled out, check valve timing: | 9.2 |
| | If engine will not turn freely, and it is known that the clutch and transmission are free, the engine must be disassembled for further evaluation: | Next Chapter |

| *Tests and Procedures* | *Results and Indications* | *Proceed to* |
|---|---|---|
| 3.1—Check the ignition switch "on" position: Connect a jumper wire between the distributor side of the coil and ground, and a 12V test lamp between the switch side of the coil and ground. Remove the high tension lead from the coil. Turn the ignition switch on and jiggle the key. | If the lamp lights: | 3.2 |
| | If the lamp flickers when the key is jiggled, replace the ignition switch: | 3.3 |
| | If the lamp doesn't light, check for loose or open connections. If none are found, remove the ignition switch and check for continuity. If the switch is faulty, replace it: | 3.3 |

Checking the ignition switch "on" position

| *Tests and Procedures* | *Results and Indications* | *Proceed to* |
|---|---|---|
| 3.2—Check the ballast resistor or resistance wire for an open circuit, using an ohmmeter. | Replace the resistor or the resistance wire if the resistance is zero. | 3.3 |
| 3.3—Visually inspect the breaker points for burning, pitting, or excessive wear. Gray coloring of the point contact surfaces is normal. Rotate the crankshaft until the contact heel rests on a high point of the distributor cam, and adjust the point gap to specifications. | If the breaker points are intact, clean the contact surfaces with fine emery cloth, and adjust the point gap to specifications. If pitted or worn, replace the points and condenser, and adjust the gap to specifications:<br>NOTE: *Always lubricate the distributor cam according to manufacturer's recommendations when servicing the breaker points.* | 3.4 |
| 3.4—Connect a dwell meter between the distributor primary lead and ground. Crank the engine and observe the point dwell angle. | If necessary, adjust the point dwell angle:<br>NOTE: *Increasing the point gap decreases the dwell angle, and vice-versa.* | 3.6 |
| | If dwell meter shows little or no reading: | 3.5 |

Dwell meter hook-up

Dwell angle

| *Tests and Procedures* | *Results and Indications* | *Proceed to* |
|---|---|---|
| 3.5—Check the condenser for short: Connect an ohmmeter across the condenser body and the pigtail lead. | If any reading other than infinite resistance is noted, replace the condenser: | 3.6 |

Checking the condenser for short

| *Test and Procedure* | *Results and Indications* | *Proceed to* |
|---|---|---|
| 3.6—Test the coil primary resistance: Connect an ohmmeter across the coil primary terminals, and read the resistance on the low scale. Note whether an external ballast resistor or resistance wire is utilized. | Coils utilizing ballast resistors or resistance wires should have approximately $1.0\Omega$ resistance; coils with internal resistors should have approximately $4.0\Omega$ resistance. If values far from the above are noted, replace the coil: | 4.1 |

**Testing the coil primary resistance**

| 4.1—Check for spark: Hold each spark plug wire approximately $\frac{1}{4}''$ from ground with gloves or a heavy, dry rag. Crank the engine, and observe the spark. | If no spark is evident: | 4.2 |
| | If spark is good in some cylinders: | 4.3 |
| | If spark is good in all cylinders: | 4.6 |

| 4.2—Check for spark at the coil high tension lead: Remove the coil high tension lead from the distributor and position it approximately $\frac{1}{4}''$ from ground. Crank the engine and observe spark. CAUTION: *This test should not be performed on cars equipped with transistorized ignition.* | If the spark is good and consistent: | 4.3 |
| | If the spark is good but intermittent, test the primary electrical system starting at 3.3: | 3.3 |
| | If the spark is weak or non-existent, replace the coil high tension lead, clean and tighten all connections and retest. If no improvement is noted: | 4.4 |

| 4.3—Visually inspect the distributor cap and rotor for burned or corroded contacts, cracks, carbon tracks, or moisture. Also check the fit of the rotor on the distributor shaft (where applicable). | If moisture is present, dry thoroughly, and retest per 4.1: | 4.1 |
| | If burned or excessively corroded contacts, cracks, or carbon tracks are noted, replace the defective part(s) and retest per 4.1: | 4.1 |
| | If the rotor and cap appear intact, or are only slightly corroded, clean the contacts thoroughly (including the cap towers and spark plug wire ends) and retest per 4.1: | |
| | If the spark is good in all cases: | 4.6 |
| | If the spark is poor in all cases: | 4.5 |

| 4.4—Check the coil secondary resistance: Connect an ohmmeter across the distributor side of the coil and the coil tower. Read the resistance on the high scale of the ohmmeter. | The resistance of a satisfactory coil should be between $4K\Omega$ and $10K\Omega$. If the resistance is considerably higher (i.e., $40K\Omega$) replace the coil, and retest per 4.1: NOTE: *This does not apply to high performance coils.* | 4.1 |

**Testing the coil secondary resistance**

| Test and Procedure | Results and Indications | Proceed to |
|---|---|---|
| 4.5—Visually inspect the spark plug wires for cracking or brittleness. Ensure that no two wires are positioned so as to cause induction firing (adjacent and parallel). Remove each wire, one by one, and check resistance with an ohmmeter. | Replace any cracked or brittle wires. If any of the wires are defective, replace the entire set. Replace any wires with excessive resistance (over 8000Ω per foot for suppression wire), and separate any wires that might cause induction firing. | 4.6 |
| 4.6—Remove the spark plugs, noting the cylinders from which they were removed, and evaluate according to the chart below. | See below. | See below. |

| | Condition | Cause | Remedy | Proceed to |
|---|---|---|---|---|
|  | Electrodes eroded, light brown deposits. | Normal wear. Normal wear is indicated by approximately .001″ wear per 1000 miles. | Clean and regap the spark plug if wear is not excessive: Replace the spark plug if excessively worn: | 4.7 |
|  | Carbon fouling (black, dry, fluffy deposits). | If present on one or two plugs: | | |
| | | Faulty high tension lead(s). | Test the high tension leads: | 4.5 |
| | | Burnt or sticking valve(s). | Check the valve train: (Clean and regap the plugs in either case.) | 9.1 |
| | | If present on most or all plugs: Overly rich fuel mixture, due to restricted air filter, improper carburetor adjustment, improper choke or heat riser adjustment or operation. | Check the fuel system: | 5.1 |
| | Oil fouling (wet black deposits) | Worn engine components. NOTE: *Oil fouling may occur in new or recently rebuilt engines until broken in.* | Check engine vacuum and compression: Replace with new spark plug | 6.1 |
|  | Lead fouling (gray, black, tan, or yellow deposits, which appear glazed or cinder-like). | Combustion by-products. | Clean and regap the plugs: (Use plugs of a different heat range if the problem recurs.) | 4.7 |

| | Condition | Cause | Remedy | Proceed to |
|---|---|---|---|---|
| | Gap bridging (deposits lodged between the electrodes). | Incomplete combustion, or transfer of deposits from the combustion chamber. | Replace the spark plugs: | 4.7 |
| | Overheating (burnt electrodes, and extremely white insulator with small black spots). | Ignition timing advanced too far. | Adjust timing to specifications: | 8.2 |
| | | Overly lean fuel mixture. | Check the fuel system: | 5.1 |
| | | Spark plugs not seated properly. | Clean spark plug seat and install a new gasket washer: (Replace the spark plugs in all cases.) | 4.7 |
| | Fused spot deposits on the insulator. | Combustion chamber blow-by. | Clean and regap the spark plugs: | 4.7 |
| | Pre-ignition (melted or severely burned electrodes, blistered or cracked insulators, or metallic deposits on the insulator). | Incorrect spark plug heat range. | Replace with plugs of the proper heat range: | 4.7 |
| | | Ignition timing advanced too far. | Adjust timing to specifications: | 8.2 |
| | | Spark plugs not being cooled efficiently. | Clean the spark plug seat, and check the cooling system: | 11.1 |
| | | Fuel mixture too lean. | Check the fuel system: | 5.1 |
| | | Poor compression. | Check compression: | 6.1 |
| | | Fuel grade too low. | Use higher octane fuel: | 4.7 |

| Test and Procedure | | Results and Indications | Proceed to |
|---|---|---|---|
| 4.7—Determine the static ignition timing: Using the flywheel or crankshaft pulley timing marks as a guide, locate top dead center on the *compression* stroke of the No. 1 cylinder. Remove the distributor cap. | | Adjust the distributor so that the rotor points toward the No. 1 tower in the distributor cap, and the points are just opening: | 4.8 |
| 4.8—Check coil polarity: Connect a voltmeter negative lead to the coil high tension lead, and the positive lead to ground (NOTE: *reverse the hook-up for positive ground cars*). Crank the engine momentarily. **Checking coil polarity** | | If the voltmeter reads up-scale, the polarity is correct: | 5.1 |
| | | If the voltmeter reads down-scale, reverse the coil polarity (switch the primary leads): | 5.1 |

| *Test and Procedure* | *Results and Indications* | *Proceed to* |
|---|---|---|
| 5.1—Determine that the air filter is functioning efficiently: Hold paper elements up to a strong light, and attempt to see light through the filter. | Clean permanent air filters in gasoline (or manufacturer's recommendation), and allow to dry. Replace paper elements through which light cannot be seen: | 5.2 |
| 5.2—Determine whether a flooding condition exists: Flooding is identified by a strong gasoline odor, and excessive gasoline present in the throttle bore(s) of the carburetor. | If flooding is not evident: <br><br> If flooding is evident, permit the gasoline to dry for a few moments and restart. <br>  If flooding doesn't recur: <br><br> If flooding is persistant: | 5.3 <br><br><br><br> 5.6 <br><br> 5.5 |
| 5.3—Check that fuel is reaching the carburetor: Detach the fuel line at the carburetor inlet. Hold the end of the line in a cup (not styrofoam), and crank the engine. | If fuel flows smoothly: <br> If fuel doesn't flow (NOTE: *Make sure that there is fuel in the tank*), or flows erratically: | 5.6 <br><br><br> 5.4 |
| 5.4—Test the fuel pump: Disconnect all fuel lines from the fuel pump. Hold a finger over the input fitting, crank the engine (with electric pump, turn the ignition or pump on); and feel for suction. | If suction is evident, blow out the fuel line to the tank with low pressure compressed air until bubbling is heard from the fuel filler neck. Also blow out the carburetor fuel line (both ends disconnected): <br><br> If no suction is evident, replace or repair the fuel pump: <br> NOTE: *Repeated oil fouling of the spark plugs, or a no-start condition, could be the result of a ruptured vacuum booster pump diaphragm, through which oil or gasoline is being drawn into the intake manifold (where applicable).* | 5.6 <br><br><br><br><br> 5.6 |
| 5.5—Check the needle and seat: Tap the carburetor in the area of the needle and seat. | If flooding stops, a gasoline additive (e.g., Gumout) will often cure the problem: <br><br> If flooding continues, check the fuel pump for excessive pressure at the carburetor (according to specifications). If the pressure is normal, the needle and seat must be removed and checked, and/or the float level adjusted: | 5.6 <br><br><br><br><br><br><br> 5.6 |
| 5.6—Test the accelerator pump by looking into the throttle bores while operating the throttle. | If the accelerator pump appears to be operating normally: <br><br> If the accelerator pump is not operating, the pump must be reconditioned. Where possible, service the pump with the carburetor(s) installed on the engine. If necessary, remove the carburetor. Prior to removal: | 5.7 <br><br><br><br><br> 5.7 |
| 5.7—Determine whether the carburetor main fuel system is functioning: Spray a commercial starting fluid into the carburetor while attempting to start the engine. | If the engine starts, runs for a few seconds, and dies: <br> If the engine doesn't start: | 5.8 <br> 6.1 |

| Test and Procedures | Results and Indications | Proceed to |
|---|---|---|
| 5.8—Uncommon fuel system malfunctions: See below: | If the problem is solved:<br><br>If the problem remains, remove and recondition the carburetor. | 6.1 |

| Condition | Indication | Test | Usual Weather Conditions | Remedy |
|---|---|---|---|---|
| Vapor lock | Car will not restart shortly after running. | Cool the components of the fuel system until the engine starts. | Hot to very hot | Ensure that the exhaust manifold heat control valve is operating. Check with the vehicle manufacturer for the recommended solution to vapor lock on the model in question. |
| Carburetor icing | Car will not idle, stalls at low speeds. | Visually inspect the throttle plate area of the throttle bores for frost. | High humidity, 32-40° F. | Ensure that the exhaust manifold heat control valve is operating, and that the intake manifold heat riser is not blocked. |
| Water in the fuel | Engine sputters and stalls; may not start. | Pump a small amount of fuel into a glass jar. Allow to stand, and inspect for droplets or a layer of water. | High humidity, extreme temperature changes. | For droplets, use one or two cans of commercial gas dryer (Dry Gas) For a layer of water, the tank must be drained, and the fuel lines blown out with compressed air. |

| Test and Procedure | Results and Indications | Proceed to |
|---|---|---|
| 6.1—Test engine compression: Remove all spark plugs. Insert a compression gauge into a spark plug port, crank the engine to obtain the maximum reading, and record. | If compression is within limits on all cylinders: | 7.1 |
| | If gauge reading is extremely low on all cylinders: | 6.2 |
| | If gauge reading is low on one or two cylinders:<br>(If gauge readings are identical and low on two or more adjacent cylinders, the head gasket must be replaced.) | 6.2 |

**Testing compression**
(© Chevrolet Div. G.M. Corp.)

**Compression pressure limits**
(© Buick Div. G.M. Corp.)

| Maxi. Press. Lbs. Sq. In. | Min. Press. Lbs. Sq. In. | Maxi. Press. Lbs. Sq. In. | Min. Press. Lbs. Sq. In. | Max. Press. Lbs. Sq. In. | Min. Press. Lbs. Sq. In. | Max. Press. Lbs. Sq. In. | Min. Press. Lbs. Sq. In. |
|---|---|---|---|---|---|---|---|
| 134 | 101 | 162 | 121 | 188 | 141 | 214 | 160 |
| 136 | 102 | 164 | 123 | 190 | 142 | 216 | 162 |
| 138 | 104 | 166 | 124 | 192 | 144 | 218 | 163 |
| 140 | 105 | 168 | 126 | 194 | 145 | 220 | 165 |
| 142 | 107 | 170 | 127 | 196 | 147 | 222 | 166 |
| 146 | 110 | 172 | 129 | 198 | 148 | 224 | 168 |
| 148 | 111 | 174 | 131 | 200 | 150 | 226 | 169 |
| 150 | 113 | 176 | 132 | 202 | 151 | 228 | 171 |
| 152 | 114 | 178 | 133 | 204 | 153 | 230 | 172 |
| 154 | 115 | 180 | 135 | 206 | 154 | 232 | 174 |
| 156 | 117 | 182 | 136 | 208 | 156 | 234 | 175 |
| 158 | 118 | 184 | 138 | 210 | 157 | 236 | 177 |
| 160 | 120 | 186 | 140 | 212 | 158 | 238 | 178 |

| Test and Procedure | Results and Indications | Proceed to |
|---|---|---|
| 6.2—Test engine compression (wet): Squirt approximately 30 cc. of engine oil into each cylinder, and retest per 6.1. | If the readings improve, worn or cracked rings or broken pistons are indicated:<br><br>If the readings do not improve, burned or excessively carboned valves or a jumped timing chain are indicated:<br>NOTE: *A jumped timing chain is often indicated by difficult cranking.* | Next Chapter<br><br><br>7.1 |
| 7.1—Perform a vacuum check of the engine: Attach a vacuum gauge to the intake manifold beyond the throttle plate. Start the engine, and observe the action of the needle over the range of engine speeds. | See below. | See below |

| | Reading | Indications | Proceed to |
|---|---|---|---|
| | Steady, from 17-22 in. Hg. | Normal. | 8.1 |
| | Low and steady. | Late ignition or valve timing, or low compression: | 6.1 |
| | Very low | Vacuum leak: | 7.2 |
| | Needle fluctuates as engine speed increases. | Ignition miss, blown cylinder head gasket, leaking valve or weak valve spring: | 6.1, 8.3 |
| | Gradual drop in reading at idle. | Excessive back pressure in the exhaust system: | 10.1 |
| | Intermittent fluctuation at idle. | Ignition miss, sticking valve: | 8.3, 9.1 |
| | Drifting needle. | Improper idle mixture adjustment, carburetors not synchronized (where applicable), or minor intake leak. Synchronize the carburetors, adjust the idle, and retest. If the condition persists: | 7.2 |
| | High and steady. | Early ignition timing: | 8.2 |

| *Test and Procedure* | *Results and Indications* | *Proceed to* |
|---|---|---|
| 7.2—Attach a vacuum gauge per 7.1, and test for an intake manifold leak. Squirt a small amount of oil around the intake manifold gaskets, carburetor gaskets, plugs and fittings. Observe the action of the vacuum gauge. | If the reading improves, replace the indicated gasket, or seal the indicated fitting or plug: | 8.1 |
| | If the reading remains low: | 7.3 |
| 7.3—Test all vacuum hoses and accessories for leaks as described in 7.2. Also check the carburetor body (dashpots, automatic choke mechanism, throttle shafts) for leaks in the same manner. | If the reading improves, service or replace the offending part(s): | 8.1 |
| | If the reading remains low: | 6.1 |
| 8.1—Check the point dwell angle: Connect a dwell meter between the distributor primary wire and ground. Start the engine, and observe the dwell angle from idle to 3000 rpm. | If necessary, adjust the dwell angle. NOTE: *Increasing the point gap reduces the dwell angle and vice-versa.* If the dwell angle moves outside specifications as engine speed increases, the distributor should be removed and checked for cam accuracy, shaft end-play and concentricity, bushing wear, and adequate point arm tension (NOTE: *Most of these items may be checked with the distributor installed in the engine, using an oscilloscope*): | 8.2 |
| 8.2—Connect a timing light (per manufacturer's recommendation) and check the dynamic ignition timing. Disconnect and plug the vacuum hose(s) to the distributor if specified, start the engine, and observe the timing marks at the specified engine speed. | If the timing is not correct, adjust to specifications by rotating the distributor in the engine: (Advance timing by rotating distributor opposite normal direction of rotor rotation, retard timing by rotating distributor in same direction as rotor rotation.) | 8.3 |
| 8.3—Check the operation of the distributor advance mechanism(s): To test the mechanical advance, disconnect all but the mechanical advance, and observe the timing marks with a timing light as the engine speed is increased from idle. If the mark moves smoothly, without hesitation, it may be assumed that the mechanical advance is functioning properly. To test vacuum advance and/or retard systems, alternately crimp and release the vacuum line, and observe the timing mark for movement. If movement is noted, the system is operating. | If the systems are functioning: | 8.4 |
| | If the systems are not functioning, remove the distributor, and test on a distributor tester: | 8.4 |
| 8.4—Locate an ignition miss: With the engine running, remove each spark plug wire, one by one, until one is found that doesn't cause the engine to roughen and slow down. | When the missing cylinder is identified: | 4.1 |

| *Test and Procedure* | *Results and Indications* | *Proceed to* |
|---|---|---|
| 9.1—Evaluate the valve train: Remove the valve cover, and ensure that the valves are adjusted to specifications. A mechanic's stethoscope may be used to aid in the diagnosis of the valve train. By pushing the probe on or near push rods or rockers, valve noise often can be isolated. A timing light also may be used to diagnose valve problems. Connect the light according to manufacturer's recommendations, and start the engine. Vary the firing moment of the light by increasing the engine speed (and therefore the ignition advance), and moving the trigger from cylinder to cylinder. Observe the movement of each valve. | See below | See below |

| *Observation* | *Probable Cause* | *Remedy* | *Proceed to* |
|---|---|---|---|
| Metallic tap heard through the stethoscope. | Sticking hydraulic lifter or excessive valve clearance. | Adjust valve. If tap persists, remove and replace the lifter: | 10.1 |
| Metallic tap through the stethoscope, able to push the rocker arm (lifter side) down by hand. | Collapsed valve lifter. | Remove and replace the lifter: | 10.1 |
| Erratic, irregular motion of the valve stem.* | Sticking valve, burned valve. | Recondition the valve and/or valve guide: | Next Chapter |
| Eccentric motion of the pushrod at the rocker arm.* | Bent pushrod. | Replace the pushrod: | 10.1 |
| Valve retainer bounces as the valve closes.* | Weak valve spring or damper. | Remove and test the spring and damper. Replace if necessary: | 10.1 |

*—When observed with a timing light.

| *Test and Procedure* | *Results and Indications* | *Proceed to* |
|---|---|---|
| 9.2—Check the valve timing: Locate top dead center of the No. 1 piston, and install a degree wheel or tape on the crankshaft pulley or damper with zero corresponding to an index mark on the engine. Rotate the crankshaft in its direction of rotation, and observe the opening of the No. 1 cylinder intake valve. The opening should correspond with the correct mark on the degree wheel according to specifications. | If the timing is not correct, the timing cover must be removed for further investigation: | |

| Test and Procedure | Results and Indications | Proceed to |
|---|---|---|
| 10.1—Determine whether the exhaust manifold heat control valve is operating: Operate the valve by hand to determine whether it is free to move. If the valve is free, run the engine to operating temperature and observe the action of the valve, to ensure that it is opening. | If the valve sticks, spray it with a suitable solvent, open and close the valve to free it, and retest. | |
| | If the valve functions properly: | 10.2 |
| | If the valve does not free, or does not operate, replace the valve: | 10.2 |
| 10.2—Ensure that there are no exhaust restrictions: Visually inspect the exhaust system for kinks, dents, or crushing. Also note that gasses are flowing freely from the tailpipe at all engine speeds, indicating no restriction in the muffler or resonator. | Replace any damaged portion of the system: | 11.1 |
| 11.1—Visually inspect the fan belt for glazing, cracks, and fraying, and replace if necessary. Tighten the belt so that the longest span has approximately ½″ play at its midpoint under thumb pressure. | Replace or tighten the fan belt as necessary: | 11.2 |

**Checking the fan belt tension**
(© Nissan Motor Co. Ltd.)

| Test and Procedure | Results and Indications | Proceed to |
|---|---|---|
| 11.2—Check the fluid level of the cooling system. | If full or slightly low, fill as necessary: | 11.5 |
| | If extremely low: | 11.3 |
| 11.3—Visually inspect the external portions of the cooling system (radiator, radiator hoses, thermostat elbow, water pump seals, heater hoses, etc.) for leaks. If none are found, pressurize the cooling system to 14-15 psi. | If cooling system holds the pressure: | 11.5 |
| | If cooling system loses pressure rapidly, reinspect external parts of the system for leaks under pressure. If none are found, check dipstick for coolant in crankcase. If no coolant is present, but pressure loss continues: | 11.4 |
| | If coolant is evident in crankcase, remove cylinder head(s), and check gasket(s). If gaskets are intact, block and cylinder head(s) should be checked for cracks or holes. | |
| | If the gasket(s) is blown, replace, and purge the crankcase of coolant: | 12.6 |
| | NOTE: *Occasionally, due to atmospheric and driving conditions, condensation of water can occur in the crankcase. This causes the oil to appear milky white. To remedy, run the engine until hot, and change the oil and oil filter.* | |

| Test and Procedure | Results and Indication | Proceed to |
|---|---|---|
| 11.4—Check for combustion leaks into the cooling system: Pressurize the cooling system as above. Start the engine, and observe the pressure gauge. If the needle fluctuates, remove each spark plug wire, one by one, noting which cylinder(s) reduce or eliminate the fluctuation.<br><br>**Radiator pressure tester**<br>(© American Motors Corp.) | Cylinders which reduce or eliminate the fluctuation, when the spark plug wire is removed, are leaking into the cooling system. Replace the head gasket on the affected cylinder bank(s). | |
| 11.5—Check the radiator pressure cap: Attach a radiator pressure tester to the radiator cap (wet the seal prior to installation). Quickly pump up the pressure, noting the point at which the cap releases.<br><br>**Testing the radiator pressure cap**<br>(© American Motors Corp.) | If the cap releases within ± 1 psi of the specified rating, it is operating properly:<br><br>If the cap releases at more than ± 1 psi of the specified rating, it should be replaced: | 11.6<br><br>11.6 |
| 11.6—Test the thermostat: Start the engine cold, remove the radiator cap, and insert a thermometer into the radiator. Allow the engine to idle. After a short while, there will be a sudden, rapid increase in coolant temperature. The temperature at which this sharp rise stops is the thermostat opening temperature. | If the thermostat opens at or about the specified temperature:<br><br>If the temperature doesn't increase:<br>(If the temperature increases slowly and gradually, replace the thermostat.) | 11.7<br><br>11.7 |
| 11.7—Check the water pump: Remove the thermostat elbow and the thermostat, disconnect the coil high tension lead (to prevent starting), and crank the engine momentarily. | If coolant flows, replace the thermostat and retest per 11.6:<br><br>If coolant doesn't flow, reverse flush the cooling system to alleviate any blockage that might exist. If system is not blocked, and coolant will not flow, recondition the water pump. | 11.6<br><br>— |
| 12.1—Check the oil pressure gauge or warning light: If the gauge shows low pressure, or the light is on, for no obvious reason, remove the oil pressure sender. Install an accurate oil pressure gauge and run the engine momentarily. | If oil pressure builds normally, run engine for a few moments to determine that it is functioning normally, and replace the sender.<br><br>If the pressure remains low:<br>If the pressure surges:<br>If the oil pressure is zero: | —<br><br>12.2<br>12.3<br>12.3 |

| Test and Procedure | Results and Indications | Proceed to |
|---|---|---|
| 12.2—Visually inspect the oil: If the oil is watery or very thin, milky, or foamy, replace the oil and oil filter. | If the oil is normal: | 12.3 |
| | If after replacing oil the pressure remains low: | 12.3 |
| | If after replacing oil the pressure becomes normal: | — |
| 12.3—Inspect the oil pressure relief valve and spring, to ensure that it is not sticking or stuck. Remove and thoroughly clean the valve, spring, and the valve body. | If the oil pressure improves: | — |
| | If no improvement is noted: | 12.4 |

**1816762**

**Oil pressure relief valve**
(© British Leyland Motors)

| | | |
|---|---|---|
| 12.4—Check to ensure that the oil pump is not cavitating (sucking air instead of oil): See that the crankcase is neither over nor underfull, and that the pickup in the sump is in the proper position and free from sludge. | Fill or drain the crankcase to the proper capacity, and clean the pickup screen in solvent if necessary. If no improvement is noted: | 12.5 |
| 12.5—Inspect the oil pump drive and the oil pump: | If the pump drive or the oil pump appear to be defective, service as necessary and retest per 12.1: | 12.1 |
| | If the pump drive and pump appear to be operating normally, the engine should be disassembled to determine where blockage exists: | Next Chapter |
| 12.6—Purge the engine of ethylene glycol coolant: Completely drain the crankcase and the oil filter. Obtain a commercial butyl cellosolve base solvent, designated for this purpose, and follow the instructions precisely. Following this, install a new oil filter and refill the crankcase with the proper weight oil. The next oil and filter change should follow shortly thereafter (1000 miles). | | |

# Chapter Three

# Engine and Engine Rebuilding

## Engine Electrical

### DISTRIBUTOR

#### Removal and Installation

1. Take off the vacuum hose at the distributor.

2. Disconnect the coil wire and remove the distributor cap.

3. Disconnect the condenser wire.

4. Bring No. 1 cylinder to top dead center (TDC) on the compression stroke by rotating the engine so that the rotor points to the No. 1 spark plug wire tower on the distributor cap and the timing marks are aligned at 0°. Mark the rotor-to-distributor relationship. Also, match mark the distributor housing-to-crankcase relationship.

5. Unscrew the distributor retaining screw on the crankcase and lift the distributor out.

6. If the engine has been rotated since the distributor was removed, bring the No. 1 cylinder to TDC on the compression stroke and align the timing marks on 0°. Align the match marks and insert the distributor into the crankcase. If the match marks are gone, have the rotor pointing to

Type 4 timing mark and rotor alignment

the No. 1 spark plug wire tower upon insertion.

7. Replace the distributor retaining screw and reconnect the condenser and coil wires. Reinstall the distributor cap.

8. Retime the engine.

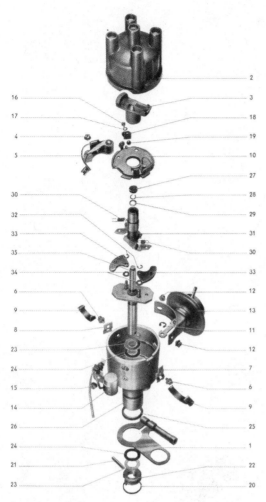

Distributor with vacuum and centrifugal advance

1. Bracket
2. Distributor cap
3. Rotor
5. Points
10. Breaker plate
13. Vacuum unit
14. Condenser
18. Ball retaining spring
19. Ball
20. Circlip for driving dog
21. Pin for driving dog
22. Driving dog
23. Shim
24. Fiber washer
25. Sealing ring
26. Distributor body
29. Thrust ring
30. Return spring
31. Cam
33. Centrifugal weight
35. Driveshaft

Fuel injection distributor

2. Distributor cap
3. Rotor
6. Points
8. Vacuum unit
9. Condenser
10. Holding spring
16. Ball retaining spring
17. Ball
18. Breaker plate
22. Return spring
23. Distributor cam
25. Flyweight
27. Circlip for drive dog
28. Pin for drive dog
29. Drive dog
30. 0.1 mm compensating washer
32. Distributor shaft
33. Distributor housing
34. Rubber sealing ring
35. Fuel injection trigger contacts

# Firing Order

### 1 - 4 - 3 - 2

No firing order diagram is shown because distributor positioning varies from model to model. All VW distributors have a scribed notch on the housing which locates the No. 1 rotor position. The firing order of all VW engines is 1-4-3-2. Correct rewiring of the distributor cap would then begin at the No. 1 notch and proceed clockwise in the firing order.

## DISTRIBUTOR DRIVESHAFT

### Removal and Installation

1. On Type 1, 2, and 3, remove the fuel pump.

2. Bring the engine to TDC on the compression stroke of No. 1 cylinder. Align the timing marks at 0°.

3. Remove the distributor.

4. Remove the spacer spring from the driveshaft.

5. Grasp the shaft and turn it slowly to the left while withdrawing it from its bore.

6. Remove the washer found under the shaft.

CAUTION: *Make sure that this washer does not fall down into the engine.*

7. To install, make sure that the engine is at TDC on the compression stroke for No. 1 cylinder with the timing marks aligned at 0°.

8. Replace the washer and insert the shaft into its bore.

NOTE: *Due to the slant of the teeth on the drive gears, the shaft must be rotated slightly to the left when it is inserted into the crankcase.*

9. When the shaft is properly inserted, the offset slot in the drive shaft of Type 1 and 2/1600 engines will be perpendicular to the crankcase joint and the slot offset will be facing the crankshaft pulley. On Type 3, the slot will form a 60° angle with the crankcase joint and the slot offset will be facing the oil cooler. On Type 4 engines, the slot should be about 12° out of parallel with the center line of the engine and the

Type 3 distributor driveshaft alignment

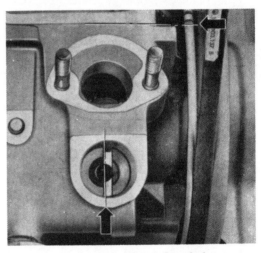

Type 1 and 2/1600 distributor driveshaft alignment

slot offset should be facing outside the engine.

10. Reinstall the spacer spring.

11. Reinstall the distributor and fuel pump, if removed.

12. Retime the engine.

## ALTERNATOR

### Alternator Precautions

1. Battery polarity should be checked before any connections, such as jumper ca-

Type 4 distributor driveshaft alignment

bles or battery charger leads, are made. Reversing the battery connections will damage the diodes in the alternator. It is recommended that the battery cables be disconnected before connecting a battery charger.

2. The battery must never be disconnected while the alternator is running.

3. Always disconnect the battery ground lead before working on the charging system, especially when replacing an alternator.

4. Do not short across or ground any alternator or regulator terminals.

5. If electric arc welding has to be done to the car, first disconnect the battery and alternator cables. Never start the car with the welding unit attached.

## Removal and Installation

### TYPE 4

The factory procedure recommends removing the engine to remove the alternator. However, it is possible to reach the alternator by first removing the right heater box which will provide access to the alternator.

1. Disconnect the battery.

2. The following is the alternator removal and installation procedure after removing the engine; however, all bolts and connections listed below must be removed, except the engine cooling fan, if the right heater box is removed to gain access to the alternator.

3. Remove the engine.

4. Remove the dipstick, if necessary, and the rear engine cover plate.

5. Remove the fan belt.

6. Remove the lower alternator bolt and the alternator cover plate.

7. Disconnect the wiring harness from the alternator.

8. Remove the allen-head screws which attach the engine cooling fan, then remove the fan.

9. Remove the rubber elbow from the fan housing.

NOTE: *This elbow must be in position upon installation because it provides cooling air for the alternator.*

10. Remove the alternator adjusting bracket.

11. Remove the alternator.

12. Installation is the reverse of the above. Make sure that the belt is properly adjusted.

## Alternator Belt Adjustment

1. Remove the insert in the cover plate and loosen the bolt in the slotted hole.

2. Move the alternator left or right to adjust the tension and then tighten the bolt. Tension is correct if the bolt can be deflected no more than ½ in. at the midpoint of the pulleys.

Alternator belt adjustment

## GENERATOR AND ALTERNATOR

### Removal and Installation

#### TYPE 1 AND 2

1. Disconnect the battery.

2. Disconnect the leads from the generator, noting their position on the generator.

3. Remove the air cleaner and the carburetor.

4. Separate the generator pulley halves, noting the number and position of the pulley shims, and remove the belt from the pulley.

5. Remove the retaining strap from the generator.

6. Remove the cooling air thermostat.

7. Remove the hot air hoses from the fan housing, take out the fan housing screws, and lift off the housing.

8. The generator, fan, and fan cover may be removed as an assembly.

9. Remove the fan from the generator by unscrewing the special nut and pulling the fan off the keyed generator shaft. Note the position of any shims found on Type 2 generators, from chassis number 219000001, as these shims are used to maintain a gap

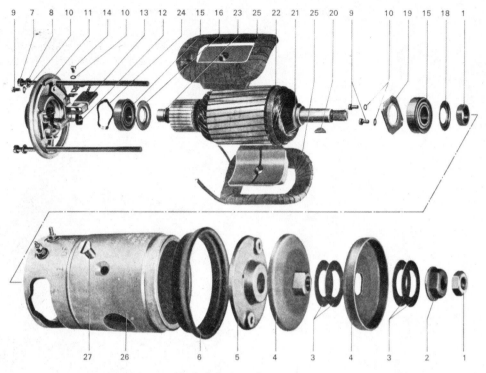

Exploded view of generator

| | | | |
|---|---|---|---|
| 1. Nut for pulley | 8. Washer | 15. Ball bearing | 22. Armature |
| 2. Special washer | 9. Screw | 16. Splash shield | 23. Armature flange |
| 3. Shim | 10. Washer | 18. Splash shield | 24. Gasket |
| 4. Pulley | 11. End plate with carbon brushes | 19. Retaining plate | 25. Field coil |
| 5. End plate | 12. Spring | 20. Woodruff key | 26. Housing |
| 6. End ring | 13. Carbon brushes | 21. Splash shield | 27. Field screw |
| 7. Through-bolt | 14. Screw | | |

of 0.047 in. between the fan and the fan cover. The Type 1 gap is 0.08 in.

10. Reverse the above steps to install. When reinstalling the generator, the cooling air intake slot in the fan cover must face downward and the generator pulley must align with the crankshaft pulley.

### TYPE 3

1. Remove the cooling air intake cover and disconnect the battery.

2. Loosen the fan belt adjustment and remove the fan belt. Removal of the belt is accomplished by removing the nut in the center of the generator pulley and removing the outer pulley half.

3. Remove the two nuts which hold the generator securing strap in place and then remove the strap.

4. Disconnect the generator wiring.

5. Remove the generator.

Alignment of Type 3 generator

6. Installation is the reverse of the above. Install the generator so that the mark on the generator housing is in line with the

notch on the clamping strap. The generator pulley must be aligned with the crankshaft pulley. Make sure that the boot which seals the generator to the air intake housing is properly placed.

### Generator Belt Adjustment

#### TYPE 1, 2, AND 3

Belt adjustment is performed by removing the nut in the center of the generator pulley and removing or installing shims between the generator pulley halves. Removing shims tightens the belt and installing shims loosens the belt.

### *REGULATOR*

### Removal and Installation

#### TYPE 1 AND 3

The regulator is located under the rear seat on the left side. It is secured to the frame by two screws. Take careful note of the wiring connections before removing the wiring from the regulator. Disconnect the battery before removing the regulator.

CAUTION: *Interchanging the connections on the regulator will destroy the regulator and generator.*

#### TYPE 2 AND 14

Disconnect the battery. The regulator is located in the engine compartment and is secured in place by two screws. Take careful note of the wiring connections before removing the wiring from the regulator.

#### TYPE 4

Disconnect the battery and do not disconnect any other wiring until the engine is turned off. Make careful note of the wiring connections. The regulator is located near the air cleaner and is mounted either on the air cleaner or on the firewall. It is secured by two screws.

### Voltage Adjustment

Volkswagen voltage regulators are sealed and cannot be adjusted.

### *STARTER*

### Removal and Installation

#### ALL TYPES

1. Disconnect the battery.
2. Disconnect the wiring from the starter.
3. The starter is held in place by two bolts. Remove the upper bolt through the engine compartment. Remove the lower bolt from underneath the car.
4. Remove the starter from the car.
5. Before installing the starter, lubricate the outboard bushing with grease. Apply sealing compound to the mating surfaces between the starter and the transmission.

## Available Starters

| Type Vehicle | Starter Number |
|---|---|
| 1 | 003 911 023A |
| | 111 911 023A |
| | 311 911 023B |
| 2 | 311 911 023B |
| 3 | 003 911 023A |
| | 111 911 023A |
| 4 | 030 911 023A |

## Alternator, Generator, and Regulator Specifications

| Year | Type | Generator Maximum Output (Amps) | Alternator Maximum Output (Amps) | Alternator Stator Winding Resistance (Ohms) | Alternator Exciter Winding Resistance (Ohms) | Regulator Load Current (Amps) | Regulator Regulating Voltage Under Load (Volts) |
|---|---|---|---|---|---|---|---|
| 1970–73 | 1 | 30 | — | — | — | 25① | 12.5–14.5 |
| 1970–73 | 2/1600 | 38 | — | — | — | 25① | 12.5–14.5 |
| 1970–73 | 2/1700 | — | 55 | $0.13 \pm 0.013$ | $4.0 \pm 0.4$ | 25–30 | 13.8–14.9② |
| 1970–73 | 3 | 30 | — | — | — | 25① | 12.5–14.5 |
| 1970–73 | 4 | — | 55 | $0.13 \pm 0.013$ | $4.0 \pm 0.4$ | 25–30 | 13.8–14.9② |

① At 2000–2500 generator rpm
② At 2000 engine rpm

## Starter Specifications

| Starter Number | Lock Test | | No-Load Test | | | Brush Spring Tension (oz) |
| | Amps | Volts | Amps | Volts | rpm | |
| --- | --- | --- | --- | --- | --- | --- |
| 003 911 023A | 250–300 | 6 | 35–50 | 12 | 6400–7900 | 42.3 |
| 111 911 023A | 270–290 | 6 | 25–40 | 12 | 6700–7800 | 42.3 |
| 311 911 023B | 250–300 | 6 | 35–45 | 12 | 7400–8100 | 42.3 |
| 003 911 023A | 250–300 | 6 | 35–50 | 12 | 6400–7900 | 42.3 |

6. Place the long starter bolt in its hole in the starter and locate the starter on the transmission housing. Install the other bolt.

7. Connect the starter wiring and battery cables.

### Solenoid Replacement

1. Remove the starter.

2. Remove the nut which secures the connector strip at the end of the solenoid.

3. Take out the two retaining screws on the mounting bracket and withdraw the solenoid after it has been unhooked from its actuating lever.

4. When replacing a defective solenoid with a new one, care should be taken to see that the distance (a) in the accompanying diagram is 19 mm when the magnet is drawn inside the solenoid.

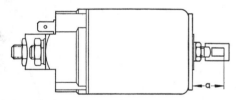

Solenoid adjustment

5. Installation is the reverse of removal. In order to facilitate engagement of the actuating rod, the pinion should be pulled out as far as possible when inserting the solenoid.

### BATTERY

The electrical system of the Volkswagen is a negative grounded type. The negative terminal of the battery, then, is grounded. In most VW models, the battery is located under the right-hand side of the rear seat. In Karmann Ghia Type 2 and 4 models, it is located in the engine compartment.

### Removal and Installation

1. Disconnect the battery cables. Note the position of the battery cables for instal-

lation. The small diameter battery post is the negative terminal. The negative battery cable is usually black.

2. Undo the battery holddown strap and lift the battery out of its holder.

CAUTION: *Do not tilt the battery as acid will spill out.*

3. Install the battery in its holder and replace the clamp. Reconnect the battery cables.

## Battery Specifications

| Year | Vehicle Type | Ampere Hour Capacity | Volts | Terminal Grounded |
| --- | --- | --- | --- | --- |
| 1970–73 | 1 | 45 | 12 | Negative |
| 1970–73 | 2 | 45 | 12 | Negative |
| 1970–73 | 3 | 45 | 12 | Negative |
| 1970–73 | 4 | 45 | 12 | Negative |

# Engine Mechanical

### DESIGN

The Volkswagen engine is a flat four cylinder design. This four cycle, overhead valve engine has two pairs of horizontally opposed cylinders. All VW engines are air cooled.

The Type 1 and 2 engine is known as an upright fan engine, that is, the engine cooling fan is mounted vertically on top of the engine and is driven by the the generator shaft. The Type 3 and 4 engine, although of the same basic design, i.e. flat four, has the cooling fan driven by the crankshaft and is therefore mounted on the front of the engine. This type of engine is known as the suitcase engine. The upright fan engine is carbureted, while the suitcase engine is available carbureted or fuel injected in the Type 3 and fuel injected in the Type 4.

Because it is air cooled, the VW engine is slightly noisier than a water cooled engine. This is due to the lack of water jacketing around the cylinders which provides sound deadening on water cooled engines. In addition, air cooled engines tend to run at somewhat higher temperatures, necessitating larger operating clearances to allow more room for the expansion of the parts. These larger operating clearances cause an increase in noise level over a water cooled engine.

The crankshaft of all Volkswagen engines is mounted in a two piece crankcase. The halves are machined to very close tolerances and line bored as a pair and, therefore, should always be replaced in pairs. When fitting them, it is necessary to coat only the mating surfaces with sealing compound and tighten them down to the correct torque. No gasket is used.

The pistons and cylinders are identical on any particular engine. However, it is not possible to interchange pistons and cylinders between engines. The four pistons each have three rings, two compression rings and one oil scraper. Each piston is attached to its connecting rod with a fully floating piston pin.

Each pair of cylinders shares a detachable cylinder head made of light aluminum alloy casting. The cylinder head contains the valves for both cylinders. Shrunk-in valve guides and valve seats are used.

## General Engine Specifications

| Year | Engine Code | Displacement (cc) | Horsepower @ rpm | Torque @ rpm (ft lbs) | Bore x Stroke (in.) | Ratio Compression | Oil Pressure @ rpm (psi) |
|------|-------------|-------------------|------------------|----------------------|---------------------|-------------------|--------------------------|
| 1970 | B | 1584 | 57/4400 | 82/3000 | 3.54 x 2.60 | 7.5:1② | 42 |
| 1970–71 | AD | 1584 | 60/4400 | 82/3000 | 3.54 x 2.60 | 7.5:1 | 42 |
| 1971–72 | AE | 1584 | 46/4000 | 72/2000 | 3.54 x 2.60 | 7.3:1 | 42 |
| 1971–72 | AK | 1584 | 46/4000 | 72/2000 | 3.54 x 2.60 | 7.3:1 | 42 |
| 1972–73 | AH | 1584 | 46/4000 | 72/2000 | 3.54 x 2.60 | 7.5:1 | 42 |
| 1972–73 | CB | 1679 | 63/4800 | 81/3200 | 3.96 x 2.72 | 7.3:1 | 42 |
| 1972–73 | CD | 1679 | 59/4200 | 82/3200 | 3.96 x 2.72 | 7.3:1 | 42 |
| 1970–73 | U | 1584 | 65/4600 | 87/2800 | 3.54 x 2.60 | 7.7:1 | 42 |
| 1972–73 | X | 1584 | 52/4000 | 77/2200 | 3.54 x 2.60 | 7.3:1 | 42 |
| 1971 | W | 1679 | 85/5000 | 99.5/3500 | 3.96 x 2.72 | 8.2:1 | 42 |
| 1972–73 | EA | 1679 | 76/4900 | 95/2700 | 3.96 x 2.72 | 8.2:1 | 42 |
| 1973 | EB① | 1679 | 69/5000 | 87/2700 | 3.96 x 2.72 | 7.3:1 | 42 |

①—California
②—Type 2 7.7:1

## Piston and Ring Specifications
### (All measurements in inches)

| Year | Type, Engine Displacement | Piston Clearance | Ring Gap | | | Ring Side Clearance | | |
|------|---------------------------|------------------|----------|---|---|--------------------|---|---|
| | | | Top Compression | Bottom Compression | Oil Control | Top Compression | Bottom Compression | Oil Control |
| 1970①–73 | 1, 2, 3 1600 | 0.0016– 0.0023 | 0.012– 0.018 | 0.012– 0.018 | 0.010– 0.016 | 0.0027– 0.0039 | 0.002– 0.0027 | 0.0011– 0.0019 |
| 1970①–73 | 2, 4 1700 | 0.0016– 0.0023 | 0.014– 0.021 | 0.012– 0.014 | 0.010– 0.016 | 0.0023– 0.0035 | 0.0016– 0.0027 | 0.0008– 0.0019 |

① This chart applies to the engines listed in the General Engines Specifications chart

## Valve Specifications

| Year | Vehicle Type Displacement | Seat Angle (deg) Intake | Seat Angle (deg) Exhaust | Face Angle (deg) Intake | Face Angle (deg) Exhaust | Valve Seat Width (in.) Intake | Valve Seat Width (in.) Exhaust | Spring Test Pressure (lbs @ in.) | Valve Guide Inside Dia (in.) Intake | Valve Guide Inside Dia (in.) Exhaust | Stem to Guide Clearance (in.) Intake | Stem to Guide Clearance (in.) Exhaust | Stem Diameter (in.) Intake | Stem Diameter (in.) Exhaust |
|---|---|---|---|---|---|---|---|---|---|---|---|---|---|---|
| 1970–73 | 1, 2, 3 1600 | 45 | 45 | 45 | 45 | 0.05–0.10 | 0.05–0.10 | 117.7–134.8 @ 1.22 | 0.3150–0.3157 | 0.3150–0.3157 | 0.009–0.010 | 0.009–0.010 | 0.3125–0.3129 | 0.3113–0.3117 |
| 1970–73 | 2, 4 1700 | 30 | 45 | 30 | 45 | 0.07–0.08 | 0.078–0.098 | 168–186 @ 1.14 | 0.3534–0.3538 | 0.3534–0.3538 | 0.018 | 0.018 | 0.3507–0.3511 | 0.3507–0.3511 |

# Crankshaft and Connecting Rod Specifications
## (All measurements are given in inches)

| | | Crankshaft | | | | | | | Connecting Rods | | |
| | | Main Bearing Journal Dia | | Main Bearing Oil Clearance | | | | | | | |
| Year | Type Engine | Types 1, 2, 3 | Type 4 | Types 1, 3 | Type 2 | Type 4 | Crankshaft End-Play | Thrust on No | Journal Dia | Oil Clearance | Endplay |
|---|---|---|---|---|---|---|---|---|---|---|---|
| 1970–73 | 1, 2, 3 1600 | 2.1640– 2.1648 | 1.5739– 1.5748 | 0.0016– 0.004 | 0.001– 0.003 | 0.002– 0.004 | 0.0027– 0.005 | 1 at flywheel | 2.1644– 2.1653 | 0.0008– 0.0027 | 0.004– 0.016 |
| 1970–73 | 2, 4 1700 | 2.3609– 2.3617 | 1.5739– 1.5748 | 0.002– 0.004 | 0.001– 0.003 | 0.002– 0.004 | 0.0027– 0.005 | 1 at flywheel | 2.1644– 2.1653 | 0.0008– 0.0027 | 0.004– 0.016 |

# Torque Specifications
## (All readings in ft lbs)

| Year | Type Vehicle | Cylinder Head Nuts | Rod Bearing Bolts | Generator Pulley | Crankshaft Pulley Bolt | Flywheel to Crankshaft Bolts | Fan to Hub | Hub to Crankshaft | Crankcase Half Nuts Sealing Nuts | Non-Sealing Nuts | Drive Plate to Crankshaft |
|---|---|---|---|---|---|---|---|---|---|---|---|
| 1970–73 | 1 | 23 | 22–25 | 40–47 | 29–36 | 253 | — | — | 18 | 14 | — |
| 1970–73 | 2/1600 | 23 | 22–25 | 40–47 | 29–36 | 253 | — | — | 18 | 14 | — |
| 1970–73 | 2/1700 | 23 | 24 | — | — | 80 | 14 | 23 | 23 | 14 | 61 |
| 1970–73 | 3 | 23 | 22–25 | 40–47 | 94–108 | 253 | — | — | 18 | 14 | — |
| 1970–73 | 4 | 23 | 24 | — | — | 80 | 14 | 23 | 23 | 14 | 61 |

## ENGINE REMOVAL AND INSTALLATION

### Type 1, 2, and 3

The Volkswagen engine is mounted on the transmission, which in turn is attached to the frame. In the Type 1 and 2 models, there are two bolts and two studs attaching the engine to the transmission. Type 3 engines have an extra mounting at the rear of the engine. Type 3 engines with automatic transmissions have front and rear engine and transmission mounts. At the front, the gearbox is supported by the rear tubular crossmember; at the rear, a crossmember is bolted to the crankcase and mounted to the body at either end.

When removing the engine from the car, it is recommended that the rear of the car be about 3 ft off the ground. Remove the engine by bringing it out from underneath the car. Proceed with the following steps to remove the engine.

1. Disconnect the battery ground cable.
2. Disconnect the generator wiring.
3. Remove the air cleaner. On Type 1 engines, remove the rear engine cover plate. On Type 2/1600 cc engines, remove the rear crossmember.

4. Disconnect the throttle cable and remove the electrical connections to the automatic choke, coil, electromagnetic cutoff jet, and the oil pressure sending unit.

5. Disconnect the fuel hose at the front engine cover plate and seal it to prevent leakage.

6. On Type 3 models, remove the oil dipstick and the rubber boot between the oil filter and the body.

7. Remove the cooling air intake bellows on Type 3 engines after loosening the clip that secures the unit.

8. On Type 3 models, remove the warm air hose.

9. On Type 3 fuel injected engines, remove and plug the pressure line to the left fuel distributor pipe and to the return line on the pressure regulator. Disconnect the fuel injection wiring harness.

10. Raise the car and support it with jackstands.

11. Remove the flexible air hoses between the engine and heat exchangers, disconnect the heater flap cables, unscrew the

two lower engine mounting nuts, and slide a jack under the engine. On Type 2 engines, remove the two bolts from the rubber engine mounts located next to the muffler.

12. On Type 1 Automatic Stick Shift models, disconnect the control valve cable and the manifold vacuum hoses. Disconnect the ATF suction line and plug it. On Type 3 fully automatic transmission models, disconnect the vacuum hose and the kickdown cable.

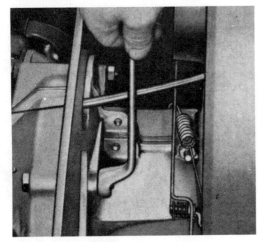

Removing upper engine mounting bolts

13. On all Automatic Stick Shift and fully automatic models, remove the four bolts from the converter drive plate through the holes in the transmission case. After the engine is removed, hold the torque converter on the transmission input shaft by using a strap bolted to the bellhousing.

Removing lower engine mounting bolts

14. Raise the jack until it just contacts the engine and have an assistant hold the two upper mounting bolts so that the nuts can be removed from the bottom.

15. When the engine mounts are disconnected and there are no remaining cables or wires left to be disconnected, move the engine toward the back of the car so that the clutch or converter plate disengages from the transmission.

16. Lower the engine out of the car.

17. Installation is the reverse of the above. When the engine is lifted into position, it should be rotated using the generator pulley so that the clutch plate hub will engage the transmission shaft splines. Tighten the upper mounting bolts first. Check the clutch, pressure plate, throwout bearing, and pilot bearing for wear.

On Type 3, synthetic washers are used to raise the engine about 3 mm when the rear engine mounting is attached and tightened. Use only enough washers in the rear mount so that the engine is lifted no more than 3 mm. Care should be used when installing the rear intake housing bellows of the Type 3 engine.

## Type 4

1. Disconnect the battery.

2. Remove the cooling air bellows, warm air hoses, cooling air intake duct, and air cleaner. On sedans, remove the cooling air fan. On station wagons, remove the dipstick tube rubber boot and the dipstick.

3. Disconnect the fuel injection wiring.

4. Disconnect the coil wires and remove the coil and its bracket.

5. Disconnect the oil pressure switch and the alternator wiring.

6. Disconnect the vacuum hose for the intake air distributor.

7. Disconnect the accelerator cable.

8. Working through the access hole at the upper right corner of the flywheel housing, remove the three screws which secure the torque converter to the drive plate. Remove the ATF oil dipstick and the rubber boot.

9. Remove the two upper engine mounting bolts.

10. Jack up the car and, working beneath the car, remove the muffler shield and the heat exchanger.

Access hole for torque converter bolts—Type 4

11. Disconnect the starter wiring.

12. Remove the heater booster exhaust pipe.

13. Remove the two lower engine mounting nuts.

14. Jack up the engine slightly and remove the four engine carrier screws.

Engine carrier screw location upon installation of engine—Type 4

NOTE: *Do not loosen the mountings on the body or the engine-transmission assembly will have to be recentralized in the chassis.*

15. Remove the engine from the car.

16. Reverse the removal procedures to install the engine. Install the engine on the lower engine mounting studs and then locate the engine in the engine carrier. When installing the engine in the carrier, lift the engine up so that the four screws

are at the top of the elongated holes and tighten them in this position. If it is necessary to raise or lower the engine for adjustment purposes, use the threaded shaft. After the engine is installed, make sure that the rubber buffer is centered in the rear axle carrier. Make sure that the engine carrier is vertical and parallel to the engine fan housing, Readjust it if necessary by moving the brackets on the side members.

Make sure the engine carrier is vertical and parallel to the fan housing

## CYLINDER HEAD

### Removal and Installation

In order to remove the cylinder head from either pair of cylinders, it is necessary to lower the engine.

1. Remove the valve cover and gasket. Remove the rocker arm assembly. Unbolt the intake manifold from the cylinder head. The cylinder head is held in place by eight studs. Since the cylinder head also holds the cylinders in place in the VW engine, and the cylinders are not going to be removed, it will be necessary to hold the cylinders in place after the head is removed.

2. After the rocker arm cover, rocker arm retaining nuts, and rocker arm assembly have been removed, the cylinder head nuts can be removed and the cylinder head lifted off.

3. When reinstalling the cylinder head, the head should be checked for cracks both in the combustion chamber and in the intake and exhaust ports. Cracked heads must be replaced.

4. Spark plug threads should be checked. New seals should be used on the pushrod tube ends and they should be checked for proper seating.

5. The pushrod tubes should be turned so that the seam faces upward. In order to ensure perfect sealing, used tubes should be stretched slightly before they are re-installed.

6. Install the cylinder head. Using new rocker shaft stud seals, install the push-rods and rocker shaft assembly.

NOTE: *Pay careful attention to the orientation of the shaft as described in the "Rocker Shaft" section.*

7. Torque the cylinder head in three stages. Adjust the valve clearance. Using a new gasket, install the rocker cover. It may be necessary to readjust the valves after the engine has been run a few minutes and allowed to cool.

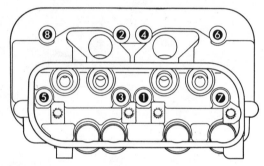

Cylinder head torque sequence

## Valve Guide Removal and Installation

Valve guide service is part of cylinder head overhauling. See the "Engine Rebuilding" section at the end of this chapter.

## Overhaul

See the "Engine Rebuilding" section at the end of this chapter.

## ROCKER SHAFTS

### Removal and Installation

Before the valve rocker assembly can be reached, it is necessary to undo the clip that retains the valve cover and then remove the valve cover. Remove the rocker arm retaining nuts, the rocker arm shaft, and the rocker arms. Remove the stud seals.

On Type 1, 2/1600, and 3, install the rocker shaft with the chamfer out and the slot up

Before installing the rocker arm mechanism, be sure that the parts are as clean as possible. Install new stud seals. On Type 1, 2, and 3, install the rocker shaft assembly with the chamfered edges of the rocker shaft supports pointing outward and the slots pointing upward. On Type 4 models, the chamfered edges must point outward and the slots must face downward.

On Type 2/1700 and 4, install the rocker shaft with the chamfer out and slots down

Tighten the retaining nuts to the proper torque. Use only the copper colored nuts that were supplied with the engine. Make sure that the ball ends of the push rods are centered in the sockets of the rocker arms. Adjust the valve clearance. Install the valve cover using a new gasket.

## INTAKE MANIFOLD

### Removal and Installation

#### TYPE 1 AND 2 SINGLE CARBURETOR

1. Disconnect the battery.
2. Disconnect the generator wiring.
3. Remove the generator. It will be necessary to loosen the fan housing and tilt it back to gain clearance to remove the generator.
4. Disconnect the choke and the accelerator cable.
5. On some models it will be necessary to remove the carburetor from the manifold.
6. Unbolt the manifold from the cylinder head and remove the manifold from the engine.
7. Reverse the above to install. Always use new gaskets.

#### FUEL INJECTED ENGINES

1. Remove the air cleaner.
2. Remove the pressure switch which is mounted under the right pair of intake manifold pipes. Disconnect the injector wiring.
3. Remove the fuel injectors by removing the two nuts which secure them in place. On Type 3, do not separate the pair of injectors; they can be removed as a pair and must be left in the injector plate. See Step 7 for proper injector installation.
4. After removing the intake manifold outer cover plate, remove the two screws which secure the manifold inner cover plate.
5. The manifold may be removed by removing the two nuts and washers which hold the manifold flange to the cylinder head.
6. Installation is the reverse of the above. The inner manifold cover should be installed first, but leave the cover loose until the outer cover and manifold are in place. Always use new gaskets. See the following step for proper injector installation.
7. Connect the fuel hoses to the injectors, if removed, after assembling the injectors with the injector retainer plate in place. Make sure that the sleeves are in place on the injector securing studs. Carefully slip the injectors into the manifold and install the securing nuts. Never force the injectors

in or out of the manifold. Reconnect the injector wiring.

## INTAKE AIR DISTRIBUTOR

### Removal and Installation

#### FUEL INJECTED ENGINES

The intake air distributor is located at the center of the engine at the junction of the intake manifold pipes.

NOTE: *It is not necessary to remove the distributor if only the manifold pipes are to be removed.*

1. Remove the air cleaner and pressure switch which are located under the right pair of manifold pipes.
2. Push the four rubber hoses onto the intake manifold pipes.
3. Remove the accelerator cable and the throttle valve switch.
4. Disconnect the accelerator cable.
5. Disconnect the vacuum hoses leading to the ignition distributor and the pressure sensor and disconnect the hose running to the auxiliary air regulator.
6. Remove those bolts under the air distributor which secure the air distributor to the crankcase and remove the air distributor.
7. Installation is the reverse of removal.

## MUFFLER, TAIL PIPES, HEAT EXCHANGERS

### Removal and Installation

#### MUFFLER, TYPE 1 AND 2

1. Working under the hood, disconnect the pre-heater hoses.
2. Remove the pre-heater pipe protection plate on each side of the engine. The plates are secured by three screws.
3. Remove the crankshaft pulley cover plate.
4. Remove the rear engine cover plate from the engine compartment. It is held in place by screws at the center, right, and left sides.
5. Remove the four intake manifold pre-heat pipe bolts. There are two bolts on each side of the engine.
6. Disconnect the warm air channel clamps at the left and right side of the engine.
7. Disconnect the heat exchanger clamps at the left and right side of the engine.

8. Remove the muffler from the engine.

9. Installation is the reverse of the above. Always use new gaskets to install the muffler.

### MUFFLER, TYPE 3

The muffler is secured to the heat exchangers with clamps and, on some models, to the body with bolts at the top and at the ends.

### MUFFLER, TYPE 4

The muffler is secured to the left and right heat exchangers by three bolts. There is a bracket at the left end of the muffler. Always use new gaskets when installing a new muffler.

### HEAT EXCHANGERS, TYPE 1, 2, AND 3

1. Disconnect the air tube at the outlet end of the exchanger.

2. Remove the clamp which secures the muffler to the exchanger.

3. Loosen the clamp which secures the exchanger to the heater hose connection at the muffler.

4. Remove the two nuts which secure the exchanger to the forward end of the cylinder head.

5. Remove the heater flap control wire.

6. Reverse the above to install. Always use new gaskets.

### HEAT EXCHANGERS, TYPE 4

1. Disconnect the air hose at the outlet of each exchanger.

2. Disconnect the warm air tube at the outside end of the exchanger.

3. Disconnect the three bolts which secure each exchanger to the muffler.

4. Remove the four nuts, two at each exhaust port, which secure the exchanger to the cylinder head.

5. Installation is the reverse of the above. Always use new gaskets.

### TAILPIPES, TYPE 1 AND 2

Loosen the clamps on the tailpipes and apply penetrating oil. Work the pipe side-to-side while trying to pull the tailpipe out of the muffler.

NOTE: *Is is often difficult to remove the tailpipes without damaging them.*

### TAILPIPE AND RESONATOR, TYPE 3

Loosen the clamp at the resonator-to-muffler connection. Remove the bolt at the bend of the tail pipe and remove the resonator and tailpipe assembly. To remove the tailpipe from the resonator, loosen the clamp which secures the tailpipe to the resonator and work them apart.

### TAILPIPE, TYPE 4

Remove the bolt which secures the pipe to the muffler. Remove the bolt which secures the pipe to the body and remove the pipe.

## *PISTONS AND CYLINDERS*

Pistons and cylinders are matched according to their size. When replacing pistons and cylinders, make sure that they are properly sized.

NOTE: *See the "Engine Rebuilding" section for cylinder refinishing.*

### Cylinder Removal and Installation

1. Remove the engine. Remove the cylinder head, pushrod tubes, and the deflector plate.

2. Slide the cylinder out of its groove in the crankcase and off of the piston. Matchmark the cylinders for reassembly. The cylinders must be returned to their original bore in the crankcase. If a cylinder is to be replaced, it must be replaced with a matching piston.

Matchmarking pistons

3. Cylinders should be checked for wear and, if necessary, replaced with another matched cylinder and piston assembly of the same size.

4. Check the cylinder seating surface on the crankcase, cylinder shoulder, and gasket, for cleanliness and deep scores. When reinstalling the cylinders, a new gasket, if required, should be used between each cylinder and the crankcase.

5. The piston, as well as the piston rings and pin must be oiled before reassembly.

6. Be sure that the ring gaps are of the correct dimension. Stagger the ring gaps around the piston, but make sure that the oil ring gap is positioned up when the pistons are in position on the connecting rods.

7. Compress the rings with a ring compressor, oil the cylinder wall, and slide the cylinder onto the piston. Make sure that the cylinder base gasket is in place.

Installing a cylinder

8. Install the deflector plates.

9. Install the pushrod tubes using new gaskets. Install the pushrods. Make sure that the seam in the pushrod tube is facing upward.

10. Install the cylinder head.

### Piston Removal and Installation

NOTE: *See the "Engine Rebuilding" section for piston ring procedures.*

1. Remove the engine. Remove the cylinder head and, after matchmarking the cylinders, remove the cylinders.

2. Matchmark the pistons to indicate the cylinder number and which side points toward the clutch.

3. Remove the circlips which retain the piston pin.

4. Heat the piston to 176 F. To heat the piston, boil a clean rag in water and wrap it around the piston. Remove the piston pin after the piston has been heated.

5. Remove the piston from the connecting rod.

6. Before installing the pistons, they should first be cleaned and checked for wear. Remove the old rings. Clean the ring grooves using a groove cleaner or a broken piece of ring. Clean the piston with solvent but do not use a wire brush or sand paper. Check for any cracks or scuff marks. Check the piston diameter with a micrometer and compare the readings to the specifications. If the running clearance between the piston and cylinder wall is 0.008 in (0.2 mm) or greater, the cylinder and piston should be replaced by a set of the same size grading. If the cylinder shows no sign of excessive wear or damage, it is permissible to install a new piston and rings of the appropriate size.

7. Place each ring in turn in its cylinder bore and check the piston ring end-gap. If the gap is too large, replace the ring. If the gap is too narrow, file the end of the ring until the proper gap is obtained.

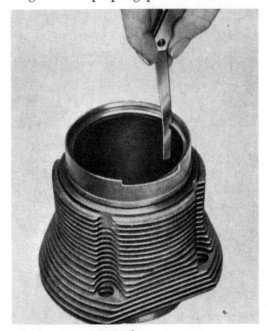

Checking piston ring end-gap

8. Insert the rings on the piston and check the ring side clearance. If the clearance is too large, replace the piston. Install the rings with the marking "Oben" or "Top" pointing upward.

Checking piston ring side clearance

9. If new rings are installed in a used piston, the ring ridge at the top of the cylinder bore must be removed with a ridge reamer.

10. Install the piston and piston pin on the connecting rod from which it originally came. Make sure that the piston is facing the proper direction.

11. Install the cylinders and the cylinder heads.

## CRANKCASE

### Disassembly and Assembly

1. Remove the engine.

2. Remove the cylinder heads, cylinders, and pistons.

3. Remove the oil strainer, oil pressure switch, and the crankcase nuts. Remove the flywheel and oil pump. The flywheel is held in place by the bolt, (Type 4 has five bolts), at the center of the flywheel. Matchmark the flywheel so that it can be replaced in the same position.

4. Keep the cam followers in the right crankcase half in position by using a retaining spring.

5. Use a rubber hammer to break the seal between the crankcase halves.

CAUTION: *Never insert sharp metal tools, wedges, or any prying device between the crankcase halves. This will ruin the gasket surface and cause serious oil leakage.*

6. After the seal between the crankcase halves is broken, remove the right hand crankcase half, the crankshaft oil seal and the camshaft end plug. The camshaft

and crankshaft can now be lifted out of the crankcase half.

7. Remove the cam followers, bearing shells, and the oil pressure relief valve.

8. Before starting reassembly, check the crankcase for any damage or cracks.

9. Flush and blow out all ducts and oil passages. Check the studs for tightness. If the tapped holes are worn install a Heli-Coil®.

10. Install the crankshaft bearing dowel pins and bearing shells for the crankshaft and camshaft. Make sure that the bearing shells with thrust flanges are installed in the proper journal.

Check dowel pins for tightness

11. Install the crankshaft and camshaft after the bearings have been well lubricated. When installing the camshaft and

Tighten this nut first on Type 1, 2/1600, and 3

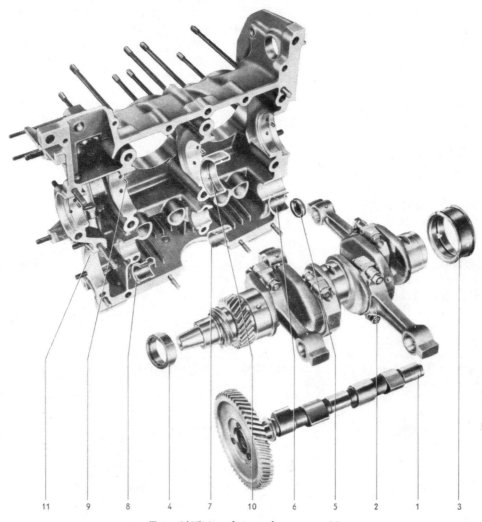

Type 2/1700 and 4 crankcase assembly

| | | |
|---|---|---|
| 1. Camshaft | 5. End cap for camshaft bore | 9. Crankshaft bearing dowel pin |
| 2. Crankshaft and connecting | 6. Camshaft No. 1 bearing shell | 10. No. 2 crankshaft bearing half |
|     rod assembly | 7. No. 2 camshaft bearing | 11. Left crankcase half |
| 3. Main bearing No. 1 | 8. No. 3 camshaft bearing | |
| 4. Main bearing No. 4 |     with shoulder for thrust | |

crankshaft, make sure that the timing marks on the timing gears are aligned.

12. Install the oil pressure relief valve.

13. Oil and install the cam followers.

14. Install the camshaft end plug using sealing compound.

15. Install the thrust washers and crankshaft oil seal. The oil seal must rest squarely on the bottom of its recess in the crankcase. The thrust washers at the flywheel end of the crankshaft are shims used to set the crankshaft end-play.

16. Spread a thin film of sealing compound on the crankcase joining faces and place the two halves together. Torque the nuts in several stages. Tighten the 8 mm nut located next to the 12 mm stud of the No. 1 crankshaft bearing first. As the crankcase halves are being torqued, continually check the crankshaft for ease of rotation.

17. Crankshaft end-play is checked when the flywheel is installed. It is adjusted by varying the number of thickness of the shims located behind the flywheel. Measure the end-play with a dial indicator mounted against the flywheel, and attached firmly to the crankcase.

*CAMSHAFT AND TIMING GEARS*

**Removal and Installation**

Removal of the camshaft requires splitting the crankcases. The camshaft and its bearing shells are then removed from the crankcase halves. Before reinstalling the camshaft, it should be checked for wear on the lobe surfaces and on the bearing surfaces. In addition, the riveted joint between the camshaft timing gear and the camshaft should be checked for tightness. The camshaft should be checked for a maximum run-out of 0.0008 in. The timing gear should be checked for the correct tooth contact and for wear. If the camshaft bearing shells are worn or damaged, new shells should be fitted. The camshaft bearing shells should be installed with the tabs engaging the notches in the crankcase. It is usually a good idea to replace the bearing shells under any circumstances. Before installing the camshaft, the bearing journals and cam lobes should be generously coated with oil. When the camshaft is installed, care should be taken to ensure that the timing gear tooth marked (O) is located between the two teeth of the crankshaft timing gear marked with a center punch. The camshaft end-play is measured at the No. 3 bearing. End-play is 0.0015–0.005 in. (0.04–0.12 mm) and the wear limit is 0.006 in. (0.16 mm).

Align valve timing marks as illustrated

*CRANKSHAFT*

**Crankshaft Pulley,
Removal and Installation**

On the Type 1 and 2, the crankshaft pulley can be removed while the engine is still in the car. However, in this instance it is necessary for the rear cover plate of the engine to be removed. Remove the cover plate after taking out the screws in the cover plate below the crankshaft pulley. Remove the fan belt and the crankshaft pulley securing screw. Using a puller, remove the crankshaft pulley. The crankshaft pulley should be checked for proper seating and belt contact. The oil return thread should be cleaned and lubricated with oil. The crankshaft pulley should be installed in the reverse sequence. Check for oil leaks after installing the pulley.

On the Type 3, the crankshaft pulley can be removed only when the engine is out of the car and the muffler, generator, and cooling air intake housing are removed. After these parts have been removed, take out the plastic cap in the pulley. Remove the crankshaft pulley retaining bolt and remove the pulley.

Type 4 removal is the same as the Type 3. However, the pulley is secured by three socket head screws and a self locking nut.

Type 2/1700 and 4 engine fan bolts

Installing for Type 3 and 4 engines is the reverse of removal. When installing, use a new paper gasket between the fan and the crankshaft pulley. If shims are used, do not forget them. Don't use more than two shims. When inserting the pulley, make sure that the pin engages the hole in the fan. Ensure that the clearance between the generator belt and the intake housing is at least 4 mm and that the belt is parallel to the housing.

## Flywheel, Removal and Installation

### TYPE 1, 2/1600, AND 3

The flywheel is attached to the crankshaft with a gland nut and is located by four dowel pins. An oil seal is recessed in the crankcase casting at No. 1 main bearing. A needle bearing, which supports the main driveshaft, is located in the gland nut. Prior to removing the flywheel, it is necessary to remove the clutch pressure plate and the clutch disc. Loosen the gland nut and remove it, using a 36 mm special wrench. Before removing the flywheel, matchmark the flywheel and the crankshaft.

Installation is the reverse of removal. Before installing the flywheel, check the flywheel teeth for any wear or damage. Check the dowel pins for correct fit in the crankshaft and in the flywheel. Adjust the crankshaft end-play and check the needle bearing in the gland nut for wear.

### TYPE 2/1700 AND 4

Removal and installation is similar to the Type 1, 2, and 3 except that the flywheel is secured to the crankshaft by five socket head screws.

## CRANKSHAFT OIL SEAL— FLYWHEEL END

### Removal and Installation

This seal is removed after removing the flywheel. After the flywheel is removed, inspect the surface on the flywheel joining flange where the seal makes contact. If there is a deep groove or any other damage, the flywheel must be replaced. Remove the oil seal by prying it out of its bore. Before installing a new seal, clean the crankcase oil seal recess and coat it thinly with a sealing compound. Be sure that the seal rests squarely on the bottom of its recess. Make sure that the correct side of the seal is facing outward, that is, the lip of the seal should be facing the inside of the crankcase. Reinstall the flywheel after coating the oil seal contact surface with oil.

NOTE: *Be careful not to damage the seal when sliding the flywheel into place.*

## CRANKSHAFT

### Removal and Installation

NOTE: *See the "Engine Rebuilding" section for crankshaft refinishing procedures.*

Removal of the crankshaft requires splitting the crankcase. After the crankcase is opened, the crankshaft can then be lifted out.

The crankshaft bearings are held in place by dowel pins. These pins must be checked for tightness.

When installing the bearings, make sure that the oil holes in the shells are properly aligned. Be sure that the bearing shells are seated properly on their dowel pins. Bearing shells are available in three undersizes. Measure the crankshaft bearing journals to determine the proper bearing size. Place one half of the No. 2 crankshaft bearing in the crankcase. Slide the No. 1 bearing on the crankshaft so that the dowel pin hole is toward the flywheel and the oil groove faces toward the fan. The No. 3 bearing is installed with the dowel pin hole facing toward the crankshaft web.

To remove the No. 3 main bearing, remove the distributor gear circlip and the distributor drive gear. Mild heat (176° F) must be applied to remove the gear. Next slide the spacer off of the crankshaft. The crankshaft timing gear should now be pressed off the crankshaft after mild heating. When the timing gear is reinstalled, the chamfer must face towards the No. 3 bearing. The No. 3 bearing can then be replaced. When removing and installing the gears on the crankshaft, be careful not to damage the No. 4 bearing journal.

When all of the crankshaft bearings are in place, lift the crankshaft and the connecting rod assembly into the crankcase and align the valve timing marks.

Install the crankcase half and reassemble the engine.

## CONNECTING RODS

### Removal and Installation

NOTE: *See the "Engine Rebuilding" section for additional information.*

After splitting the crankcase, remove the crankshaft and the connecting rod assembly. Remove the connecting rods, clamping bolts, and the connecting rod caps. Inspect the piston pin bushing. With a new bushing, the correct clearance is indicated by a light finger push fit of the pin at room temperature. Reinsert the new connecting rod bearings after all parts have been thoroughly cleaned. Assemble the con-

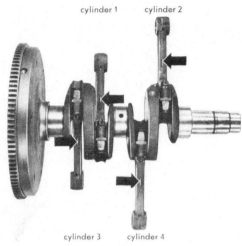

cylinder 1    cylinder 2

cylinder 3    cylinder 4

Forge marks on connecting rods must face up

Staking the connecting rod bolt

Tapping the connecting rod cap to relieve pre-tension

Measuring the connecting rod side clearance

necting rods on the crankshaft, making sure that the rods are oriented properly on the crankshaft. The identification numbers stamped on the connecting rods and connecting rod caps must be on the same side. Note that the marks on the connecting rods are pointing upward, while the rods are pointing toward their respective cylinders. Lubricate the bearing shells before installing them.

Tighten the connecting rod bolts to the specified torque. A slight pre-tension be-

tween the bearing halves, which is likely to occur when tightening the connecting rod bolts, can be eliminated by gently striking the side of the bearing cap with a hammer. Do not install the connecting rod in the engine unless it swings freely on its journal. Using a peening chisel, secure the connecting rod bolts in place.

Failure to swing freely on the journal may be caused by improper side clearance, improper bearing clearance, or failure to lubricate the rod before assembly.

## Engine Lubrication

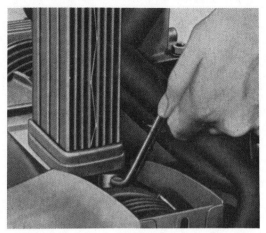

Removing oil cooler mounting nuts with a ring wrench

### OIL STRAINER

#### Removal and Installation

The oil strainer can be easily removed by removing the retaining nuts, washers, oil strainer plate, strainer, and gaskets. The Type 4 strainer is secured by a single bolt at the center of the strainer. Once taken out, the strainer must be thoroughly cleaned and all traces of old gaskets removed prior to fitting new ones. The suction pipe should be checked for tightness and proper position. When the strainer is installed, be sure that the suction pipe is correctly seated in the strainer. If necessary, the strainer may be bent slightly. The measurement from the strainer flange to the tip of the suction pipe should be 10 mm. The measurement from the flange to the bottom of the strainer should be 6 mm. The cap nuts on Types 1, 2, and 3 must not be overtightened. The Type 4 has a spin-off replaceable oil filter as well as the strainer in the crankcase. The oil filter is located at the left rear corner of the engine.

### OIL COOLER

#### Removal and Installation

The Type 1 and 2 oil cooler is located under the engine cooling fan housing at the left side of the engine. The Type 3 cooler is located at the same position but is mounted horizontally. The Type 4 cooler is mounted near the oil filter, at the left corner of the engine.

The oil cooler may be removed without taking the engine out of the car. On Types 1 and 2, the engine fan housing must be removed. On the Type 3, the cooler is accessible through the left-hand cylinder cover plate. The Type 4 cooler is accessible through the left side engine cowling, working either in the engine compartment or from underneath the car.

The oil cooler can be removed after the three retaining nuts have been taken off. The gaskets should be removed along with the cooler and replaced with new gaskets. If the cooler is leaking, check the oil pressure relief valve. The studs and bracket on the cooler should be checked for tightness.

Make certain that the hollow ribs of the cooler do not touch one another. The cooler must not be clogged with dirt. Clean the contact surfaces on the crankcase, install new gaskets, and attach the oil cooler. Type 3 and 4 have a spacer ring between the crankcase and the cooler at each securing screw. If these rings are omitted, the seals may be squeezed too tightly, resulting in oil stoppage and resultant engine damage.

Oil cooler spacers

### OIL PUMP

#### Removal and Installation

On Types 1 and 2, the pump can be removed while the engine is in the car, but it is first necessary to remove the cover plate, the crankshaft pulley, and the cover

Removing oil pump housing—Type 1, 2, 3

Disassembling Type 4 oil pump assembly

plate under the pulley. On Types 3 and 4, the oil pump can be taken out only after the engine is removed from the car and the air intake housing, the belt pulley fan housing, and fan are dismantled. On the Automatic Stick Shift models, the torque converter oil pump is driven by the engine oil pump.

On Type 1, 2, and 3 remove the nuts from the oil pump cover and then remove the cover and its gasket. Remove the gears and take out the pump with a special extractor that pulls the body out of the crankcase. Care should be taken so as not to damage the inside of the pump housing.

On Type 4 engines, remove the four pump securing nuts and, prying on either side of the pump, pry the pump assembly out of the crankcase. To disassemble the pump, the pump cover must be pressed apart.

Prior to assembly, check the oil pump body for wear, especially the gear seating surface. If the pump body is worn, the result will be loss of oil pressure. Check the driven gear shaft for tightness and, if necessary, peen it tightly into place or replace the pump housing. The gears should be checked for excessive wear, backlash, and end-play. Maximum end-play without a gasket is 1 mm (0.004 in.). The end-play can be checked using a T-square and a feeler gauge. Check the mating surfaces of the pump body and the crankcase for damage and cleanliness. Install the pump into the crankcase with a new gasket. Do not use any sealing compound. Turn the camshaft several revolutions in order to center the pump body opposite the slot in the camshaft. On Type 1, 2, and 3 the cover may now be installed. On Type 4, the pump was installed complete. Tighten the securing nuts.

Removing Type 4 oil pump assembly

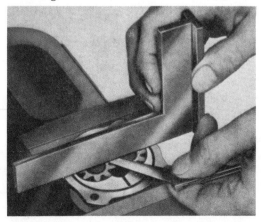

Checking oil pump end-play

## OIL PRESSURE RELIEF VALVE

### Removal and Installation

The oil pressure relief valve is removed by unscrewing the end plug and removing the gasket ring, spring, and plunger. If the plunger sticks in its bore, it can be removed by screwing a 10 mm tap into it.

On 1600 cc engines, the valve is located to the left of the oil pump. On Automatic Stick Shift models, it is located in the oil pump housing. On 1700 engines, the valve is located beside the oil filter.

Before installing the valve, check the plunger for any signs of seizure. If necessary, the plunger should be replaced. If there is any doubt about the condition of the spring, it should also be replaced. When installing the relief valve, be careful that you do not scratch the bore. Reinstall the plug with a new gasket.

Type 4 engines have a second oil pressure relief valve located just to the right of, and below the oil filler.

---

# Engine Cooling

---

## FAN HOUSING

### Removal and Installation

#### TYPE 1 AND 2/1600

1. Remove the two heater hoses and the generator strap.
2. Pull out the lead wire from the coil. Remove the distributor cap and take off the spark plug connectors.
3. Remove the retaining screws that are located on both sides of the fan housing. Remove the rear hood.
4. Remove the outer half of the generator pulley and remove the fan belt.
5. Remove the thermostat securing screw and take out the thermostat.
6. Remove the lower part of the carburetor pre-heater duct.
7. The fan housing can now be removed with the generator. After removal, check the fan housing for damage and for loose air deflector plates.
8. Installation is the reverse of the above.
9. Make sure that the thermostat connecting rod is inserted into its hole in the cylinder head. The fan housing should be fitted properly on the cylinder cover plates so that there is no loss of cooling air.

## FAN HOUSING AND FAN

### Removal and Installation

#### TYPE 3

1. Remove the crankshaft pulley, the rear fan housing half, and the fan.
2. Unhook the linkage and spring at the right-hand air control flap.
3. Remove the screws for the front half of the housing and remove the housing.
4. Install the front half and ensure the correct sealing of the cylinder cover plates.
5. Replace and tighten the two lower mounting screws slightly.
6. Turn the two halves of the fan housing to the left until the left crankcase half is contacted by the front lug.
7. Fully tighten the two lower mounting screws.
8. Loosen the nuts at the breather support until it can be moved.
9. Insert and tighten the mounting screws of the upper fan housing half. Tighten the breather support nuts fully.
10. Connect the linkage and spring to the right-hand air control flap.
11. Install the fan and the rear half of the fan housing.

Type 3 fan housing nuts

#### TYPE 4

1. Remove the engine. Remove the fan belt.
2. Remove the allen head screws and re-

move the belt pulley and fan as an assembly.

NOTE: *It is not necessary to remove the alternator to remove the fan housing.*

3. Remove the spacer and the alternator cover plate.

4. Disconnect the cooling air regulating cable at the shaft.

5. Remove the nuts and remove both halves of the fan housing at the same time.

6. Installation is the reverse of the above.

### FAN

#### Removal and Installation

##### TYPE 1 AND 2/1600

1. Remove the generator and fan assembly as described in the "Generator Removal and Installation" section.

2. While holding the fan, unscrew the fan retaining nut and take off the fan, spacer washers, and the hub.

3. To install, place the hub on the generator shaft, making sure that the woodruff key is securely positioned.

4. Insert the spacer washers. The clearance between the fan and the fan cover is 0.06–0.07 in. Place the fan into position and tighten its retaining nut. Correct the spacing by inserting the proper number of spacer washers. Place any extra washers between the lockwasher and the fan.

5. Reinstall the generator and the fan assembly.

### AIR FLAPS AND THERMOSTAT

#### Adjustment

##### TYPE 1 AND 2

1. Loosen the thermostat bracket securing nut and disconnect the thermostat from the bracket.

2. Push the thermostat upwards to fully open the air flaps.

3. Reposition the thermostat bracket so that the thermostat contacts the bracket at the upper stop, and then tighten the bracket nut.

4. Reconnect the thermostat to the bracket.

Engine cooling air thermostat

##### TYPE 3

1. Loosen the clamp screw on the relay lever.

2. Place the air flaps in the closed position. Make sure that the flaps close evenly. To adjust a flap, loosen its securing screw and turn it on its shaft.

3. With the flaps closed, tighten the clamp screw on the relay lever.

##### TYPE 4

1. Loosen the cable control.
2. Push the air flaps completely closed.
3. Tighten the cable control.

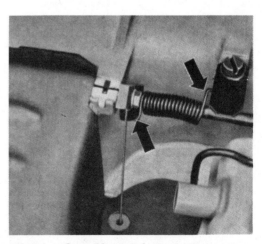

Type 4 air flap cable control

# Engine Rebuilding

This section describes, in detail, the procedures involved in rebuilding a typical engine. The procedures specifically refer to an inline engine, however, they are basically identical to those used in rebuilding engines of nearly all design and configurations. Procedures for servicing atypical engines (i.e., horizontally opposed) are described in the appropriate section, although in most cases, cylinder head reconditioning procedures described in this chapter will apply.

The section is divided into two sections. The first, Cylinder Head Reconditioning, assumes that the cylinder head is removed from the engine, all manifolds are removed, and the cylinder head is on a workbench. The camshaft should be removed from overhead cam cylinder heads. The second section, Cylinder Block Reconditioning, covers the block, pistons, connecting rods and crankshaft. It is assumed that the engine is mounted on a work stand, and the cylinder head and all accessories are removed.

Procedures are identified as follows:

*Unmarked*—Basic procedures that must be performed in order to successfully complete the rebuilding process.

*Starred* (*)—Procedures that should be performed to ensure maximum performance and engine life.

*Double starred* (**)—Procedures that may be performed to increase engine performance and reliability. These procedures are usually reserved for extremely heavy-duty or competition usage.

In many cases, a choice of methods is also provided. Methods are identified in the same manner as procedures. The choice of method for a procedure is at the discretion of the user.

The tools required for the basic rebuilding procedure should, with minor exceptions, be those

## TORQUE (ft. lbs.)*

### U.S.

| Bolt Diameter (inches) | Bolt Grade (SAE) | | | | Wrench Size (inches) | |
|---|---|---|---|---|---|---|
| | 1 and 2 | 5 | 6 | 8 | Bolt | Nut |
| 1/4 | 5 | 7 | 10 | 10.5 | 3/8 | 7/16 |
| 5/16 | 9 | 14 | 19 | 22 | 1/2 | 9/16 |
| 3/8 | 15 | 25 | 34 | 37 | 9/16 | 5/8 |
| 7/16 | 24 | 40 | 55 | 60 | 5/8 | 3/4 |
| 1/2 | 37 | 60 | 85 | 92 | 3/4 | 13/16 |
| 9/16 | 53 | 88 | 120 | 132 | 7/8 | 7/8 |
| 5/8 | 74 | 120 | 167 | 180 | 15/16 | 1 |
| 3/4 | 120 | 200 | 280 | 296 | 1-1/8 | 1-1/8 |
| 7/8 | 190 | 302 | 440 | 473 | 1-5/16 | 1-5/16 |
| 1 | 282 | 466 | 660 | 714 | 1-1/2 | 1-1/2 |

### Metric

| Bolt Diameter (mm) | Bolt Grade | | | | Wrench Size (mm) |
|---|---|---|---|---|---|
| | 5D | 8G | 10K | 12K | Bolt and Nut |
| 6 | 5 | 6 | 8 | 10 | 10 |
| 8 | 10 | 16 | 22 | 27 | 14 |
| 10 | 19 | 31 | 40 | 49 | 17 |
| 12 | 34 | 54 | 70 | 86 | 19 |
| 14 | 55 | 89 | 117 | 137 | 22 |
| 16 | 83 | 132 | 175 | 208 | 24 |
| 18 | 111 | 182 | 236 | 283 | 27 |
| 22 | 182 | 284 | 394 | 464 | 32 |
| 24 | 261 | 419 | 570 | 689 | 36 |

*—Torque values are for lightly oiled bolts. CAUTION: Bolts threaded into aluminum require much less torque.

**General Torque Specifications**

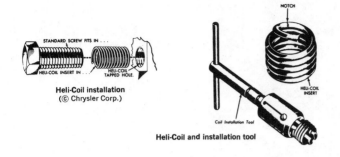

**Heli-Coil installation**
(© Chrysler Corp.)

**Heli-Coil and installation tool**

| Heli-Coil Insert | | | Drill | Tap | Insert. Tool | Extract- ing Tool |
|---|---|---|---|---|---|---|
| Thread Size | Part No. | Insert Length (In.) | Size | Part No. | Part No. | Part No. |
| 1/2 -20 | 1185-4 | 3/8 | 17/64 (.266) | 4 CPB | 528-4N | 1227-6 |
| 5/16-18 | 1185-5 | 15/32 | Q (.332) | 5 CPB | 528-5N | 1227-6 |
| 3/8 -16 | 1185-6 | 9/16 | X (.397) | 6 CPB | 528-6N | 1227-6 |
| 7/16-14 | 1185-7 | 21/32 | 29/64 (.453) | 7 CPB | 528-7N | 1227-16 |
| 1/2 -13 | 1185-8 | 3/4 | 33/64 (.516) | 8 CPB | 528-8N | 1227-16 |

**Heli-Coil Specifications**

included in a mechanic's tool kit. An accurate torque wrench, and a dial indicator (reading in thousandths) mounted on a universal base should be available. Bolts and nuts with no torque specification should be tightened according to size (see chart). Special tools, where required, all are readily available from the major tool suppliers (i.e., Craftsman, Snap-On, K-D). The services of a competent automotive machine shop must also be readily available.

When assembling the engine, any parts that will be in frictional contact must be pre-lubricated, to provide protection on initial start-up. Vortex Pre-Lube, STP, or any product specifically formulated for this purpose may be used. NOTE: *Do not use engine oil.* Where semi-permanent (locked but removable) installation of bolts or nuts is desired, threads should be cleaned and coated with Loctite. Studs may be permanently installed using Loctite Stud and Bearing Mount.

Aluminum has become increasingly popular for use in engines, due to its low weight and excellent heat transfer characteristics. The following precautions

must be observed when handling aluminum engine parts:

—Never hot-tank aluminum parts.

—Remove all aluminum parts (identification tags, etc.) from engine parts before hot-tanking (otherwise they will be removed during the process).

—Always coat threads lightly with engine oil or anti-seize compounds before installation, to prevent seizure.

—Never over-torque bolts or spark plugs in aluminum threads. Should stripping occur, threads can be restored according to the following procedure, using Heli-Coil thread inserts:

Tap drill the hole with the stripped threads to the specified size (see chart). Using the specified tap (NOTE: *Heli-Coil tap sizes refer to the size thread being replaced, rather than the actual tap size*), tap the hole for the Heli-Coil. Place the insert on the proper installation tool (see chart). Apply pressure on the insert while winding it clockwise into the hole, until the top of the insert is one turn below the surface. Remove the installation tool, and break the installation tang from the bottom of the in-

sert by moving it up and down. If the Heli-Coil must be removed, tap the removal tool firmly into the hole, so that it engages the top thread, and turn the tool counter-clockwise to extract the insert.

Snapped bolts or studs may be removed, using a stud extractor (unthreaded) or Vise-Grip pliers (threaded). Penetrating oil (e.g., Liquid Wrench) will often aid in breaking frozen threads. In cases where the stud or bolt is flush with, or below the surface, proceed as follows:

Drill a hole in the broken stud or bolt, approximately ½ its diameter. Select a screw extractor (e.g., Easy-Out) of the proper size, and tap it into the stud or bolt. Turn the extractor counter-clockwise to remove the stud or bolt.

Magnaflux and Zyglo are inspection techniques used to locate material flaws, such as stress cracks. Magnafluxing coats the part with fine magnetic particles, and subjects the part to a magnetic field. Cracks cause breaks

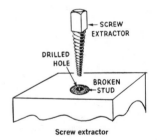

**Screw extractor**

in the magnetic field, which are outlined by the particles. Since Magnaflux is a magnetic process, it is applicable only to ferrous materials. The Zyglo process coats the material with a fluorescent dye penetrant, and then subjects it to blacklight inspection, under which cracks glow bright-

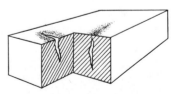

**Magnaflux indication of cracks**

ly. Parts made of any material may be tested using Zyglo. While Magnaflux and Zyglo are excellent for general inspection, and locating hidden defects, specific checks of suspected cracks may be made at lower cost and more readily using spot check dye. The dye is sprayed onto the suspected area, wiped off, and the area is then sprayed with a developer. Cracks then will show up brightly. Spot check dyes will only indicate surface cracks; therefore, structural cracks below the surface may escape detection. When questionable, the part should be tested using Magnaflux or Zyglo.

## CYLINDER HEAD RECONDITIONING

| Procedure | Method |
| --- | --- |
| Identify the valves:  **Valve identification** (© SAAB) | Invert the cylinder head, and number the valve faces front to rear, using a permanent felt-tip marker. |
| Remove the rocker arms: | Remove the rocker arms with shaft(s) or balls and nuts. Wire the sets of rockers, balls and nuts together, and identify according to the corresponding valve. |
| Remove the valves and springs: | Using an appropriate valve spring compressor (depending on the configuration of the cylinder head), compress the valve springs. Lift out the keepers with needlenose pliers, release the compressor, and remove the valve, spring, and spring retainer. |
| Check the valve stem-to-guide clearance: 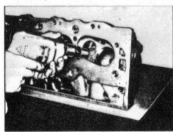 **Checking the valve stem-to-guide clearance** (© American Motors Corp.) | Clean the valve stem with lacquer thinner or a similar solvent to remove all gum and varnish. Clean the valve guides using solvent and an expanding wire-type valve guide cleaner. Mount a dial indicator so that the stem is at 90° to the valve stem, as close to the valve guide as possible. Move the valve off its seat, and measure the valve guide-to-stem clearance by moving the stem back and forth to actuate the dial indicator. Measure the valve stems using a micrometer, and compare to specifications, to determine whether stem or guide wear is responsible for excessive clearance. |
| De-carbon the cylinder head and valves: **Removing carbon from the cylinder head** (© Chevrolet Div. G.M. Corp.) | Chip carbon away from the valve heads, combustion chambers, and ports, using a chisel made of hardwood. Remove the remaining deposits with a stiff wire brush. NOTE: *Ensure that the deposits are actually removed, rather than burnished.* |

| Procedure | Method |
|---|---|
| Hot-tank the cylinder head: | Have the cylinder head hot-tanked to remove grease, corrosion, and scale from the water passages. NOTE: *In the case of overhead cam cylinder heads, consult the operator to determine whether the camshaft bearings will be damaged by the caustic solution.* |
| Degrease the remaining cylinder head parts: | Using solvent (i.e., Gunk), clean the rockers, rocker shaft(s) (where applicable), rocker balls and nuts, springs, spring retainers, and keepers. Do not remove the protective coating from the springs. |
| Check the cylinder head for warpage:<br><br>①③CHECK DIAGONALLY<br>②CHECK ACROSS CENTER  A 2895-A<br>**Checking the cylinder head<br>for warpage**<br>(ⓒ Ford Motor Co.) | Place a straight-edge across the gasket surface of the cylinder head. Using feeler gauges, determine the clearance at the center of the straight-edge. Measure across both diagonals, along the longitudinal centerline, and across the cylinder head at several points. If warpage exceeds .003″ in a 6″ span, or .006″ over the total length, the cylinder head must be resurfaced. NOTE: *If warpage exceeds the manufacturers maximum tolerance for material removal, the cylinder head must be replaced.* When milling the cylinder heads of V-type engines, the intake manifold mounting position is altered, and must be corrected by milling the manifold flange a proportionate amount. |
| ** Porting and gasket matching:<br><br>**Marking the cylinder head for<br>gasket matching**<br>(ⓒ Petersen Publishing Co.)<br><br>**Port configuration before and after<br>gasket matching**<br>(ⓒ Petersen Publishing Co.) | ** Coat the manifold flanges of the cylinder head with Prussian blue dye. Glue intake and exhaust gaskets to the cylinder head in their installed position using rubber cement and scribe the outline of the ports on the manifold flanges. Remove the gaskets. Using a small cutter in a hand-held power tool (i.e., Dremel Moto-Tool), gradually taper the walls of the port out to the scribed outline of the gasket. Further enlargement of the ports should include the removal of sharp edges and radiusing of sharp corners. Do not alter the valve guides. NOTE: *The most efficient port configuration is determined only by extensive testing. Therefore, it is best to consult someone experienced with the head in question to determine the optimum alterations.* |

| *Procedure* | *Method* |
|---|---|

** Polish the ports:

Relieved and polished ports
(© Petersen Publishing Co.)

Polished combustion chamber
(© Petersen Publishing Co.)

** Using a grinding stone with the above mentioned tool, polish the walls of the intake and exhaust ports, and combustion chamber. Use progressively finer stones until all surface imperfections are removed. NOTE: *Through testing, it has been determined that a smooth surface is more effective than a mirror polished surface in intake ports, and vice-versa in exhaust ports.*

* Knurling the valve guides:

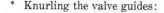

Cut-away view of a knurled valve guide
(© Petersen Publishing Co.)

* Valve guides which are not excessively worn or distorted may, in some cases, be knurled rather than replaced. Knurling is a process in which metal is displaced and raised, thereby reducing clearance. Knurling also provides excellent oil control. The possibility of knurling rather than replacing valve guides should be discussed with a machinist.

Replacing the valve guides: NOTE: *Valve guides should only be replaced if damaged or if an oversize valve stem is not available.*

A-VALVE GUIDE I.D.
B-SLIGHTLY SMALLER THAN VALVE GUIDE O.D.

Valve guide removal tool

A-VALVE GUIDE I.D.
B-LARGER THAN THE VALVE GUIDE O.D.

Valve guide installation tool (with washers used during installation)

Depending on the type of cylinder head, valve guides may be pressed, hammered, or shrunk in. In cases where the guides are shrunk into the head, replacement should be left to an equipped machine shop. In other cases, the guides are replaced as follows: Press or tap the valve guides out of the head using a stepped drift (see illustration). Determine the height above the boss that the guide must extend, and obtain a stack of washers, their I.D. similar to the guide's O.D., of that height. Place the stack of washers on the guide, and insert the guide into the boss. NOTE: *Valve guides are often tapered or beveled for installation.* Using the stepped installation tool (see illustration), press or tap the guides into position. Ream the guides according to the size of the valve stem.

| *Procedure* | *Method* |
|---|---|
| Replacing valve seat inserts: | Replacement of valve seat inserts which are worn beyond resurfacing or broken, if feasible, must be done by a machine shop. |
| Resurfacing (grinding) the valve face:  **Grinding a valve** (© Subaru) 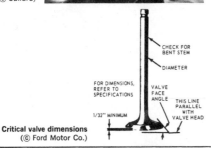 **Critical valve dimensions** (© Ford Motor Co.) | Using a valve grinder, resurface the valves according to specifications. CAUTION: *Valve face angle is not always identical to valve seat angle.* A minimum margin of 1/32″ should remain after grinding the valve. The valve stem tip should also be squared and resurfaced, by placing the stem in the V-block of the grinder, and turning it while pressing lightly against the grinding wheel. |
| Resurfacing the valve seats using reamers:  **Reaming the valve seat** (© S.p.A. Fiat)  **Valve seat width and centering** (© Ford Motor Co.) | Select a reamer of the correct seat angle, slightly larger than the diameter of the valve seat, and assemble it with a pilot of the correct size. Install the pilot into the valve guide, and using steady pressure, turn the reamer clockwise. CAUTION: *Do not turn the reamer counter-clockwise.* Remove only as much material as necessary to clean the seat. Check the concentricity of the seat (see below). If the dye method is not used, coat the valve face with Prussian blue dye, install and rotate it on the valve seat. Using the dye marked area as a centering guide, center and narrow the valve seat to specifications with correction cutters. NOTE: *When no specifications are available, minimum seat width for exhaust valves should be 5/64″, intake valves 1/16″.* After making correction cuts, check the position of the valve seat on the valve face using Prussian blue dye. |
| * Resurfacing the valve seats using a grinder:  **Grinding a valve seat** (© Subaru) | Select a pilot of the correct size, and a coarse stone of the correct seat angle. Lubricate the pilot if necessary, and install the tool in the valve guide. Move the stone on and off the seat at approximately two cycles per second, until all flaws are removed from the seat. Install a fine stone, and finish the seat. Center and narrow the seat using correction stones, as described above. |

| Procedure | Method |
|---|---|

Checking the valve seat concentricity:

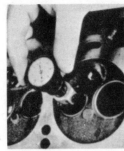

**Checking the valve seat concentricity using a dial gauge** (© American Motors Corp.)

Coat the valve face with Prussian blue dye, install the valve, and rotate it on the valve seat. If the entire seat becomes coated, and the valve is known to be concentric, the seat is concentric.

\* Install the dial gauge pilot into the guide, and rest the arm on the valve seat. Zero the gauge, and rotate the arm around the seat. Run-out should not exceed .002″.

---

\* Lapping the valves: NOTE: *Valve lapping is done to ensure efficient sealing of resurfaced valves and seats. Valve lapping alone is not recommended for use as a resurfacing procedure.*

**Hand lapping the valves**

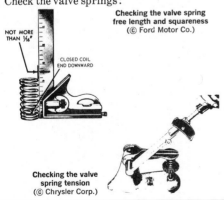

HAND DRILL

ROD

SUCTION CUP

**Home made mechanical valve lapping tool**

\* Invert the cylinder head, lightly lubricate the valve stems, and install the valves in the head as numbered. Coat valve seats with fine grinding compound, and attach the lapping tool suction cup to a valve head (NOTE: *Moisten the suction cup*). Rotate the tool between the palms, changing position and lifting the tool often to prevent grooving. Lap the valve until a smooth, polished seat is evident. Remove the valve and tool, and rinse away all traces of grinding compound.

\*\* Fasten a suction cup to a piece of drill rod, and mount the rod in a hand drill. Proceed as above, using the hand drill as a lapping tool. CAUTION: *Due to the higher speeds involved when using the hand drill, care must be exercised to avoid grooving the seat.* Lift the tool and change direction of rotation often.

---

Check the valve springs:

NOT MORE THAN 1/16″

**Checking the valve spring free length and squareness** (© Ford Motor Co.)

CLOSED COIL END DOWNWARD

**Checking the valve spring tension** (© Chrysler Corp.)

Place the spring on a flat surface next to a square. Measure the height of the spring, and rotate it against the edge of the square to measure distortion. If spring height varies (by comparison) by more than 1/16″ or if distortion exceeds 1/16″, replace the spring.

\*\* In addition to evaluating the spring as above, test the spring pressure at the installed and compressed (installed height minus valve lift) height using a valve spring tester. Springs used on small displacement engines (up to 3 liters) should be ± 1 lb. of all other springs in either position. A tolerance of ± 5 lbs. is permissible on larger engines.

| Procedure | Method |
|---|---|

\* Install valve stem seals:

**Valve stem seal installation**
(© Ford Motor Co.)     SEAL

\* Due to the pressure differential that exists at the ends of the intake valve guides (atmospheric pressure above, manifold vacuum below), oil is drawn through the valve guides into the intake port. This has been alleviated somewhat since the addition of positive crankcase ventilation, which lowers the pressure above the guides. Several types of valve stem seals are available to reduce blow-by. Certain seals simply slip over the stem and guide boss, while others require that the boss be machined. Recently, Teflon guide seals have become popular. Consult a parts supplier or machinist concerning availability and suggested usages. NOTE: *When installing seals, ensure that a small amount of oil is able to pass the seal to lubricate the valve guides; otherwise, excessive wear may result.*

Install the valves:

Lubricate the valve stems, and install the valves in the cylinder head as numbered. Lubricate and position the seals (if used, see above) and the valve springs. Install the spring retainers, compress the springs, and insert the keys using needlenose pliers or a tool designed for this purpose. NOTE: *Retain the keys with wheel bearing grease during installation.*

Checking valve spring installed height:

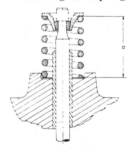

**Valve spring installed height dimension**
(© Porsche)

**Measuring valve spring installed height**
(© Petersen Publishing Co.)

Measure the distance between the spring pad and the lower edge of the spring retainer, and compare to specifications. If the installed height is incorrect, add shim washers between the spring pad and the spring. CAUTION: *Use only washers designed for this purpose.*

\*\* CC'ing the combustion chambers:

\*\* Invert the cylinder head and place a bead of sealer around a combustion chamber. Install an apparatus designed for this purpose (burette mounted on a clear plate; see illustration) over the combustion chamber, and fill with the specified fluid to an even mark on the burette. Record the burette reading, and fill the combustion chamber with fluid. (NOTE: *A hole drilled in the plate will permit air to escape*). Subtract the burette reading, with the combustion chamber filled, from the previous reading, to determine combustion chamber volume in cc's. Duplicate this procedure in all combustion

| *Procedure* | *Method* |
|---|---|

CC'ing the combustion chamber
(© Petersen Publishing Co.)

chambers on the cylinder head, and compare the readings. The volume of all combustion chambers should be made equal to that of the largest. Combustion chamber volume may be increased in two ways. When only a small change is required (usually), a small cutter or coarse stone may be used to remove material from the combustion chamber. NOTE: *Check volume frequently.* Remove material over a wide area, so as not to change the configuration of the combustion chamber. When a larger change is required, the valve seat may be sunk (lowered into the head). NOTE: *When altering valve seat, remember to compensate for the change in spring installed height.*

---

Inspect the rocker arms, balls, studs, and nuts (where applicable):

Stress cracks in rocker nuts
(© Ford Motor Co.)

Visually inspect the rocker arms, balls, studs, and nuts for cracks, galling, burning, scoring, or wear. If all parts are intact, liberally lubricate the rocker arms and balls, and install them on the cylinder head. If wear is noted on a rocker arm at the point of valve contact, grind it smooth and square, removing as little material as possible. Replace the rocker arm if excessively worn. If a rocker stud shows signs of wear, it must be replaced (see below). If a rocker nut shows stress cracks, replace it. If an exhaust ball is galled or burned, substitute the intake ball from the same cylinder (if it is intact), and install a new intake ball. NOTE: *Avoid using new rocker balls on exhaust valves.*

---

Replacing rocker studs:

Reaming the stud bore for oversize rocker studs
(© Buick Div. G.M. Corp.)

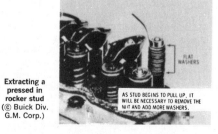

Extracting a pressed in rocker stud
(© Buick Div. G.M. Corp.)

In order to remove a threaded stud, lock two nuts on the stud, and unscrew the stud using the lower nut. Coat the lower threads of the new stud with Loctite, and install.

Two alternative methods are available for replacing pressed in studs. Remove the damaged stud using a stack of washers and a nut (see illustration). In the first, the boss is reamed .005-.006″ oversize, and an oversize stud pressed in. Control the stud extension over the boss using washers, in the same manner as valve guides. Before installing the stud, coat it with white lead and grease. To retain the stud more positively, drill a hole through the stud and boss, and install a roll pin. In the second method, the boss is tapped, and a threaded stud installed. Retain the stud using Loctite Stud and Bearing Mount.

| *Procedure* | *Method* |
|---|---|
| Inspect the rocker shaft(s) and rocker arms (where applicable): <br><br>Disassembled rocker shaft parts arranged for inspection<br>(© American Motors Corp.)<br><br>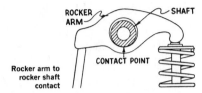<br>ROCKER ARM — SHAFT<br>CONTACT POINT<br>Rocker arm to rocker shaft contact | Remove rocker arms, springs and washers from rocker shaft. NOTE: *Lay out parts in the order they are removed.* Inspect rocker arms for pitting or wear on the valve contact point, or excessive bushing wear. Bushings need only be replaced if wear is excessive, because the rocker arm normally contacts the shaft at one point only. Grind the valve contact point of rocker arm smooth if necessary, removing as little material as possible. If excessive material must be removed to smooth and square the arm, it should be replaced. Clean out all oil holes and passages in rocker shaft. If shaft is grooved or worn, replace it. Lubricate and assemble the rocker shaft. |
| Inspect the camshaft bushings and the camshaft (overhead cam engines): | See next section. |
| Inspect the pushrods: | Remove the pushrods, and, if hollow, clean out the oil passages using fine wire. Roll each pushrod over a piece of clean glass. If a distinct clicking sound is heard as the pushrod rolls, the rod is bent, and must be replaced. |
|  | * The length of all pushrods must be equal. Measure the length of the pushrods, compare to specifications, and replace as necessary. |
| Inspect the valve lifters: 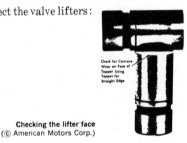<br>Check for Concave Wear on Face of Tappet Using Tappet for Straight Edge<br><br>Checking the lifter face<br>(© American Motors Corp.) | Remove lifters from their bores, and remove gum and varnish, using solvent. Clean walls of lifter bores. Check lifters for concave wear as illustrated. If face is worn concave, replace lifter, and carefully inspect the camshaft. Lightly lubricate lifter and insert it into its bore. If play is excessive, an oversize lifter must be installed (where possible). Consult a machinist concerning feasibility. If play is satisfactory, remove, lubricate, and reinstall the lifter. |
| * Testing hydraulic lifter leak down: 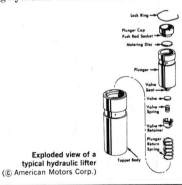<br>Lock Ring<br>Plunger Cap<br>Push Rod Socket<br>Metering Disc<br>Plunger<br>Valve Seat<br>Valve<br>Valve Spring<br>Valve Retainer<br>Plunger Return Spring<br>Tappet Body<br><br>Exploded view of a typical hydraulic lifter<br>(© American Motors Corp.) | Submerge lifter in a container of kerosene. Chuck a used pushrod or its equivalent into a drill press. Position container of kerosene so pushrod acts on the lifter plunger. Pump lifter with the drill press, until resistance increases. Pump several more times to bleed any air out of lifter. Apply very firm, constant pressure to the lifter, and observe rate at which fluid bleeds out of lifter. If the fluid bleeds very quickly (less than 15 seconds), lifter is defective. If the time exceeds 60 seconds, lifter is sticking. In either case, recondition or replace lifter. If lifter is operating properly (leak down time 15-60 seconds), lubricate and install it. |

## CYLINDER BLOCK RECONDITIONING

| *Procedure* | *Method* |
|---|---|
| Checking the main bearing clearance: | Invert engine, and remove cap from the bearing to be checked. Using a clean, dry rag, thoroughly clean all oil from crankshaft journal and bearing insert. NOTE: *Plastigage is soluble in oil; therefore, oil on the journal or bearing could result in erroneous readings.* Place a piece of Plastigage along the full length of journal, reinstall cap, and torque to specifications. Remove bearing cap, and determine bearing clearance by comparing width of Plastigage to the scale on Plastigage envelope. Journal taper is determined by comparing width of the Plastigage strip near its ends. Rotate crankshaft 90° and retest, to determine journal eccentricity. NOTE: *Do not rotate crankshaft with Plastigage installed.* If bearing insert and journal appear intact, and are within tolerances, no further main bearing service is required. If bearing or journal appear defective, cause of failure should be determined before replacement. |

Plastigage installed on main bearing journal
(© Chevrolet Div. G.M. Corp.)

Measuring Plastigage to determine
main bearing clearance
(© Chevrolet Div. G.M. Corp.)

Causes of bearing failure
(© Ford Motor Co.)

\* Remove crankshaft from block (see below). Measure the main bearing journals at each end twice (90° apart) using a micrometer, to determine diameter, journal taper and eccentricity. If journals are within tolerances, reinstall bearing caps at their specified torque. Using a telescope gauge and micrometer, measure bearing I.D. parallel to piston axis and at 30° on each side of piston axis. Subtract journal O.D. from bearing I.D. to determine oil clearance. If crankshaft journals appear defective, or do not meet tolerances, there is no need to measure bearings; for the crankshaft will require grinding and/or undersize bearings will be required. If bearing appears defective, cause for failure should be determined prior to replacement.

| Checking the connecting rod bearing clearance: | Connecting rod bearing clearance is checked in the same manner as main bearing clearance, using Plastigage. Before removing the crankshaft, connecting rod side clearance also should be measured and recorded. |
|---|---|

Plastigage installed on connecting rod
bearing journal
(© Chevrolet Div. G.M. Corp.)

\* Checking connecting rod bearing clearance, using a micrometer, is identical to checking main bearing clearance. If no other service

| Procedure | Method |
|---|---|

**Measuring Plastigage to determine
connecting rod bearing clearance**
(© Chevrolet Div. G.M. Corp.)

is required, the piston and rod assemblies need not be removed.

Removing the crankshaft:

**Connecting rod matching marks**
(© Ford Motor Co.)

Using a punch, mark the corresponding main bearing caps and saddles according to position (i.e., one punch on the front main cap and saddle, two on the second, three on the third, etc.). Using number stamps, identify the corresponding connecting rods and caps, according to cylinder (if no numbers are present). Remove the main and connecting rod caps, and place sleeves of plastic tubing over the connecting rod bolts, to protect the journals as the crankshaft is removed. Lift the crankshaft out of the block.

Remove the ridge from the top of the cylinder:

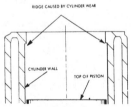

RIDGE CAUSED BY CYLINDER WEAR

CYLINDER WALL    TOP OF PISTON

**Cylinder bore ridge**
(© Pontiac Div. G.M. Corp.)

In order to facilitate removal of the piston and connecting rod, the ridge at the top of the cylinder (unworn area; see illustration) must be removed. Place the piston at the bottom of the bore, and cover it with a rag. Cut the ridge away using a ridge reamer, exercising extreme care to avoid cutting too deeply. Remove the rag, and remove cuttings that remain on the piston. CAUTION: *If the ridge is not removed, and new rings are installed, damage to rings will result.*

Removing the piston and connecting rod:

**Removing the piston**
(© SAAB)

Invert the engine, and push the pistons and connecting rods out of the cylinders. If necessary, tap the connecting rod boss with a wooden hammer handle, to force the piston out. CAUTION: *Do not attempt to force the piston past the cylinder ridge* (see above).

| Procedure | Method |
|---|---|
| Service the crankshaft: | Ensure that all oil holes and passages in the crankshaft are open and free of sludge. If necessary, have the crankshaft ground to the largest possible undersize. |
| | ** Have the crankshaft Magnafluxed, to locate stress cracks. Consult a machinist concerning additional service procedures, such as surface hardening (e.g., nitriding, Tuftriding) to improve wear characteristics, cross drilling and chamfering the oil holes to improve lubrication, and balancing. |
| Removing freeze plugs: | Drill a hole in the center of the freeze plugs, and pry them out using a screwdriver or drift. |
| Remove the oil gallery plugs: | Threaded plugs should be removed using an appropriate (usually square) wrench. To remove soft, pressed in plugs, drill a hole in the plug, and thread in a sheet metal screw. Pull the plug out by the screw using pliers. |
| Hot-tank the block: | Have the block hot-tanked to remove grease, corrosion, and scale from the water jackets. NOTE: *Consult the operator to determine whether the camshaft bearings will be damaged during the hot-tank process.* |
| Check the block for cracks: | Visually inspect the block for cracks or chips. The most common locations are as follows: Adjacent to freeze plugs. Between the cylinders and water jackets. Adjacent to the main bearing saddles. At the extreme bottom of the cylinders. Check only suspected cracks using spot check dye (see introduction). If a crack is located, consult a machinist concerning possible repairs. |
| | ** Magnaflux the block to locate hidden cracks. If cracks are located, consult a machinist about feasibility of repair. |
| Install the oil gallery plugs and freeze plugs: | Coat freeze plugs with sealer and tap into position using a piece of pipe, slightly smaller than the plug, as a driver. To ensure retention, stake the edges of the plugs. Coat threaded oil gallery plugs with sealer and install. Drive replacement soft plugs into block using a large drift as a driver. |
| | * Rather than reinstalling lead plugs, drill and tap the holes, and install threaded plugs. |

| *Procedure* | *Method* |
|---|---|

Check the bore diameter and surface:

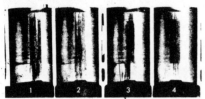

1, 2, 3 Piston skirt seizure resulted in this pattern. Engine must be rebored
4. Piston skirt and oil ring seizure caused this damage. Engine must be rebored

5, 6 Score marks caused by a split piston skirt. Damage is not serious enough to warrant reboring
7. Ring seized longitudinally, causing a score mark 1 3/16" wide, on the land side of the piston groove. The honing pattern is destroyed and the cylinder must be rebored

8. Result of oil ring seizure. Engine must be rebored
9. Oil ring seizure here was not serious enough to warrant reboring. The honing marks are still visible

**Cylinder wall damage**
(© Daimler-Benz A.G.)

Visually inspect the cylinder bores for roughness, scoring, or scuffing. If evident, the cylinder bore must be bored or honed oversize to eliminate imperfections, and the smallest possible oversize piston used. The new pistons should be given to the machinist with the block, so that the cylinders can be bored or honed exactly to the piston size (plus clearance). If no flaws are evident, measure the bore diameter using a telescope gauge and micrometer, or dial gauge, parallel and perpendicular to the engine centerline, at the top (below the ridge) and bottom of the bore. Subtract the bottom measurements from the top to determine taper, and the parallel to the centerline measurements from the perpendicular measurements to determine eccentricity. If the measurements are not within specifications, the cylinder must be bored or honed, and an oversize piston installed. If the measurements are within specifications the cylinder may be used as is, with only finish honing (see below). NOTE: *Prior to submitting the block for boring, perform the following operation(s).*

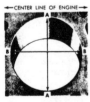

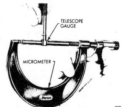

Cylinder bore measuring positions
(© Ford Motor Co.)

Measuring the cylinder bore with a telescope gauge
(© Buick Div. G.M. Corp.)

Determining the cylinder bore by measuring the telescope gauge with a micrometer
(© Buick Div. G.M. Corp.)

Measuring the cylinder bore with a dial gauge
(© Chevrolet Div. G.M. Corp.)

| Procedure | Method |
|---|---|
| Check the block deck for warpage: | Using a straightedge and feeler gauges, check the block deck for warpage in the same manner that the cylinder head is checked (see Cylinder Head Reconditioning). If warpage exceeds specifications, have the deck resurfaced. NOTE: *In certain cases a specification for total material removal (Cylinder head and block deck) is provided. This specification must not be exceeded.* |
| * Check the deck height: | The deck height is the distance from the crankshaft centerline to the block deck. To measure, invert the engine, and install the crankshaft, retaining it with the center main cap. Measure the distance from the crankshaft journal to the block deck, parallel to the cylinder centerline. Measure the diameter of the end (front and rear) main journals, parallel to the centerline of the cylinders, divide the diameter in half, and subtract it from the previous measurement. The results of the front and rear measurements should be identical. If the difference exceeds .005", the deck height should be corrected. NOTE: *Block deck height and warpage should be corrected concurrently.* |
| Check the cylinder block bearing alignment:  Checking main bearing saddle alignment (© Petersen Publishing Co.) | Remove the upper bearing inserts. Place a straightedge in the bearing saddles along the centerline of the crankshaft. If clearance exists between the straightedge and the center saddle, the block must be align-bored. |
| Clean and inspect the pistons and connecting rods: 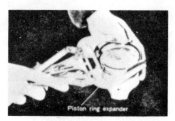 Removing the piston rings (© Subaru) | Using a ring expander, remove the rings from the piston. Remove the retaining rings (if so equipped) and remove piston pin. NOTE: *If the piston pin must be pressed out, determine the proper method and use the proper tools; otherwise the piston will distort.* Clean the ring grooves using an appropriate tool, exercising care to avoid cutting too deeply. Thoroughly clean all carbon and varnish from the piston with solvent. CAUTION: *Do not use a wire brush or caustic solvent on pistons.* Inspect the pistons for scuffing, scoring, cracks, pitting, or excessive ring groove wear. If wear is evident, the piston must be replaced. Check the connecting rod length by measuring the rod from the inside of the large end to the inside of the small end using calipers (see |

| Procedure | Method |
|---|---|

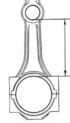

Cleaning the piston ring grooves
(© Ford Motor Co.)

Connecting rod
length checking
dimension

illustration). All connecting rods should be equal length. Replace any rod that differs from the others in the engine.

\* Have the connecting rod alignment checked in an alignment fixture by a machinist. Replace any twisted or bent rods.

\* Magnaflux the connecting rods to locate stress cracks. If cracks are found, replace the connecting rod.

---

Fit the pistons to the cylinders:

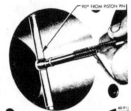

Measuring the cylinder
with a telescope gauge
for piston fitting
(© Buick Div.
G.M. Corp.)

Measuring the piston
for fitting
(© Buick Div.
G.M. Corp.)

Using a telescope gauge and micrometer, or a dial gauge, measure the cylinder bore diameter perpendicular to the piston pin, $2\frac{1}{2}''$ below the deck. Measure the piston perpendicular to its pin on the skirt. The difference between the two measurements is the piston clearance. If the clearance is within specifications or slightly below (after boring or honing), finish honing is all that is required. If the clearance is excessive, try to obtain a slightly larger piston to bring clearance within specifications. Where this is not possible, obtain the first oversize piston, and hone (or if necessary, bore) the cylinder to size.

---

Assemble the pistons and connecting rods:

Installing piston pin lock rings
(© Nissan Motor Co., Ltd.)

Inspect piston pin, connecting rod small end bushing, and piston bore for galling, scoring, or excessive wear. If evident, replace defective part(s). Measure the I.D. of the piston boss and connecting rod small end, and the O.D. of the piston pin. If within specifications, assemble piston pin and rod. CAUTION: *If piston pin must be pressed in, determine the proper method and use the proper tools; otherwise the piston will distort.* Install the lock rings; ensure that they seat properly. If the parts are not within specifications, determine the service method for the type of engine. In some cases, piston and pin are serviced as an assembly when either is defective. Others specify reaming the piston and connecting rods for an oversize pin. If the connecting rod bushing is worn, it may in many cases be replaced. Reaming the piston and replacing the rod bushing are machine shop operations.

| *Procedure* | *Method* |
|---|---|

Clean and inspect the camshaft:

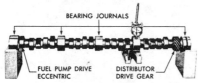

BEARING JOURNALS

FUEL PUMP DRIVE ECCENTRIC    DISTRIBUTOR DRIVE GEAR

**Checking the camshaft for straightness**
(© Chevrolet Motor Div. G.M. Corp.)

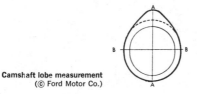

**Camshaft lobe measurement**
(© Ford Motor Co.)

Degrease the camshaft, using solvent, and clean out all oil holes. Visually inspect cam lobes and bearing journals for excessive wear. If a lobe is questionable, check all lobes as indicated below. If a journal or lobe is worn, the camshaft must be reground or replaced. NOTE: *If a journal is worn, there is a good chance that the bushings are worn.* If lobes and journals appear intact, place the front and rear journals in V-blocks, and rest a dial indicator on the center journal. Rotate the camshaft to check straightness. If deviation exceeds .001", replace the camshaft.

\* Check the camshaft lobes with a micrometer, by measuring the lobes from the nose to base and again at 90° (see illustration). The lift is determined by subtracting the second measurement from the first. If all exhaust lobes and all intake lobes are not identical, the camshaft must be reground or replaced.

Replace the camshaft bearings:

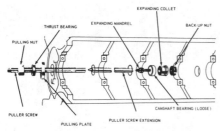

EXPANDING COLLET

THRUST BEARING    EXPANDING MANDREL    BACK-UP NUT

PULLING NUT

PULLER SCREW

PULLING PLATE    PULLER SCREW EXTENSION

CAMSHAFT BEARING (LOOSE)

**Camshaft removal and installation tool (typical)**
(© Ford Motor Co.)

If excessive wear is indicated, or if the engine is being completely rebuilt, camshaft bearings should be replaced as follows: Drive the camshaft rear plug from the block. Assemble the removal puller with its shoulder on the bearing to be removed. Gradually tighten the puller nut until bearing is removed. Remove remaining bearings, leaving the front and rear for last. To remove front and rear bearings, reverse position of the tool, so as to pull the bearings in toward the center of the block. Leave the tool in this position, pilot the new front and rear bearings on the installer, and pull them into position. Return the tool to its original position and pull remaining bearings into position. NOTE: *Ensure that oil holes align when installing bearings.* Replace camshaft rear plug, and stake it into position to aid retention.

Finish hone the cylinders:

CROSS-HATCH PATTERN

**Finish honed cylinder**
(© Chrysler Corp.)

Chuck a flexible drive hone into a power drill, and insert it into the cylinder. Start the hone, and move it up and down in the cylinder at a rate which will produce approximately a 60° cross-hatch pattern (see illustration). NOTE: *Do not extend the hone below the cylinder bore.* After developing the pattern, remove the hone and recheck piston fit. Wash the cylinders with a detergent and water solution to remove abrasive dust, dry, and wipe several times with a rag soaked in engine oil.

| *Procedure* | *Method* |
|---|---|
| Check piston ring end-gap:<br><br>**Checking ring end-gap**<br>(© Chevrolet Motor Div. G.M. Corp.) | Compress the piston rings to be used in a cylinder, one at a time, into that cylinder, and press them approximately 1″ below the deck with an inverted piston. Using feeler gauges, measure the ring end-gap, and compare to specifications. Pull the ring out of the cylinder and file the ends with a fine file to obtain proper clearance. CAUTION: *If inadequate ring end-gap is utilized, ring breakage will result.* |
| Install the piston rings:<br>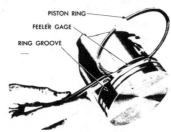<br>**Checking ring side clearance**<br>(© Chrysler Corp.)<br>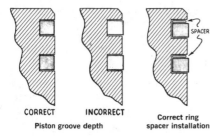<br>CORRECT     INCORRECT     Correct ring spacer installation<br>Piston groove depth | Inspect the ring grooves in the piston for excessive wear or taper. If necessary, recut the groove(s) for use with an overwidth ring or a standard ring and spacer. If the groove is worn uniformly, overwidth rings, or standard rings and spacers may be installed without recutting. Roll the outside of the ring around the groove to check for burrs or deposits. If any are found, remove with a fine file. Hold the ring in the groove, and measure side clearance. If necessary, correct as indicated above. NOTE: *Always install any additional spacers above the piston ring.* The ring groove must be deep enough to allow the ring to seat below the lands (see illustration). In many cases, a "go-no-go" depth gauge will be provided with the piston rings. Shallow grooves may be corrected by recutting, while deep grooves require some type of filler or expander behind the piston. Consult the piston ring supplier concerning the suggested method. Install the rings on the piston, lowest ring first, using a ring expander. NOTE: *Position the ring markings as specified by the manufacturer (see car section).* |
| Install the camshaft: | Liberally lubricate the camshaft lobes and journals, and slide the camshaft into the block. CAUTION: *Exercise extreme care to avoid damaging the bearings when inserting the camshaft.* Install and tighten the camshaft thrust plate retaining bolts. |
| Check camshaft end-play:<br><br>**Checking camshaft end-play with a feeler gauge**<br>(© Ford Motor Co.) | Using feeler gauges, determine whether the clearance between the camshaft boss (or gear) and backing plate is within specifications. Install shims behind the thrust plate, or reposition the camshaft gear and retest end-play. |

| *Procedure* | *Method* |
|---|---|

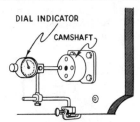

DIAL INDICATOR

CAMSHAFT

**Checking camshaft end-play with a dial indicator**

\* Mount a dial indicator stand so that the stem of the dial indicator rests on the nose of the camshaft, parallel to the camshaft axis. Push the camshaft as far in as possible and zero the gauge. Move the camshaft outward to determine the amount of camshaft end-play. If the end-play is not within tolerance, install shims behind the thrust plate, or reposition the camshaft gear and retest.

---

Install the rear main seal (where applicable):

**Seating the rear main seal**
(© Buick Div. G.M. Corp.)

Position the block with the bearing saddles facing upward. Lay the rear main seal in its groove and press it lightly into its seat. Place a piece of pipe the same diameter as the crankshaft journal into the saddle, and firmly seat the seal. Hold the pipe in position, and trim the ends of the seal flush if required.

---

Install the crankshaft:

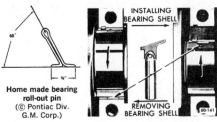

**Home made bearing roll-out pin**
(© Pontiac Div. G.M. Corp.)

INSTALLING BEARING SHELL

REMOVING BEARING SHELL

**Removal and installation of upper bearing insert using a roll-out pin**
(© Buick Div. G.M. Corp.)

Thoroughly clean the main bearing saddles and caps. Place the upper halves of the bearing inserts on the saddles and press into position. NOTE: *Ensure that the oil holes align.* Press the corresponding bearing inserts into the main bearing caps. Lubricate the upper main bearings, and lay the crankshaft in position. Place a strip of Plastigage on each of the crankshaft journals, install the main caps, and torque to specifications. Remove the main caps, and compare the Plastigage to the scale on the Plastigage envelope. If clearances are within tolerances, remove the Plastigage, turn the crankshaft 90°, wipe off all oil and retest. If all clearances are correct, remove all Plastigage, thoroughly

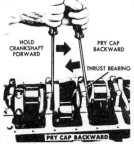
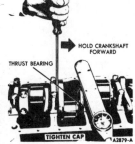

PRY FORWARD

THRUST BEARING

PRY CRANKSHAFT FORWARD

HOLD CRANKSHAFT FORWARD

PRY CAP BACKWARD

THRUST BEARING

PRY CAP BACKWARD

THRUST BEARING

HOLD CRANKSHAFT FORWARD

TIGHTEN CAP

**Aligning the thrust bearing**
(© Ford Motor Co.)

| Procedure | Method |
|---|---|
| | lubricate the main caps and bearing journals, and install the main caps. If clearances are not within tolerance, the upper bearing inserts may be removed, without removing the crankshaft, using a bearing roll out pin (see illustration). Roll in a bearing that will provide proper clearance, and retest. Torque all main caps, excluding the thrust bearing cap, to specifications. Tighten the thrust bearing cap finger tight. To properly align the thrust bearing, pry the crankshaft the extent of its axial travel several times, the last movement held toward the front of the engine, and torque the thrust bearing cap to specifications. Determine the crankshaft end-play (see below), and bring within tolerance with thrust washers. |
| Measure crankshaft end-play:<br><br>**Checking crankshaft end-play with a dial indicator**<br>(© Ford Motor Co.)<br><br>**Checking crankshaft end-play with a feeler gauge**<br>(© Chevrolet Div. (G.M. Corp.)) | Mount a dial indicator stand on the front of the block, with the dial indicator stem resting on the nose of the crankshaft, parallel to the crankshaft axis. Pry the crankshaft the extent of its travel rearward, and zero the indicator. Pry the crankshaft forward and record crankshaft end-play. NOTE: *Crankshaft end-play also may be measured at the thrust bearing, using feeler gauges* (see illustration). |
| Install the pistons: | Press the upper connecting rod bearing halves into the connecting rods, and the lower halves into the connecting rod caps. Position the piston ring gaps according to specifications (see car section), and lubricate the pistons. Install a ring compresser on a piston, and press two long (8″) pieces of plastic tubing over the rod bolts. Using the plastic tubes as a guide, press the pistons into the bores and onto the crankshaft with a wooden hammer handle. After seating the rod on the crankshaft journal, remove the tubes and install the cap finger tight. Install the remaining pistons in the same man- |

| *Procedure* | *Method* |
|---|---|

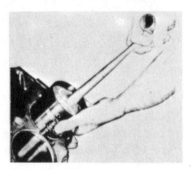

Tubing used as guide when installing
a piston
(© Oldsmobile Div. G.M. Corp.)

ner. Invert the engine and check the bearing clearance at two points (90° apart) on each journal with Plastigage. NOTE: *Do not turn the crankshaft with Plastigage installed.* If clearance is within tolerances, remove *all* Plastigage, thoroughly lubricate the journals, and torque the rod caps to specifications. If clearance is not within specifications, install different thickness bearing inserts and recheck. CAUTION: *Never shim or file the connecting rods or caps.* Always install plastic tube sleeves over the rod bolts when the caps are not installed, to protect the crankshaft journals.

Installing a piston
(© Chevrolet Div. G.M. Corp.)

Check connecting rod side clearance:

Checking connecting rod side clearance
(© Chevrolet Div. G.M. Corp.)

Determine the clearance between the sides of the connecting rods and the crankshaft, using feeler gauges. If clearance is below the minimum tolerance, the rod may be machined to provide adequate clearance. If clearance is excessive, substitute an unworn rod, and recheck. If clearance is still outside specifications, the crankshaft must be welded and reground, or replaced.

Inspect the timing chain:

Visually inspect the timing chain for broken or loose links, and replace the chain if any are found. If the chain will flex sideways, it must be replaced. Install the timing chain as specified. NOTE: *If the original timing chain is to be reused, install it in its original position.*

| Procedure | Method |
|---|---|
| Check timing gear backlash and runout:<br><br><br><br>**Checking camshaft gear backlash**<br>(© Chevrolet Div. G.M. Corp.)<br><br><br><br>**Checking camshaft gear runout**<br>(© Chevrolet Div. G.M. Corp.) | Mount a dial indicator with its stem resting on a tooth of the camshaft gear (as illustrated). Rotate the gear until all slack is removed, and zero the indicator. Rotate the gear in the opposite direction until slack is removed, and record gear backlash. Mount the indicator with its stem resting on the edge of the camshaft gear, parallel to the axis of the camshaft. Zero the indicator, and turn the camshaft gear one full turn, recording the runout. If either backlash or runout exceed specifications, replace the worn gear(s). |

## Completing the Rebuilding Process

Following the above procedures, complete the rebuilding process as follows:

Fill the oil pump with oil, to prevent cavitating (sucking air) on initial engine start up. Install the oil pump and the pickup tube on the engine. Coat the oil pan gasket as necessary, and install the gasket and the oil pan. Mount the flywheel and the crankshaft vibrational damper or pulley on the crankshaft. NOTE: *Always use new bolts when installing the flywheel.* Inspect the clutch shaft pilot bushing in the crankshaft. If the bushing is excessively worn, remove it with an expanding puller and a slide hammer, and tap a new bushing into place.

Position the engine, cylinder head side up. Lubricate the lifters, and install them into their bores. Install the cylinder head, and torque it as specified in the car section. Insert the pushrods (where applicable), and install the rocker shaft(s) (if so equipped) or position the rocker arms on the pushrods. If solid lifters are utilized, adjust the valves to the "cold" specifications.

Mount the intake and exhaust manifolds, the carburetor(s), the distributor and spark plugs. Adjust the point gap and the static ignition timing. Mount all accessories and install the engine in the car. Fill the radiator with coolant, and the crankcase with high quality engine oil.

## Break-in Procedure

Start the engine, and allow it to run at low speed for a few minutes, while checking for leaks. Stop the engine, check the oil level, and fill as necessary. Restart the engine, and fill the cooling system to capacity. Check the point dwell angle and adjust the ignition timing and the valves. Run the engine at low to medium speed (800-2500 rpm) for approximately ½ hour, and retorque the cylinder head bolts. Road test the car, and check again for leaks.

Follow the manufacturer's recommended engine break-in procedure and maintenance schedule for new engines.

# Chapter Four

# Emission Controls and Fuel System

## Emission Controls

### CRANKCASE VENTILATION SYSTEM

All models are equipped with a crankcase ventilation system. The purpose of the crankcase ventilation system is twofold. It keeps harmful vapors from escaping into the atmosphere and prevents the buildup of crankcase pressure. Prior to the 1960s, most cars employed a vented oil filler cap and road draft tube to dispose of crankcase vapor. The crankcase ventilation systems now in use are improvement over the old method and, when functioning properly, will not reduce engine efficiency.

Type 1 and 2 crankcase vapors are recirculated from the oil breather through a rubber hose to the air cleaner. The vapors then join the air/fuel mixture and are burned in the engine. Fuel injected cars, Type 4 and some Type 3, mix crankcase vapors into the air/fuel mixture to be burned in the combustion chambers. Fresh air is forced through the engine to evacuate vapors and recirculate them into the oil breather, intake air distributor, and then to be burned.

The only maintenance required on the crankcase ventilation system is a periodic check. At every tune-up, examine the hoses for clogging or deterioration. Clean or replace the hoses as required.

### EVAPORATIVE EMISSION CONTROL SYSTEM

Required by law since 1971, this system prevents raw fuel vapors from entering the atmosphere. The various systems for different models are similar. They consist of an expansion chamber, activated charcoal filter, and connecting lines. Fuel vapors are vented to the charcoal filter where hydrocarbons are deposited on the element. The engine fan forces fresh air into the filter when the engine is running. The air purges the filter and the hydrocarbons are forced into the air cleaner to become part of the air/fuel mixture and burned.

Maintenance of this system consists of checking the condition of the various connecting lines and the charcoal filter at 10,000 mile intervals. The charcoal filter, which is located under the engine compartment, should be replaced at 48,000 mile intervals.

### AIR INJECTION SYSTEM

Type 2 vehicles, beginning in 1973, are equipped with the air injection system, or air pump as it is sometimes called. In this system, an engine driven air pump delivers fresh air to the engine exhaust ports. The additional air is used to promote after-burning of any unburned mixture as they leave the combustion chamber. In addition, the system supplies fresh air to the intake manifold during gear changes to provide more complete combustion of the air/fuel mixture.

Check the air pump belt tension and examine the hoses for deterioration as a regular part of your tune-up procedure. The filter element in the pump should be replaced every 18,000 miles or at least every two years.

### EXHAUST GAS RECIRCULATION

This system is used to reduce nitrous oxide emissions ($NO_x$) by lowering peak flame temperature during combustion. Exhaust gases are routed into the intake manifold through an EGR control valve. On Type 1 Automatic Stick Shift cars, exhaust gas is diverted, cleaned in a filter, and routed to the intake manifold by the EGR valve. The valve is vacuum operated to control gas flow according to engine demand. EGR introduced in 1973.

Type 2 vehicles are equipped with two EGR valves, one for each intake manifold. On manual transmission models, the valves open and close according to engine vacuum. On automatic transmission vehicles, the valves open and close according to the throttle position and engine temperature.

Type 3 cars with automatic transmissions are equipped with EGR. Exhaust gases are recirculated via a filter and an EGR valve. The valve is electromagnetically operated, receiving engine condition inputs to determine its opening and closing. Manual transmission Type 1 and Type 4 cars are not equipped with EGR.

Replace the filter and check the EGR valve every 24,000 miles.

### EGR Valve Checking

#### TYPE 1 AND 3

1. Remove the EGR valve.
2. Reconnect the vacuum hose and place the valve on the base.
3. Start the engine. If it doesn't stall, the vacuum line between the valve base and the intake manifold is clogged and must be cleaned.
4. Run the engine at 2000–3000 rpm. The closing pin of the EGR valve should pull in 0.15 in. (4 mm) and immediately return to its original position at idle. Replace the EGR valve if it doesn't operate correctly.
5. Install the EGR valve using new seals.

#### TYPE 2

1. Remove the EGR valve.
2. Inspect the valve for cleanliness.
3. Check the valve for freedom of movement by pressing in on the valve pin.
4. Connect the valve to the vacuum hose of another engine or vacuum source and start the engine. At 1500–2000 rpm the valve pin should be pulled in and when the speed is reduced it should return to its original position. Replace the EGR valve if it doesn't operate correctly.
5. Replace the washer and install the valve.
6. Repeat this operation on the second valve.

### THROTTLE REGULATOR

Type 1 and 2 vehicles are equipped with a throttle regulator which holds the throttle slightly open during deceleration to prevent an excessively rich mixture. The throttle regulator consists of two parts, connected by a hose. The operating part is mounted at the carburetor. The control section is located on the left side of the engine compartment.

Throttle valve positioner with securing screws and push rod indicated

### Adjustment

1. The engine must be at operating temperature, with the automatic choke fully open.

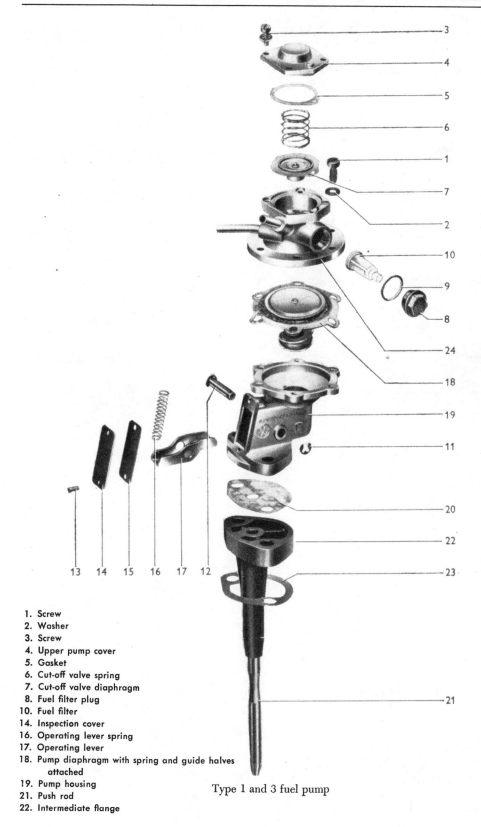

1. Screw
2. Washer
3. Screw
4. Upper pump cover
5. Gasket
6. Cut-off valve spring
7. Cut-off valve diaphragm
8. Fuel filter plug
10. Fuel filter
14. Inspection cover
16. Operating lever spring
17. Operating lever
18. Pump diaphragm with spring and guide halves
        attached
19. Pump housing
21. Push rod
22. Intermediate flange

Type 1 and 3 fuel pump

2. Start the engine. Turn the regulator adjusting screw clockwise until the control rod just starts to move the throttle valve lever. The stop collar on the control rod will be against the regulator body. Engine speed should be 1,700–1,800 rpm.

3. If speed is too high, shorten the control rod.

4. After adjustment, tighten the locknuts on the control rod.

5. Turn the regulator adjusting screw counterclockwise until an idle speed of 850 rpm is obtained.

6. Increase the engine speed to 3,000 rpm, then release the throttle valve lever. The engine should take 3–4 seconds to return to idle.

Incorrect throttle regulator adjustment may cause erratic idle, excessively high idle speed, and backfiring on deceleration.

## Fuel System

### MECHANICAL FUEL PUMP

There are two types of fuel pumps. They are identified by the cover on the top of the pump. The fuel filter is found under this cover.

Types 1 and 3, with carburetors, have fuel pumps with the cover secured by four screws. The Type 2 fuel pump has a cover secured by a single screw.

The Type 4 and fuel injected Type 3 have an electric pump.

The removal and installation procedures for both mechanical fuel pumps are the same.

#### Removal and Installation

1. Disconnect the fuel lines at the pump and plug them to prevent leakage.

2. Remove the two securing nuts.

3. Remove the fuel pump. If necessary, the pushrod, gaskets, and intermediate flange may also be removed.

4. When installing the fuel pump, it is necessary to check the fuel pump pushrod stroke. This is done by measuring the distance that the pushrod projects above the intermediate flange when both gaskets are in place. The rod must project ½ in.

5. Fill the cavity in the lower part of the fuel housing with grease.

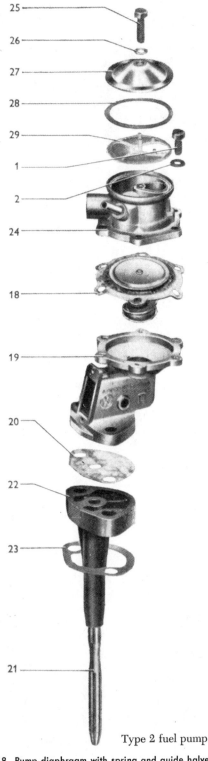

Type 2 fuel pump

18. Pump diaphragm with spring and guide halves attached
21. Push rod
22. Intermediate flange
27. Fuel filter cover
28. Fuel filter cover gasket
29. Fuel filter screen

6. Using new gaskets, install the fuel pump and tighten the two securing nuts.

7. Install the fuel hoses.

### Testing and Adjusting

The maximum fuel pump pressure developed by the Type 1 and 2 fuel pump is 3.5 psi, at 3,400 rpm for the Type 1 and 3,800 rpm for the Type 2. The Type 3 develops 5 psi at 3,800 rpm.

All fuel pumps deliver 400 cc of fuel per minute.

The only adjustment possible is performed by varying the thickness of the fuel pump flange gaskets. Varying the thickness of the gaskets will change the stroke of the fuel pump pushrod. This adjustment is not meant to compensate for a pump in bad condition; therefore, do not attempt to vary the height of the pushrod to any great extent.

## Electric Fuel Pump

### Location and Type

Only the Type 3 with the fuel injected engine and the Type 4 have an electric pump. The fuel pump is located near the front axle.

Type 3 electric fuel pump

### Removal and Installation

1. Disconnect the fuel pump wiring. Pull the plug from the pump but do not pull on the wiring.

2. Disconnect the fuel hoses and plug them to prevent any leakage.

3. Remove the two nuts which secure the pump and then remove the pump.

4. Reconnect the fuel pump hoses and wiring and install the pump on the vehicle.

### Adjustments

Electric fuel pump pressure is 28 psi. Fuel pump pressure is determined by a pressure regulator which diverts part of the fuel pump output to the gas tank when 28 psi is reached. The regulator, located on the engine firewall, has a screw and lock nut on its end. Loosen the lock nut and adjust the screw to adjust the pressure. Do not force the screw in or out if it does not turn.

Fuel pressure regulator with lock nut and adjusting screw at the left end of the regulator

### CARBURETORS

Types 1 and 2 are available in carbureted form. Types 1 and 2/1600 have a single carburetor while the Type 2/1700 has two carburetors.

The carburetor used by VW is a single barrel downdraft type. It is designated as the 34 PDSIT-2 and 34 PDSIT-3. The -2 means that the carburetor is used on the left cylinder head and the -3 is the designation for the right cylinder head. Single carburetor engines use the -3 carburetor.

### Removal and Installation

#### TYPE 1, 2, AND 3

1. Remove the air cleaner.

2. Disconnect the fuel hose.

3. Disconnect the vacuum hoses.

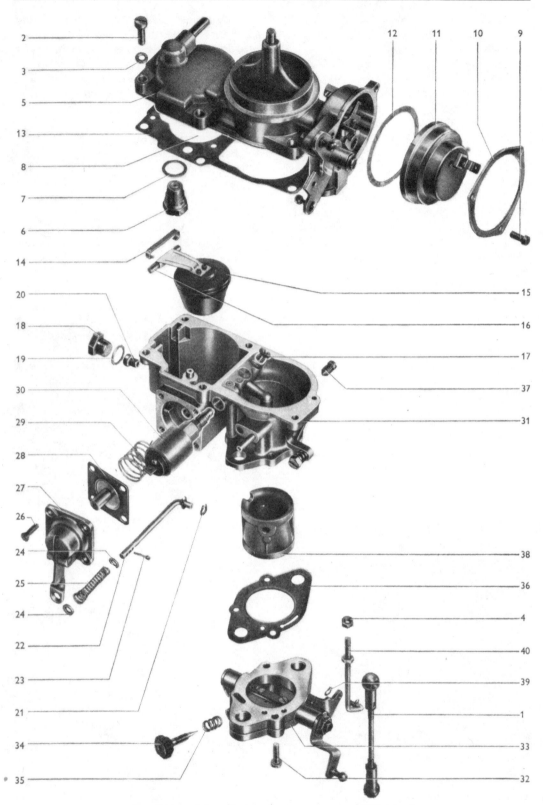

Typical single barrel downdraft carburetor—Type 3 32 PDSIT shown

4. Remove the automatic choke cable and remove the wire for the electromagnetic pilot jet.

5. Disconnect the accelerator cable at the throttle valve lever, on Type 1 and 2. On Type 3, disconnect the carburetor linkage return spring and connecting rod.

6. Remove the two nuts securing the carburetor on the intake manifold and then remove the carburetor from the engine.

7. Using a new gasket, install the carburetor on the manifold.

8. Reconnect the fuel and vacuum hoses, the automatic choke cable, and the wiring for the pilot jet.

9. Reconnect the throttle cable and adjust it so that at full throttle there is a gap of 0.04 in. between the throttle valve lever and its stop on the lower portion of the carburetor body.

NOTE: *Open the throttle valve by hand and tighten the adjustment screw, then have an assistant open the throttle and recheck the adjustment.*

**Overhaul**

### ALL TYPES

NOTE: *Overhaul kits contain specific procedures for overhauling the carburetor.*

Efficient carburetion depends greatly upon careful cleaning and inspection during overhaul, since dirt, gum, water, or varnish in or on the carburetor parts are often responsible for poor performance.

Overhaul your carburetor in a clean, dust-free area. Carefully disassemble the carburetor, referring often to the exploded views. Keep all similar and look-alike parts segregated during disassembly and cleaning to avoid accidential interchange during assembly. Make a note of all jet sizes.

When the carburetor is disassembled, wash all of the parts (except diaphragms,

electric choke units, pump plunger, and any other plastic, leather, fiber, or rubber parts) in clean carburetor solvent. Do not leave parts in the solvent any longer than is necessary to sufficiently loosen the deposits. Excessive cleaning may remove the special finish from the float bowl and choke valve bodies, leaving these parts unfit for service. Rinse all parts in clean solvent and blow them dry with compressed air or allow them to air dry. Wipe clean all cork, plastic, leather, and fiber parts with a clean, lint-free cloth.

Blow out all passages and jets with compressed air and be sure that there are no restrictions or blockages. Never use wire or similar tools to clean jets, fuel passages, or air bleeds. Clean all jets and valves separately to avoid accidental interchange.

Check all parts for wear or damage. If any wear or damage is found, replace defective parts. Especially check the following:

1. Check the float needle and seat for wear. If wear is found, replace the complete assembly with new parts.

2. Check the float hinge pin for wear and the float(s) for dents or distortion. Replace the float if fuel has leaked into it.

3. Check the throttle and choke shaft bores for wear or an out-of-round condition. Damage or wear to the throttle arm, shaft, or shaft bore often requires replacement of the throttle body. These parts require a close tolerance of fit; wear may allow air leakage, which could affect starting and idling.

NOTE: *Throttle shafts and bushings are not included in overhaul kits. They can be purchased separately.*

4. Inspect the idle mixture adjusting needles for burrs or grooves. Any such condition requires replacement of the needle, since you will not be able to obtain a satisfactory idle.

5. Test the accelerator pump check

| | | |
|---|---|---|
| 1. Pull rod | 16. Float pin | 29. Accelerator pump spring |
| 4. Adjusting nut for connecting rod | 17. Air correction jet | 30. Pilot jet and cut-off valve |
| 6. Float needle valve assembly | 18. Plug for main jet | 33. Throttle valve housing |
| 7. Needle valve assembly washer | 20. Main jet | 34. Volume control screw |
| 10. Choke cover retaining ring | 22. Connecting link | 37. Venturi screw |
| 11. Choke cover | 25. Spring for connecting link | 38. Venturi |
| 14. Spring for float pin | 27. Accelerator pump cover | 40. Connecting rod |
| 15. Float | 28. Accelerator pump diaphragm | |

valves. They should pass air one way but not the other. Test for proper seating by blowing and sucking on the valve. Replace the valve if necessary. If the valve is satisfactory, wash the valve again to remove breath moisture.

6. Check the bowl cover for warped surfaces with a straightedge.

7. Closely inspect the valves and seats for wear or damage, replacing as necessary.

8. After the carburetor is assembled, check the choke valve for freedom of operation.

Carburetor overhaul kits are recommended for each overhaul. These kits contain all gaskets and new parts to replace those that deteriorate most rapidly. Failure to replace all parts supplied with the kit, especially gaskets, can result in poor performance later.

Some carburetor manufacturers supply overhaul kits of three basic types; minor repair, major repair, and gasket kits. Basically, they contain the following:

Minor Repair Kits:
    All gaskets
    Float needle valve
    Volume control screw
    All diaphragms
    Spring for the pump diaphragm

Major Repair Kits:
    All jets and gaskets
    All diaphragms
    Float needle valve
    Volume control screw
    Pump ball valve
    Main jet carrier
    Float
    Complete intermediate rod
    Intermediate pump lever
    Complete injector tube
    Several cover hold-down screws and washers

Gasket Kits:
    All gaskets

After cleaning and checking all of the components, reassemble the carburetor using new parts and referring to the exploded view. When reassembling, make sure that all screws and jets are tight in their seats, but do not overtighten, as the tips will be distorted. Tighten all of the screws gradually in rotation. Do not tighten the needle valves into their seats; uneven jetting will result. Always use new gaskets.

### Throttle Linkage Adjustment

#### TYPE 1 AND 2

1. Loosen the cable adjusting screw found in the bottom on the throttle lever.

2. The throttle lever has a rigid cylinder attached to its end. Move the rigid portion in or out of the end of the throttle lever to obtain the proper adjustment and tighten the adjusting screw. The proper adjustment is reached when there is a gap of 0.04 in. between the throttle valve lever and its stop on the lower portion of the carburetor body. See the note at the end of the "Carburetor Removal and Installation" procedure.

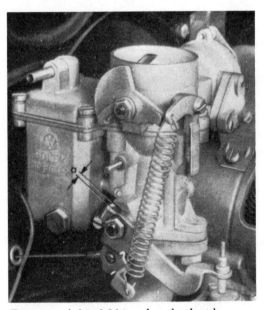

Dimension (a) is 0.04 in. when the throttle linkage is properly adjusted

#### TYPE 3

1. Have an assistant open the throttle with the gas pedal to the wide open position.

2. Measure the distance between the throttle valve lever and its stop at the lower portion of the carburetor body. The distance should be 0.04 in.

3. To obtain the proper adjustment, adjust the length of the short rod between the base of the throttle lever and the bellcrank that is attached to the carburetor.

### Accelerator Pump Adjustment

Improper accelerator pump adjustment is characterized by flat spots during acceleration or a severe hesitation when the throttle is first depressed.

1. Remove the carburetor from the engine and remove the upper half of the carburetor.

2. Support the carburetor securely in a vise without damaging the carburetor body.

3. Fill the float chamber with gasoline and attach a rubber tube to the injector tube. Place the open end of the tube into a millileter measuring tube.

Measuring acceleration pump output

4. Move the throttle lever several strokes until all of the air is forced out of the tube. Move the throttle lever an additional ten full strokes and measure the quanity of gas in the measuring tube. Multiply the accelerator pump quantity injected specification by 10 and compare this figure to the amount of gas in the measuring tube.

5. To decrease the amount injected, reduce the number of washers between the cotter pin and the pump lever. To increase the amount, increase the number of washers. If varying the number of washers will not yield enough adjustment, move the cotter pin in the connecting link.

### Float and Fuel Level Adjustment

A properly assembled carburetor has a preset float level. For the float level to be correct the fiber washer under the needle

valve seat must be installed and be of the proper thickness, 1 mm or 0.039 in.

The only way to adjust the float level, if it is absolutely necessary, and still retain proper seating of the needle in the needle valve seat, is to vary the thickness of the fiber washer beneath the seat.

### Throttle Valve Gap

#### CARBURETOR REMOVED

1. Remove the carburetor from the car.

2. Loosen the two nuts on the automatic choke connecting rod and insert a 0.028 in. wire gauge or drill between the throttle valve and the side of the venturi.

3. Move the two nuts up or down on the connecting rod until the throttle valve gap is adjusted and tighten the two nuts.

NOTE: *The choke valve must be closed for proper adjustment.*

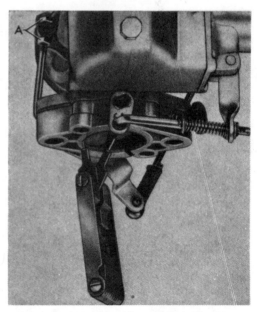

Adjust nuts (A) when adjusting throttle valve gap

#### CARBURETOR INSTALLED

1. Back out the idle speed screw until the throttle valve is completely closed.

2. Turn the idle speed screw until it just touches the throttle lever.

3. Close the choke valve.

4. Place a 0.09 in. drill or wire gauge between the idle screw and the throttle valve lever. Adjust the two nuts on the automatic choke connecting rod either up

## Carburetor Specifications
### ( all measurements are in metric units )

| Type | Engine | Carburetor | Venturi Diameter (mm) | Main Jet | Air Correction Jet | Pilot Jet | Aux. Fuel Jet | Aux. Air Jet | Power Fuel Jet | Needle Valve Washer Thickness (mm) | Accelerator Pump Injection Quantity (cc³/stroke) | Throttle Valve Gap (mm) |
|---|---|---|---|---|---|---|---|---|---|---|---|---|
| 1/1600 | AE | 34 PICT-3 | 26 | 130 | 75Z② | g60 | 47.5 | 90 | 100/100 | 0.5 | 1.45/1.75 | — |
| 1/1600 | AH, AK | 34 PICT-3 | 26 | 127.5/130 | 75Z/80Z | g55 | 42.5 | 90 | 100/100 | 0.5 | 1.3-1.6 | — |
| 2/1600 | AE | 34 PICT-3 | 26 | 125 | 60Z | g60 | 47.5 | 90 | 95/95 | 0.5 | 1.45 ± 0.15 | — |
| 2/1700 | CB | 34 PDICT-3, 2 | 26 | 137.5 | 155/050 | 55 | 45① | 0.7① | — | 0.5 | 0.45 ± 0.1 | 0.8 |
| 2/1700 | CB (1973) | 34 PDSIT-3, 2 | 26 | x130 | 140 | — | 45① | 0.7① | — | 1.0 | 0.7 ± 0.1 | 0.6 |
| 2/1700 | CD | 34 PDSIT-3, 2 | 26 | x132.5 | 155 | — | 45① | 0.7① | — | 1.0 | 0.5 ± 0.1 | 0.6 |

① This jet not found in 34 PDSIT-3 carburetors
② Karmann Ghia—80Z

or down until the drill can be easily pulled out.

5. It will be necessary to rebalance the carburetors on dual carburetor models.

## Fast Idle Adjustment

The fast idle speed is adjusted by means of a screw located at the upper end of the throttle valve arm. This screw rests against a cam with steps cut into its edge.

To adjust the fast idle, start the engine and rotate the cam so that the fast idle screw is resting against the highest step on the fast idle cam. The fast idle speed should be approximately 1500 rpm. Turn the fast idle screw either in or out until the proper idle speed is obtained.

On dual carburetor engines it is necessary to adjust the fast idle on only one of the carburetors. There is a direct mechanical connection between the two carburetors and if one carburetor is adjusted the other will automatically be adjusted.

## Accelerator Cable

### Removal and Installation

1. Disconnect the cable from the accelerator pedal.

2. Disconnect the cable from the throttle lever.

3. Pull the cable from the accelerator pedal end and then remove it from the car.

4. Grease the cable before sliding it into its housing.

5. Slide the cable into its housing and push it through its guide tubes. It may be necessary to raise the car and start the cable into the segments of guide tube found under the car.

6. Install one cable end into the accelerator cable. Slip the other end into the throttle valve lever and adjust the cable.

NOTE: *Make sure that the rubber boot at the rear end of the cable is properly seated so that water will not enter the guide tubes.*

## FUEL INJECTION

The Volkswagen fuel injection system consists of two parts. One part consists of the actual injection components: the injectors, the fuel pump, pressure regulator, and related wiring and hoses. The second part consists of the injection controls and engine operating characteristics sensors: a manifold vacuum sensor that monitors engine load, trigger contacts used to determine when and which pair of injectors will operate, three temperature sensors used to control air fuel mixture enrichment, a cold starting valve for additional cold starting fuel enrichment, a throttle valve switch used to cut off fuel during deceleration, and the brain box used to analyze information about engine operating characteristics and, after processing this information, to control the electrically operated injectors.

It is absolutely imperative that no ad-

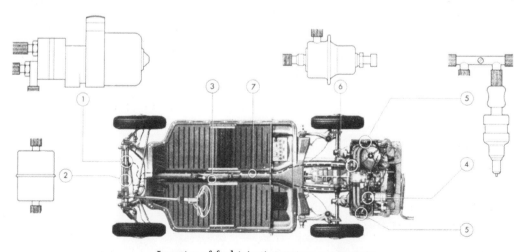

Location of fuel injection system components

1. Fuel pump
2. Fuel filter
3. Pressure line
4. Ring main
5. Injectors
6. Pressure regulator
7. Return line (not pressurized)

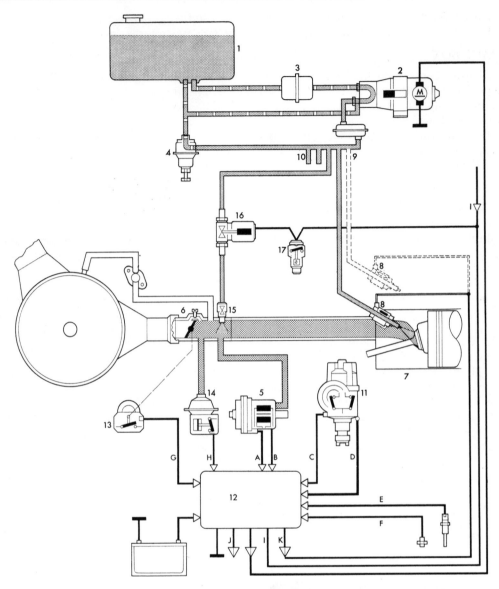

Schematic of fuel injection system

1. Fuel tank
2. Fuel pump
3. Fuel filter
4. Pressure regulator
5. Pressure sensor
6. Intake air distributor
7. Cylinder head

8. Injectors
9. Fuel distributor pipe
10. Fuel distributor pipe with connection for cold starting device
11. Distributor with trigger contacts
12. Electronic control unit
13. Throttle valve switch

14. Pressure switch
15. Cold starting jet
16. Electro magnetic valve for cold starting device
17. Thermostat for cold starting device
E. and F. Wiring from temperature sensors to control box

justments other than those found in the following pages be performed. The controls for this fuel injection system are extremely sensitive and easily damaged when subject to abuse. Never attempt to test the brain box without proper training and the proper equipment. The dealer is the best place to have any needed work performed.

CAUTION: *Whenever a fuel injection component is to be removed or installed, the battery should be disconnected and the ignition turned OFF.*

It is not recommended that the inex-

perienced mechanic work on any portion
of the fuel injection system.

## BRAIN BOX

All work concerning the brain box is to
be performed by the dealer. Do not remove
the brain box and take it to a dealer because the dealer will not be able to test it
without the vehicle. Do not disconnect the
brain box unless the battery is disconnected and the ignition is OFF.

## FUEL INJECTORS

There are two types of injectors. One
type is secured in place by a ring that holds
a single injector. The second type of injector is secured to the intake manifold in
pairs by a common bracket.

**Removal and Installation**

### SINGLE INJECTORS

1. Remove the nut which secures the injector bracket to the manifold.

2. If the injector is not going to be replaced, do not disconnect the fuel line.
Disconnect the injector wiring.

3. Gently slide the injector bracket up
the injector and pull the injector from the
intake manifold. Be careful not to damage
the inner and outer rubber sealing rings.
These sealing rings are used to seal the
injector to the manifold and must be replaced if they show any sign of deterioration.

4. Installation is the reverse of removal.

Be careful not to damage the injector tip
or contaminate the injector with dirt.

### PAIRED INJECTORS

1. Disconnect the injector wiring.

2. Remove the two nuts which secure
the injector bracket to the manifold. Slide
the bracket up the injector. Do not disconnect the fuel lines if the injector is not
going to be replaced.

3. Gently slide the pair of injectors out
of their bores along with the rubber sealing
rings, injector plate, and the inner and
outer injector locating bushings. It may be
necessary to remove the inner bushings
from the intake manifold after the injectors
are removed since they sometimes lodge
within the manifold.

NOTE: *There are two sleeves that fit
over the injector bracket studs. Be careful not to lose them.*

4. Upon installation, place the injector
bracket, the outer locating bushings, the
injector plate, and the inner locating bushings on the pair of injectors in that order.

5. Gently slip the injector assembly into
the manifold and install the bracket nuts.
Be careful not to damage the injector tips
or contaminate the injectors with dirt.

6. Reconnect the injector wiring.

## THROTTLE VALVE SWITCH

**Removal and Installation**

1. Remove the air filter.

2. The switch is located on the throttle

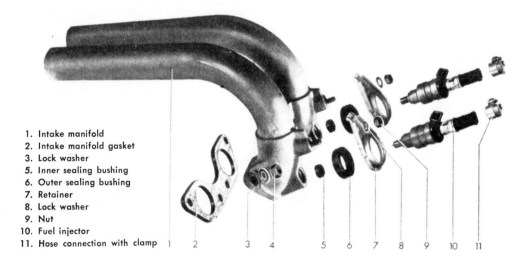

1. Intake manifold
2. Intake manifold gasket
3. Lock washer
5. Inner sealing bushing
6. Outer sealing bushing
7. Retainer
8. Lock washer
9. Nut
10. Fuel injector
11. Hose connection with clamp

Individually mounted fuel injectors

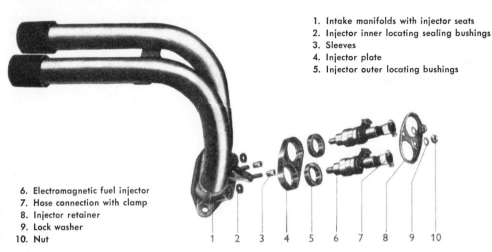

1. Intake manifolds with injector seats
2. Injector inner locating sealing bushings
3. Sleeves
4. Injector plate
5. Injector outer locating bushings

6. Electromagnetic fuel injector
7. Hose connection with clamp
8. Injector retainer
9. Lock washer
10. Nut

Paired fuel injectors

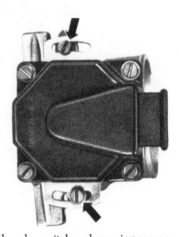

Throttle valve switch and securing screws

Pressure sensor and securing screws

valve housing. Disconnect the throttle valve return spring.

3. Remove the throttle valve assembly but do not disconnect the bowden wire for the throttle valve or the connecting hoses to the ignition distributor.

4. Remove the throttle valve switch securing screws and remove the switch.

5. Reverse the above steps to install. It will be necessary to adjust the switch after installation.

## PRESSURE SENSOR

### Removal and Installation

The sensor is secured to the firewall by two screws. Remove the screws and disconnect the wiring.

Remove the pressure connection and immediately plug the connection into the sensor. Always keep the connection plugged as the bellows inside the sensor is sensitive to the smallest pieces of dirt. Reverse the above steps to install.

Do not disassemble the sensor. There are no adjustments possible for the sensor.

NOTE: *Do not reverse the square electrical plug when reconnecting the sensor wiring.*

## FUEL PRESSURE REGULATOR

### Removal and Installation

Disconnect the hoses from the regulator and remove the regulator from its bracket. The fuel pump pressure is adjustable; however, lack of fuel pressure is usually due to other defects in the system and the regulator should be adjusted only as a last resort.

## TEMPERATURE SENSORS

### Removal and Installation

The air temperature sensor is located in the air distributor housing and may be unscrewed from the housing. The second temperature switch is located in the cylinder head on the left side. It is removed with a special wrench. To test these switches, attach an ohmmeter and measure the resistance of the switch as the temperature is raised gradually to 212°. As the temperature rises, the resistance of the first switch should drop from about 200 ohms to 80 ohms. The cylinder head switch resistance should drop from about 1700 ohms to 190 ohms at 212°.

The third switch is actually a thermo-switch and is an ON/OFF type switch. Below 41° it is ON to activate the cold

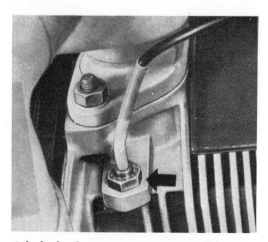

Cylinder head temperature sensing switch

Thermo switch

starting valve. The switch is located next to the distributor and may be removed with a 24 mm wrench.

## COLD START VALVE

### Removal and Installation

The cold start valve is located near the thermo-switch and is secured to the air intake distributor by two screws. This valve sometimes jams open and causes excessive consumption, rough idle, and low power output.

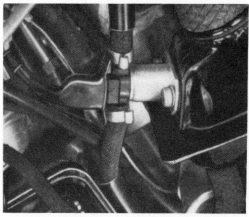

Cold start valve

## TRIGGER CONTACTS

### Removal and Installation

The trigger contacts are located in the base of the distributor and are secured by

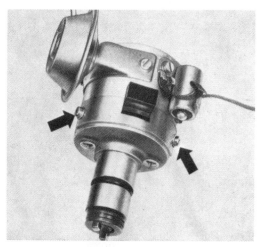

Trigger contact assembly securing screw in the base of the distributor

two screws. These contacts are supplied in pairs and are not adjustable. Do not attempt to replace just one set of contacts.

One set of contacts controls a pair of injectors and tells the injectors when to fire.

## TROUBLESHOOTING

There are very few items to check without the special tester used by the dealer.

It is possible to check the fuel pressure by inserting a fuel pressure gauge in the line after the pressure regulator. Insert the gauge using a T-fitting. Turn on the key and check the pressure. If the pressure is low, check for leaking injectors, restricted lines, clogged fuel filters, damaged pressure regulator, bad fuel pump, water in the gas and resultant corrosion of the injectors, or a leaking or jammed cold start valve.

## ADJUSTMENTS

### Throttle Valve Switch

The throttle valve switch is used to shut off the fuel supply during deceleration. The switch is supposed to operate when the throttle valve is opened 2°. A degree scale is stamped into the attachment plate for adjustment purposes.

1. Completely close the throttle valve.
2. Loosen the switch attaching screws

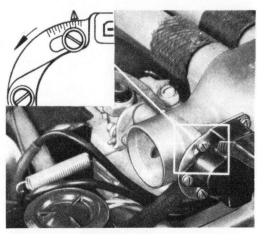

Throttle valve switch degree scale and location

and turn the switch carefully to the right until it hits its stop.

3. Turn the switch slowly to the left until it can be heard to click and then note the position of the switch according to the degree scale.

4. Continue to turn the switch another 2°. The distance between any two marks on the degree scale is 2°.

5. Tighten the screws and recheck the adjustment.

### Engine Idle Speed

Engine idle speed adjustment is given in the "Tune-Up" section.

# Chapter Five

# Chassis Electrical

## Heater

The Volkswagen heating system has no electrical blower. The engine cooling fan blows air over the engine and out through the cooling ducts. If the heater flaps are opened, then a portion of the heated air from the engine is diverted to the passenger compartment. An auxiliary gas heater is optional on Types 1, 2, and 3, and standard on Type 4.

Procedures for removing the heat exchangers and heater flap assemblies are given in Chapter Three.

*CABLE FOR HEATER OUTLET*

**Removal and Installation**

1. Remove the rear air outlet, hose, and heater pipe as an assembly.
2. Remove the hose from the outlet and from the pipe.
3. Remove the pin which attaches the cable to the flap in the heater pipe.
   NOTE: *The pin is push-fit.*
4. Remove the heater pipe from the outlet.
5. Bend up the tabs which secure the cable shielding to the outlet.

6. Disconnect the opposite end from the heater controls and remove the cable.
7. Reverse the above steps to install.

## Windshield Wipers

*MOTOR*

**Removal and Installation**

### TYPE 1

1. Disconnect the battery ground cable.
2. Loosen the clamp screws and remove the wiper arms.
3. Remove the wiper bearing nuts as well as the washers. Take off the outer bearing seals.
4. Remove the back of the instrument panel from the luggage compartment.
5. Disconnect the cable from the wiper motor.
6. Remove the glove compartment box.
7. Remove the screw which secures the wiper frame to the body.
8. Remove the frame and motor with the linkage.
   NOTE: *The ball joints at the ends of the linkage may be slipped apart by gently popping the ball and socket apart with a*

Typical wiper linkage ball joint—Type 4 illustrated

*screwdriver. Always lubricate the joints upon reassembly.*

9. Remove the lock and spring washers from the motor drive shaft and remove the connecting rod. Matchmark the motor and frame to ensure proper realignment when the motor is reinstalled.

10. Remove the nut located at the base of the motor drive shaft, and the nut at the side of the driveshaft, and remove the motor from the frame.

11. To install, reverse the above steps and heed the following reminders.

12. The pressed lug on the wiper frame must engage the groove in the wiper bearing. Make sure that the wiper spindles are perpendicular to the plane of the windshield.

13. Check the linkage bushings for wear.

14. The hollow side of the links must face toward the frame with the angled end of the driving link toward the right bearing.

15. The inner bearing seal should be placed so that the shoulder of the rubber molding faces the wiper arm.

### TYPE 2

1. Disconnect the ground wire from the battery.

2. Remove both wiper arms.

3. Remove the bearing cover and nut.

4. Remove the heater branch connections under the instrument panel.

5. Disconnect the wiper motor wiring.

6. Remove the wiper motor securing screw and remove the motor.

7. Reverse the above steps to install.

### TYPE 3

1. Disconnect the negative battery cable.

2. Remove the ashtray and glove compartment.

3. Remove the fresh air controls.

4. Remove the cover for the heater and water drainage hoses.

5. Disconnect the motor wiring.

6. Remove the wiper arms.

7. Remove the bearing covers and nuts, washers, and outer bearing seals.

8. Remove the wiper motor securing screws and remove the motor.

9. Reverse the above steps to install.

### TYPE 4

1. Disconnect the negative battery cable.

2. Remove the wiper arms.

3. Remove the bearing cover and remove the nut under it.

4. Remove the steering column cover and the hoses running between the fresh air control box and the vents.

5. Remove the clock but do not disconnect the wiring.

6. Remove the left fresh air and defroster vent. Disconnect the air hose from the vent.

7. Disconnect the wiring for the motor at the windshield wiper switch. Remove the ground wire from the motor gear cover.

8. Remove the motor securing screw and remove the motor frame and motor assembly downward and to the right.

9. Reverse the above steps to install.

### *LINKAGE*

#### Removal and Installation

The windshield wiper linkage is secured at the ends by a ball and socket type joint. The ball and joint may be gently pried apart with the aid of a screwdriver. Always lubricate the joints with grease before reassembly.

#### WIPER ARM SHAFT

1. Remove the wiper arm.

2. Remove the bearing cover or the shaft seal depending on the type.

3. On Type 4, remove the shaft circlip.

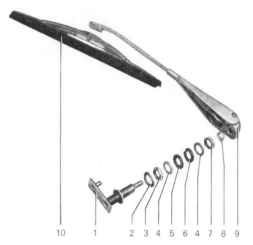

Type 1, 2, and 3 wiper shaft assembly

1. Wiper shaft with crank
2. Spring washer
3. Brass nut
4. Washer
5. Inner bearing seal
6. Outer bearing seal
7. Nut
8. Wiper shaft seal
9. Bracket and arm
10. Windshield wiper blade

4. Remove the large wiper shaft bearing securing nut and remove the accompanying washer and rubber seal.

5. Disconnect the wiper linkage from the wiper arm shaft.

6. Working from inside the car, slide the shaft out of its bearing.

NOTE: *It may be necessary to lightly tap the shaft out of its bearing. Use a soft face hammer.*

7. Reverse the above steps to install.

## Instrument Cluster

### Removal and Installation

#### SPEEDOMETER

1. Disconnect the negative battery cable.

2. Disconnect the speedometer light bulb wires.

3. Unscrew the knurled nut which secures the speedometer cable to the back of the speedometer. Pull the cable from the back of the speedometer.

4. Using a 4 mm allen wrench, remove the two knurled nuts which secure the speedometer brackets. Remove the brackets.

5. Remove the speedometer from the dashboard by sliding it out toward the steering wheel.

6. Reverse the above steps to install. Before fully tightening the nuts for the speedometer brackets, make sure the speedometer is correctly positioned in the dash.

#### CLOCK AND FUEL GAUGE ASSEMBLY

1. Disconnect the negative battery cable.

2. Disconnect the wiring from the back of the assembly.

3. Remove the knurled nuts and brackets which secure the assembly in the dash. Use a 4 mm allen wrench.

4. Remove the assembly by gently slid-

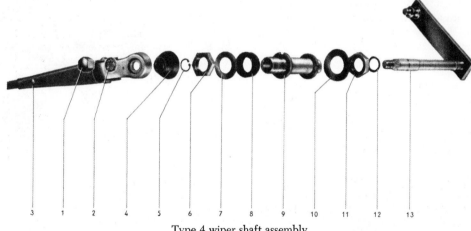

Type 4 wiper shaft assembly

1. Cap nut
2. Lock washer
3. Wiper arm
4. Bearing cover
5. Circlip
6. Nut
7. Washer
8. Seal
9. Shaft bearing
10. Spring washer
11. Brass nut
12. Spring washer
13. Wiper shaft

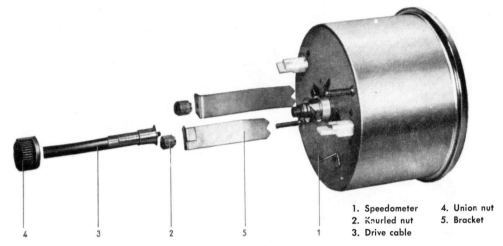

1. Speedometer    4. Union nut
2. Knurled nut    5. Bracket
3. Drive cable

Speedometer and brackets

ing it toward the steering wheel and out of the dash.

5. The fuel gauge is secured into the base of the clock by two screws. Remove the screws and slip the fuel gauge out of the clock.

6. Reverse the above steps to install. Make sure the clock and fuel gauge assembly is properly centered in the dash before fully tightening the nuts.

## IGNITION SWITCH

### Removal and Installation

1. Disconnect the steering column wiring at the block located behind the instrument panel and pull the column wiring harness into the passenger compartment.

2. Remove the steering wheel.

3. Remove the circlip on the steering shaft.

4. Disconnect the negative battery cable.

5. Insert the key and turn the switch to the ON position. On Type 3 vehicles it is necessary to remove the fuse box.

6. Remove the three securing screws and slide the switch assembly from the steering column tube.

NOTE: *It is not necessary to remove the turn signal switch at this time. If it is necessary to remove the switch from the housing, continue with the disassembly procedure.*

7. Remove the turn signal switch.

8. After removing the wiring retainer, press the ignition switch wiring block up-

ward and out of the housing and disconnect the wiring.

9. Remove the lock cylinder and the steering lock mechanism.

10. Remove the ignition switch screw and pull the ignition switch rearward.

11. Reverse the above steps to install. When reinstalling the turn signal switch, make sure the lever is in the center position.

NOTE: *The distance (a) between the steering wheel and the ignition switch housing is 2–3 mm (0.08–0.12 in.).*

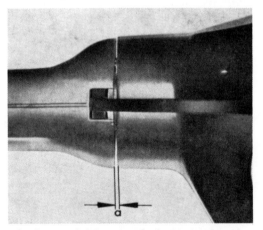

The distance (a) between the housing and steering wheel is 0.08–0.12 in.

## LOCK CYLINDER

### Removal and Installation

1. Proceed with Steps 1–8 in the "Ignition Switch" procedure.

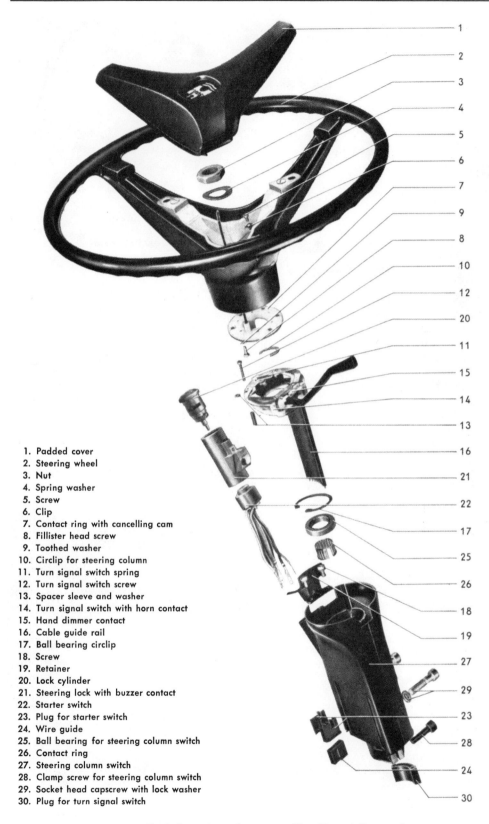

1. Padded cover
2. Steering wheel
3. Nut
4. Spring washer
5. Screw
6. Clip
7. Contact ring with cancelling cam
8. Fillister head screw
9. Toothed washer
10. Circlip for steering column
11. Turn signal switch spring
12. Turn signal switch screw
13. Spacer sleeve and washer
14. Turn signal switch with horn contact
15. Hand dimmer contact
16. Cable guide rail
17. Ball bearing circlip
18. Screw
19. Retainer
20. Lock cylinder
21. Steering lock with buzzer contact
22. Starter switch
23. Plug for starter switch
24. Wire guide
25. Ball bearing for steering column switch
26. Contact ring
27. Steering column switch
28. Clamp screw for steering column switch
29. Socket head capscrew with lock washer
30. Plug for turn signal switch

Typical steering column assembly—Type 4 illustrated

2. With the key in the cylinder and turned to the ON position, pull the lock cylinder out far enough so the securing pin can be depressed through a hole in the side of the lock cylinder housing. Use a steel wire to depress the pin.

3. As the pin is depressed, pull the lock cylinder out of its housing.

Turn signal switch retaining screws

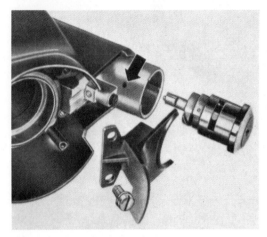

Access hole for depressing lock cylinder retaining pin

4. To install the lock cylinder, gently push the cylinder into its housing. Make sure the pin engages correctly and that the retainer fits easily in place. Do not force any parts together; when they are correctly aligned, they will fit easily together.

*TURN SIGNAL SWITCH*

#### Removal and Installation

1. Disconnect the negative battery cable.
2. Remove the steering wheel.
3. Disconnect the switch wiring at the base of the switch housing.
4. Remove the four screws which secure the turn signal switch and pull the switch and wiring outward.
5. Reverse the above steps to install.

## Lighting

### Removal and Installation

#### TYPE 1, 2, AND 3

1. Remove the screw which secures the headlight ring and remove the ring.
2. The sealed beam is held in place by a ring secured by three screws. Remove the screws and the ring. Do not confuse the headlight aiming screws with the screws for the ring. There are only two screws used for aiming.
3. Pull the wiring off the back of the sealed beam and remove the beam.
4. Reverse the above steps to install.

#### TYPE 4

This is the same procedure as above except that the headlight ring is secured by two screws.

*FUSES*

All fuses are either 8 amp or 16 amp. White colored fuses are 8 amp and red fuses are 16 amp.

# Light Bulb Specifications

| Bulb | Type 1 | Type 2 | Type 3 | Type 4 |
|------|--------|--------|--------|--------|
| Sealed beam unit | 12.8V;50/40W | 12.8V;50/40W | 12.8V;50/40W | 12.8V;37.5/50W |
| Turn signal | 12V;21W | 12V;21W | 12V;21W | —— |
| Stop/tail light | 12V;21/5W | 12V;21/5W | 12V;21/5W | 12V;32/4 cp |
| License plate | 12V;10W | 12V;10W | 12V;5W① | 12V;6 cp |
| Back-up light | 12V;25W | 12V;25W | 12V;25W | 12V;25W |
| Interior light | 12V;10W | 12V;10W | 12V;10W | 10V;10W |
| Parking light | 12V;4W | 12V;4W | 12V;4W | —— |
| Warning light | 12V;2W | 12V;1.2W | 12V;2W | 12V;1.2W |
| Side marker light | 12V;2 cp | 12V;2 cp | 12V;2 cp | 12V;2 cp |
| Turn signal parking light | —— | —— | —— | 32/4 cp |

V—Volts    cp—Candle Power
W—Watts    ① Squareback Sedan—12V;10W

# Fuses

## Type 1

| Circuit | Fuse |
|---------|------|
| Left parking, side marker, and tail lights | 8 amps |
| Right parking, side marker, and tail lights | 8 amps |
| Left low beam | 8 amps |
| Right low beam | 8 amps |
| Left high beam | 8 amps |
| Right high beam, high beam indicator | 8 amps |
| License plate light | 8 amps |
| Emergency flasher system | 8 amps |
| Interior lights | 16 amps |
| Windshield wiper, rear window defogger, fresh air fan | 16 amps |
| Horn, stop lights, ATF warning light | 8 amps |
| Fuel gauge, turn signals, brake warning light, oil pressure, turn signal and generator warning lights | 8 amps |

## Type 2

| Circuit | Fuse |
|---------|------|
| Left tail and side marker lights | 8 amps |
| Right tail and marker lights, license light, parking lights | 8 amps |
| Left low beam | 8 amps |
| Right low beam | 8 amps |
| Left high beam, high beam indicator | 8 amps |

## Type 2

| Circuit | Fuse |
|---------|------|
| Right high beam | 8 amps |
| Accessories | 8 amps |
| Emergency flasher, front interior light | 8 amps |
| Rear interior light, buzzer alarm, auxiliary heater | 16 amps |
| Windshield wipers, rear window defogger | 16 amps |
| Turn signals, warning lamps for alternator, oil pressure, fuel gauge, kickdown, and back-up lights | 8 amps |
| Horn, stop lights, brake warning light | 8 amps |

## Type 3

| Circuit | Fuse |
|---------|------|
| Right tail light, license plate light, parking and side marker light, luggage compartment light | 8 amps |
| Left tail light | 8 amps |
| Left low beam | 8 amps |
| Right low beam | 8 amps |
| Left high beam, high beam indicator | 8 amps |
| Right high beam | 8 amps |
| Electric fuel pump | 8 amps |
| Emergency flasher, interior light | 8 amps |
| Buzzer | 16 amps |

# Fuses (cont.)

## Type 3

| Circuit | Fuse |
|---|---|
| Windshield wipers, fresh air fan, rear window defogger | 16 amps |
| Stop lights, turn signals, horn, brake warning light, back-up lights | 8 amps |
| Accessories | 8 amps |

## Type 4

| Circuit | Fuse |
|---|---|
| Parking lights, left tail and left rear side marker lights | 8 amps |
| Right tail light, right rear side marker light, license plate light, selector lever console light | 8 amps |

## Type 4

| Circuit | Fuse |
|---|---|
| Left low beam | 8 amps |
| Right low beam | 8 amps |
| Left high beam | 8 amps |
| Right high beam, high beam indicator | 8 amps |
| Fuel pump | 8 amps |
| Interior light, emergency flasher, buzzer | 8 amps |
| Cigarette lighter, heater | 16 amps |
| Window wiper, fresh air fan, heater, rear window defogger | 16 amps |
| Turn signals, back-up lights, warning lights for alternator, oil pressure, fuel gauge | 8 amps |
| Horn, brake warning light, stop lights | 8 amps |

| | |
|---|---|
| A | Battery |
| B | Starter |
| C | Generator |
| $C^1$ | Regulator |
| D | Ignition/starter switch |
| E | Windshield wiper switch |
| $E^1$ | Light switch |
| $E^2$ | Turn signal and headlight dimmer switch |
| $E^3$ | Emergency flasher switch |
| F | Brake light switch with warning switch |
| $F^1$ | Oil pressure switch |
| $F^2$ | Door contact switch, left, with contact for buzzer $H^5$ |
| $F^3$ | Door contact switch, right |
| $F^4$ | Back-up light switch |
| G | Fuel gauge sending unit |
| $G^1$ | Fuel gauge |
| H | Horn button |
| $H^1$ | Horn |
| $H^5$ | Ignition key warning buzzer |
| J | Dimmer relay |
| $J^2$ | Emergency flasher relay |
| $J^6$ | Vibrator for fuel gauge |
| $K^1$ | High beam warning light |
| $K^2$ | Generator charging warning light |
| $K^3$ | Oil pressure warning light |
| $K^5$ | Turn signal warning light |
| $K^6$ | Emergency flasher warning light |
| $K^7$ | Dual circuit brake system warning light |
| $L^1$ | Sealed beam unit, left headlight |
| $L^2$ | Sealed beam unit, right headlight |
| $L^{10}$ | Instrument panel light |
| $M^2$ | Tail and brake light, right |
| $M^4$ | Tail and brake light, left |

| | |
|---|---|
| $M^5$ | Turn signal and parking light, front, left |
| $M^6$ | Turn signal, rear, left |
| $M^7$ | Turn signal and parking light, front, right |
| $M^8$ | Turn signal, rear, right |
| $M^{11}$ | Side marker light, front |
| N | Ignition coil |
| $N^1$ | Automatic choke |
| $N^3$ | Electro-magnetic pilot jet |
| O | Ignition distributor |
| $P^1$ | Spark plug connector, No. 1 cylinder |
| $P^2$ | Spark plug connector, No. 2 cylinder |
| $P^3$ | Spark plug connector, No. 3 cylinder |
| $P^4$ | Spark plug connector, No. 4 cylinder |
| $Q^1$ | Spark plug, No. 1 cylinder |
| $Q^2$ | Spark plug, No. 2 cylinder |
| $Q^3$ | Spark plug, No. 3 cylinder |
| $Q^4$ | Spark plug, No. 4 cylinder |
| R | Radio connection |
| S | Fuse box |
| $S^1$ | Back-up light fuse |
| T | Cable adapter |
| $T^1$ | Cable connector, single |
| $T^2$ | Cable connector, double |
| $T^3$ | Cable connector, triple |
| $T^4$ | Cable connector (four connections) |
| V | Windshield wiper motor |
| W | Interior light |
| X | License plate light |
| $X^1$ | Back-up light, left |
| $X^2$ | Back-up light, right |
| ① | Battery to frame ground strap |
| ② | Transmission to frame ground strap |

# Wiring Diagrams

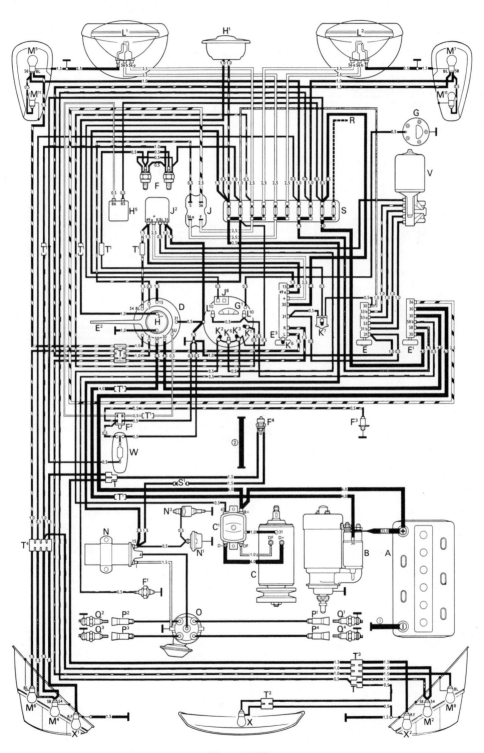

Type 1 1970

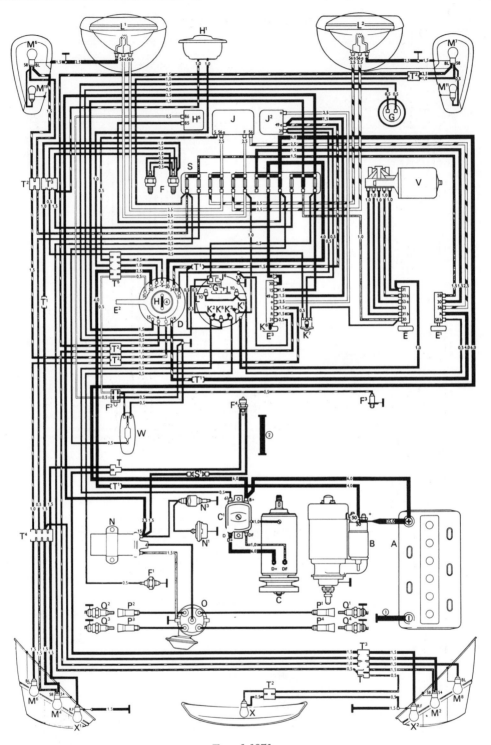

Type 1 1971

| | |
|---|---|
| A | Battery |
| B | Starter |
| C | Generator |
| $C^1$ | Regulator |
| D | Ignition/starter switch |
| E | Windshield wiper switch |
| $E^1$ | Light switch |
| $E^2$ | Turn signal and headlight dimmer switch |
| $E^3$ | Emergency flasher switch |
| F | Brake light switch |
| $F^1$ | Oil pressure switch |
| $F^2$ | Door contact and buzzer alarm switch, left |
| $F^3$ | Door contact switch, right |
| $F^4$ | Back-up light switch |
| G | Fuel gauge sending unit |
| $G^1$ | Fuel gauge |
| H | Horn button |
| $H^1$ | Horn |
| $H^5$ | Ignition key warning buzzer |
| J | Dimmer relay |
| $J^2$ | Emergency flasher relay |
| $J^6$ | Fuel gauge vibrator |
| $K^1$ | High beam warning light |
| $K^2$ | Generator charging warning light |
| $K^3$ | Oil pressure warning light |
| $K^5$ | Turn signal warning light |
| $K^6$ | Emergency flasher warning light |
| $K^7$ | Dual circuit brake warning light |
| $L^1$ | Sealed-Beam unit, left headlight |
| $L^2$ | Sealed-Beam unit, right headlight |
| $L^{10}$ | Instrument panel light |
| $M^1$ | Parking light, left |
| $M^2$ | Tail/brake light, right |
| $M^4$ | Tail/brake light, left |

| | |
|---|---|
| $M^5$ | Turn signal and parking light front left |
| $M^6$ | Turn signal, rear, left |
| $M^7$ | Turn signal and parking light front right |
| $M^8$ | Turn signal, rear, right |
| $M^{11}$ | Side marker light, front |
| N | Ignition coil |
| $N^1$ | Automatic choke |
| $N^3$ | Electro-magnetic pilot jet |
| O | Distributor |
| $P^1$ | Spark plug connector, No. 1 cylinder |
| $P^2$ | Spark plug connector, No. 2 cylinder |
| $P^3$ | Spark plug connector, No. 3 cylinder |
| $P^4$ | Spark plug connector, No. 4 cylinder |
| $Q^1$ | Spark plug, No. 1 cylinder |
| $Q^2$ | Spark plug, No. 2 cylinder |
| $Q^3$ | Spark plug, No. 3 cylinder |
| $Q^4$ | Spark plug, No. 4 cylinder |
| S | Fuse box |
| $S^1$ | Back-up light in-line fuse |
| T | Cable adapter |
| $T^1$ | Cable connector, single |
| $T^2$ | Cable connector, double |
| $T^3$ | Cable connector, triple |
| $T^4$ | Cable connector (four connections) |
| $T^5$ | Cable connector (five connections) |
| V | Windshield wiper motor |
| W | Interior light |
| X | License plate light |
| $X^1$ | Back-up light, left |
| $X^2$ | Back-up light, right |

| | |
|---|---|
| ① | Ground strap from battery to frame |
| ② | Ground strap from transmission to frame |
| ④ | Ground cable from front axle to frame |

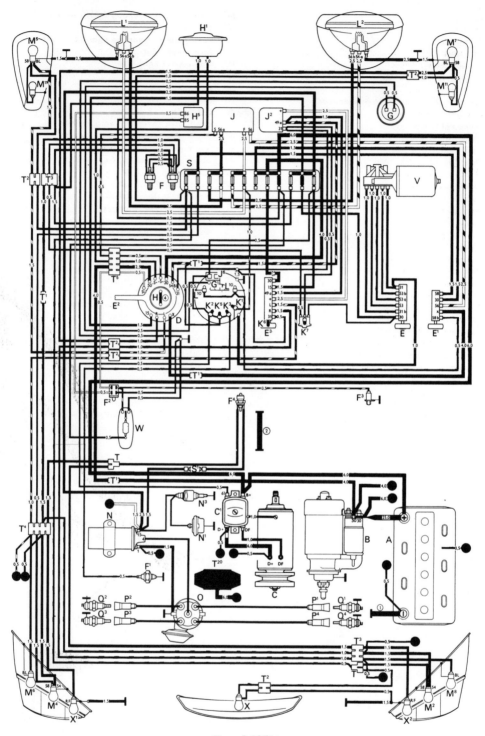

Type 1 1972

| | |
|---|---|
| A | Battery |
| B | Starter |
| C | Generator |
| $C^1$ | Regulator |
| D | Ignition/starter switch |
| E | Windshield wiper switch |
| $E^1$ | Light switch |
| $E^2$ | Turn signal and headlight dimmer switch |
| $E^3$ | Emergency flasher switch |
| F | Brake light switch |
| $F^1$ | Oil pressure switch |
| $F^2$ | Door contact and buzzer alarm switch, left |
| $F^3$ | Door contact switch, right |
| $F^4$ | Back-up light switch |
| G | Fuel gauge sending unit |
| $G^1$ | Fuel gauge |
| H | Horn button |
| $H^1$ | Horn |
| $H^5$ | Ignition key warning buzzer |
| J | Dimmer relay |
| $J^2$ | Emergency flasher relay |
| $J^6$ | Fuel gauge vibrator |
| $K^1$ | High beam warning light |
| $K^2$ | Generator charging warning light |
| $K^3$ | Oil pressure warning light |
| $K^5$ | Turn signal warning light |
| $K^6$ | Emergency flasher warning light |
| $K^7$ | Dual circuit brake warning light |
| $L^1$ | Sealed-Beam unit, left headlight |
| $L^2$ | Sealed-Beam unit, right headlight |
| $L^{10}$ | Instrument panel light |
| $M^1$ | Parking light, left |
| $M^2$ | Tail/brake light, right |
| $M^4$ | Tail/brake light, left |

| | |
|---|---|
| $M^5$ | Turn signal and parking light front left |
| $M^6$ | Turn signal, rear, left |
| $M^7$ | Turn signal and parking light front right |
| $M^8$ | Turn signal, rear, right |
| $M^{11}$ | Side marker light, front |
| N | Ignition coil |
| $N^1$ | Automatic choke |
| $N^3$ | Electro-magnetic pilot jet |
| O | Distributor |
| $P^1$ | Spark plug connector, No. 1 cylinder |
| $P^2$ | Spark plug connector, No. 2 cylinder |
| $P^3$ | Spark plug connector, No. 3 cylinder |
| $P^4$ | Spark plug connector, No. 4 cylinder |
| $Q^1$ | Spark plug, No. 1 cylinder |
| $Q^2$ | Spark plug, No. 2 cylinder |
| $Q^3$ | Spark plug, No. 3 cylinder |
| $Q^4$ | Spark plug, No. 4 cylinder |
| S | Fuse box |
| $S^1$ | Back-up light in-line fuse |
| T | Cable adapter |
| $T^1$ | Cable connector, single |
| $T^2$ | Cable connector, double |
| $T^3$ | Cable connector, triple |
| $T^4$ | Cable connector (four connections) |
| $T^5$ | Cable connector (five connections) |
| $T^{20}$ | Test network, central plug |
| V | Windshield wiper motor |
| W | Interior light |
| X | License plate light |
| $X^1$ | Back-up light, left |
| $X^2$ | Back-up light, right |
| ① | Ground strap from battery to frame |
| ② | Ground strap from transmission to frame |
| ④ | Ground cable from front axle to frame |

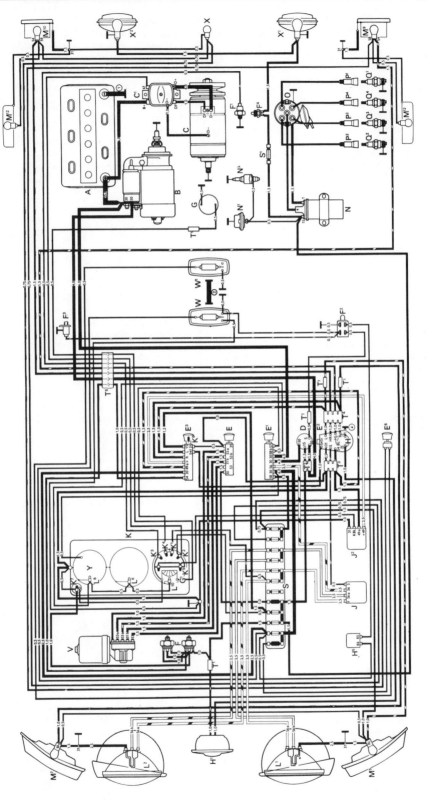

Type 2 1970

| | |
|---|---|
| A | Battery |
| B | Starter |
| C | Generator |
| $C^1$ | Regulator |
| D | Ignition/starter switch |
| E | Windshield wiper switch |
| $E^1$ | Light switch |
| $E^2$ | Turn signal and headlight dimmer switch |
| $E^3$ | Emergency flasher switch |
| $E^6$ | Switch for interior light, rear |
| F | Brake light switch |
| $F^1$ | Oil pressure switch |
| $F^2$ | Door contact switch, left with contact for buzzer $H^5$ |
| $F^3$ | Door contact switch, right |
| $F^4$ | Switch for back-up lights |
| G | Fuel gauge sending unit |
| $G^1$ | Fuel gauge |
| H | Horn button |
| $H^1$ | Horn |
| $H^5$ | Ignition key warning buzzer |
| J | Dimmer relay |
| $J^2$ | Emergency flasher relay |
| K | Instrument panel insert |
| $K^1$ | High beam warning light |
| $K^2$ | Generator charging warning light |
| $K^3$ | Oil pressure warning light |
| $K^4$ | Parking light warning light |
| $K^5$ | Turn signal warning light |
| $K^6$ | Emergency flasher warning light |
| $K^7$ | Dual circuit brake system warning light |
| $L^1$ | Sealed beam light, left headlight |
| $L^2$ | Sealed beam light, right headlight |
| $L^6$ | Speedometer light |
| $L^8$ | Clock light |

| | |
|---|---|
| $L^{10}$ | Instrument panel light |
| $M^5$ | Turn signal and parking light, front, left |
| $M^7$ | Turn signal and parking light, front, right |
| $M^9$ | Tail/brake/turn signal light, left |
| $M^{10}$ | Tail/brake/turn signal light, right |
| $M^{12}$ | Side marker lights, rear |
| N | Ignition coil |
| $N^1$ | Automatic choke |
| $N^3$ | Electro-magnetic pilot jet |
| O | Distributor |
| $P^1$ | Spark plug connector, No. 1 cylinder |
| $P^2$ | Spark plug connector, No. 2 cylinder |
| $P^3$ | Spark plug connector, No. 3 cylinder |
| $P^4$ | Spark plug connector, No. 4 cylinder |
| $Q^1$ | Spark plug, No. 1 cylinder |
| $Q^2$ | Spark plug, No. 2 cylinder |
| $Q^3$ | Spark plug, No. 3 cylinder |
| $Q^4$ | Spark plug, No. 4 cylinder |
| S | Fuse box |
| $S^1$ | In-line fuse for back-up lights |
| $T^1$ | Cable connector, single |
| $T^2$ | Cable connector, double |
| $T^3$ | Cable connector, triple |
| $T^4$ | Cable connector (four connections) |
| $T^5$ | Push-on connector |
| V | Windshield wiper motor |
| W | Interior light, front |
| $W^1$ | Interior light, rear |
| X | License plate light |
| $X^1$ | Back-up light, left |
| $X^2$ | Back-up light, right |
| Y | Clock |
| ① | Ground strap from battery to frame |
| ② | Ground strap from transmission to the frame |
| ④ | Ground cable from horn button |

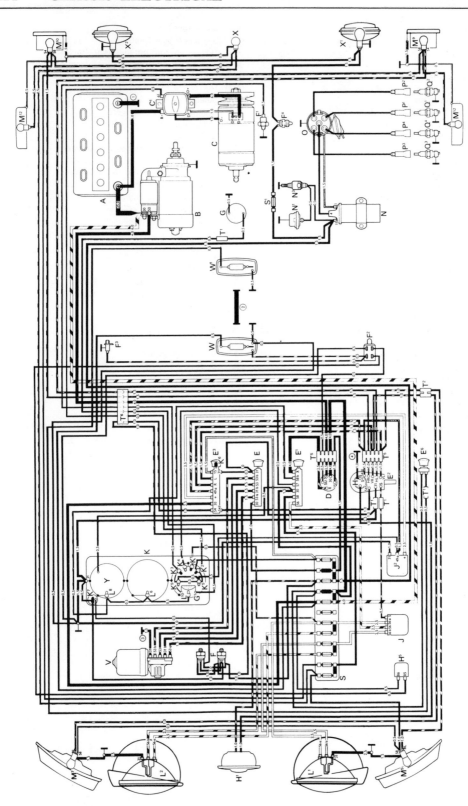

Type 2 1971

| | |
|---|---|
| A | Battery |
| B | Starter |
| C | Generator |
| $C^1$ | Regulator |
| D | Ignition/starter switch |
| E | Windshield wiper switch |
| $E^1$ | Light switch |
| $E^2$ | Turn signal and headlight dimmer switch |
| $E^3$ | Emergency flasher switch |
| $E^6$ | Interior light switch, rear |
| F | Brake light switch with warning switch |
| $F^1$ | Oil pressure switch |
| $F^2$ | Door contact switch, left, with contact for buzzer |
| $F^3$ | Door contact switch, right |
| $F^4$ | Back-up light switch |
| G | Fuel gauge sending unit |
| $G^1$ | Fuel gauge |
| H | Horn button |
| $H^1$ | Horn |
| $H^5$ | Ignition key warning buzzer |
| J | Dimmer relay |
| $J^2$ | Emergency flasher relay |
| K | Instrument panel insert |
| $K^1$ | High beam warning light |
| $K^2$ | Generator charging warning light |
| $K^3$ | Oil pressure warning light |
| $K^4$ | Parking light warning light |
| $K^5$ | Turn signal warning light |
| $K^6$ | Emergency flasher warning light |
| $K^7$ | Dual circuit brake system warning light |
| $L^1$ | Sealed beam unit, left headlight |
| $L^2$ | Sealed beam unit, right headlight |
| $L^6$ | Speedometer light |

| | |
|---|---|
| $L^8$ | Clock light |
| $L^{10}$ | Instrument panel light |
| $M^5$ | Turn signal and parking light, front, left |
| $M^7$ | Turn signal and parking light, front, right |
| $M^9$ | Tail/brake/turn signal light, left |
| $M^{10}$ | Tail/brake/turn signal light, right |
| $M^{12}$ | Sidemarker light, rear |
| N | Ignition coil |
| $N^1$ | Automatic choke |
| O | Ignition distributor |
| $P^1$ | Spark plug connector, No. 1 cylinder |
| $P^2$ | Spark plug connector, No. 2 cylinder |
| $P^3$ | Spark plug connector, No. 3 cylinder |
| $P^4$ | Spark plug connector, No. 4 cylinder |
| $Q^1$ | Spark plug, No. 1 cylinder |
| $Q^2$ | Spark plug, No. 2 cylinder |
| $Q^3$ | Spark plug, No. 3 cylinder |
| $Q^4$ | Spark plug, No. 4 cylinder |
| S | Fuse box |
| $S^1$ | Fuse for back-up light |
| $T^1$ | Cable connector, single |
| $T^5$ | Cable connector, five connections |
| $T^6$ | Cable connector, seven connections |
| V | Windshield wiper motor |
| W | Interior light, front |
| $W^1$ | Interior light, rear |
| X | License plate light |
| $X^1$ | Back-up light, left |
| $X^2$ | Back-up light, right |
| Y | Clock |
| ① | Ground strap battery to frame |
| ② | Ground strap transmission to frame |
| ③ | Ground strap windshield wiper |
| ④ | Ground strap horn button to steering coupling |

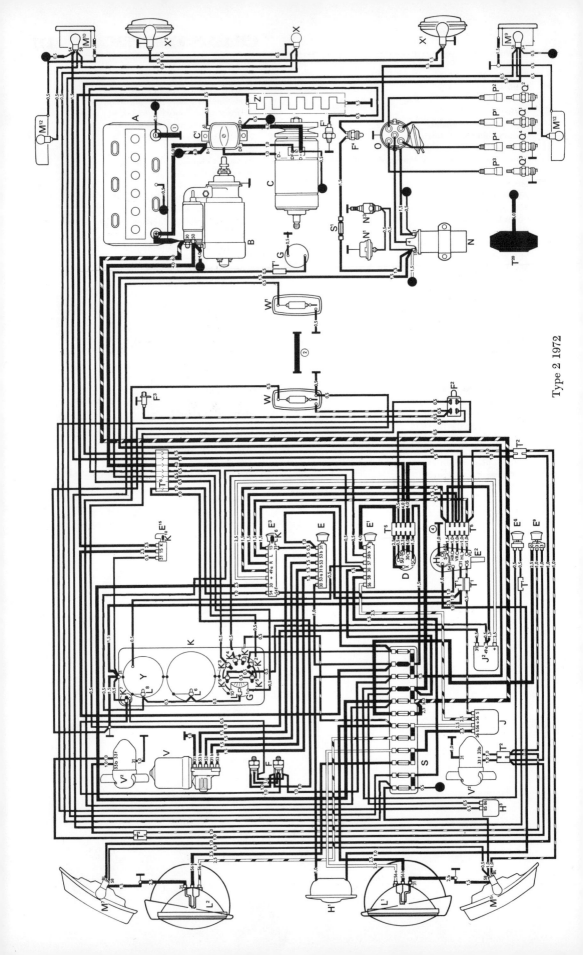

Type 2 1972

| | |
|---|---|
| A | Battery |
| B | Starter |
| C | Generator |
| $C^1$ | Regulator |
| D | Ignition/starter switch |
| E | Windshield wiper switch |
| $E^1$ | Light switch |
| $E^2$ | Turn signal and headlight dimmer switch |
| $E^3$ | Emergency flasher switch |
| $E^6$ | Interior light switch, rear |
| $E^9$ | Switch for fan motors |
| $E^{15}$ | Rear window defogger switch |
| F | Brake light switch with warning switch |
| $F^1$ | Oil pressure switch |
| $F^2$ | Door contact switch, left, with contact for buzzer |
| $F^3$ | Door contact switch, right |
| $F^4$ | Back-up light switch |
| G | Fuel gauge sending unit |
| $G^1$ | Fuel gauge |
| H | Horn button |
| $H^1$ | Horn |
| $H^3$ | Ignition key warning buzzer |
| J | Dimmer relay |
| $J^2$ | Emergency flasher relay |
| K | Instrument panel insert |
| $K^1$ | High beam warning light |
| $K^2$ | Generator charging warning light |
| $K^3$ | Oil pressure warning light |
| $K^4$ | Parking light warning light |
| $K^5$ | Turn signal warning light |
| $K^6$ | Emergency flasher warning light |
| $K^7$ | Dual circuit brake system warning light |
| $K^{10}$ | Rear window defogger warning light |
| $L^1$ | Sealed beam unit, left headlight |
| $L^2$ | Sealed beam unit, right headlight |
| $L^6$ | Speedometer light |
| $L^8$ | Clock light |

| | |
|---|---|
| $L^{10}$ | Instrument panel light |
| $M^5$ | Turn signal and parking light, front, left |
| $M^7$ | Turn signal and parking light, front, right |
| $M^9$ | Tail/brake/turn signal light, left |
| $M^{10}$ | Tail/brake/turn signal light, right |
| $M^{12}$ | Sidemarker light, rear |
| N | Ignition coil |
| $N^1$ | Automatic choke |
| $N^3$ | Electro-magnetic pilot jet |
| O | Ignition distributor |
| $P^1$ | Spark plug connector, No. 1 cylinder |
| $P^2$ | Spark plug connector, No. 2 cylinder |
| $P^3$ | Spark plug connector, No. 3 cylinder |
| $P^4$ | Spark plug connector, No. 4 cylinder |
| $Q^1$ | Spark plug, No. 1 cylinder |
| $Q^2$ | Spark plug, No. 2 cylinder |
| $Q^3$ | Spark plug, No. 3 cylinder |
| $Q^4$ | Spark plug, No. 4 cylinder |
| S | Fuse box |
| $S^1$ | Fuse for back-up light |
| $T^1$ | Cable connector, single |
| $T^2$ | Cable connector, double |
| $T^5$ | Cable connector, five connections |
| $T^6$ | Cable connector, eight connections |
| $T^{20}$ | Test network, central plug |
| V | Windshield wiper motor |
| $Y^2$ | Fan motor, front |
| W | Interior light, front |
| $W^1$ | Interior light, rear |
| X | License plate light |
| $X^1$ | Back-up light, left |
| $X^2$ | Back-up light, right |
| Y | Clock |
| $Z^1$ | Rear window defogger heating element |
| ① | Ground strap from battery to frame |
| ② | Ground strap from transmission to the frame |
| ④ | Ground cable from horn button to steering coupling |

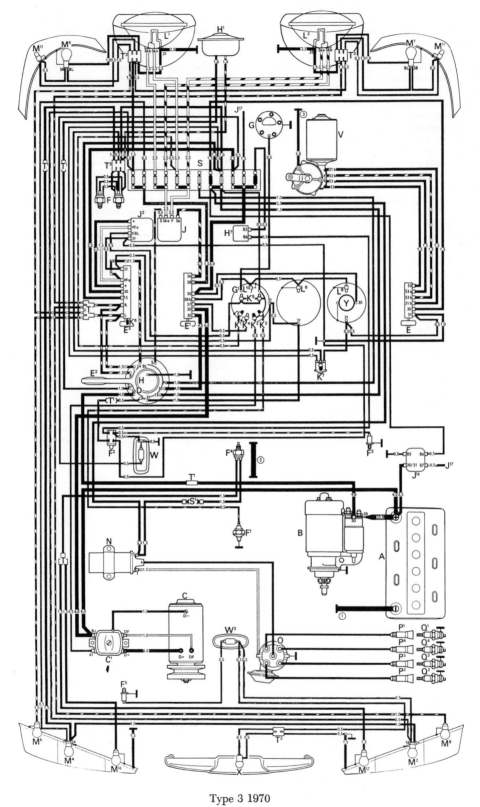

Type 3 1970

| | |
|---|---|
| A | Battery |
| B | Starter |
| C | Generator |
| $C^1$ | Regulator |
| D | Ignition/starter switch |
| E | Windshield wiper switch |
| $E^1$ | Light switch |
| $E^2$ | Turn signal and head light dimmer switch |
| $E^3$ | Emergency flasher switch |
| F | Brake light switch |
| $F^1$ | Oil pressure switch |
| $F^2$ | Door contact switch, left, with contact for buzzer |
| $F^3$ | Door contact switch, right |
| $F^4$ | Back-up light switch |
| $F^5$ | Luggage compartment light switch |
| G | Fuel gauge sending unit |
| $G^1$ | Fuel gauge |
| H | Horn button |
| $H^1$ | Horn |
| $H^5$ | Ignition key warning buzzer |
| J | Dimmer relay |
| $J^2$ | Emergency flasher relay |
| $J^{16}$ | Power supply relay for fuel injection system |
| $J^{17}$ | To fuel pump relay |
| $K^1$ | High beam warning light |
| $K^2$ | Generator charging warning light |
| $K^3$ | Oil pressure warning light |
| $K^4$ | Parking light warning light |
| $K^5$ | Turn signal warning lights |
| $K^6$ | Hazard warning light |
| $K^7$ | Dual circuit brake system warning light |
| $L^1$ | Sealed beam unit, left |
| $L^2$ | Sealed beam unit, right |
| $L^6$ | Speedometer light |

| | |
|---|---|
| $L^8$ | Clock light |
| $L^{10}$ | Instrument panel light |
| $M^2$ | Tail and brake light, right |
| $M^4$ | Tail and brake light, left |
| $M^5$ | Turn signal and parking light, front, left |
| $M^6$ | Turn signal, rear, left |
| $M^7$ | Turn signal and parking light, front, right |
| $M^8$ | Turn signal, rear, right |
| $M^{11}$ | Side marker light, front |
| $M^{16}$ | Back-up light, left |
| $M^{17}$ | Back-up light, right |
| N | Ignition coil |
| O | Distributor |
| $P^1$ | Spark plug connector, No. 1 cylinder |
| $P^2$ | Spark plug connector, No. 2 cylinder |
| $P^3$ | Spark plug connector, No. 3 cylinder |
| $P^4$ | Spark plug connector, No. 4 cylinder |
| $Q^1$ | Spark plug, No. 1 cylinder |
| $Q^2$ | Spark plug, No. 2 cylinder |
| $Q^3$ | Spark plug, No. 3 cylinder |
| $Q^4$ | Spark plug, No. 4 cylinder |
| S | Fuse box |
| $S^1$ | Back-up light in-line fuse |
| T | Cable adapter |
| $T^1$ | Cable connector, single |
| $T^2$ | Cable connector, double |
| $T^3$ | Cable connector, triple |
| V | Windshield wiper motor |
| W | Interior light |
| $W^3$ | Luggage compartment light |
| X | License plate light |

| | |
|---|---|
| ① | Battery to frame ground strap |
| ② | Transmission to frame ground strap |
| ③ | Windshield wiper motor to body ground strap |

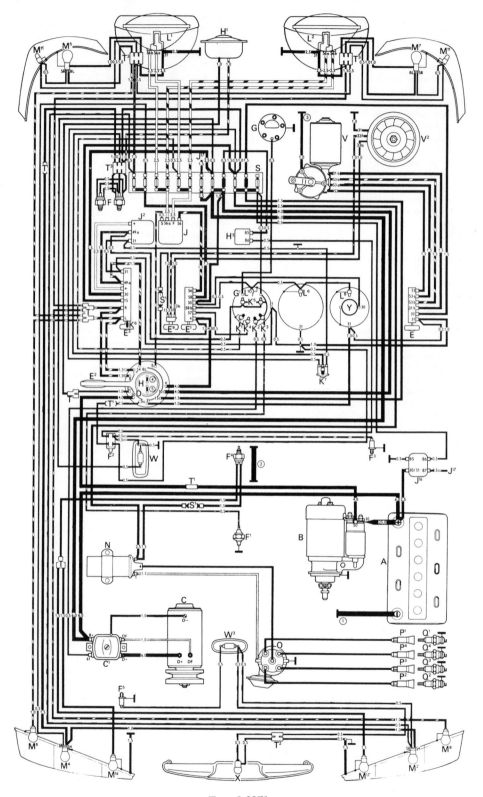

Type 3 1971

| | |
|---|---|
| A | Battery |
| B | Starter |
| C | Generator |
| $C^1$ | Regulator |
| D | Ignition/starter switch |
| E | Windshield wiper switch |
| $E^1$ | Light switch |
| $E^2$ | Turn signal and headlight dimmer switch |
| $E^3$ | Emergency flasher switch |
| $E^9$ | Fresh air fan motor switch |
| F | Brake light switch |
| $F^1$ | Oil pressure switch |
| $F^2$ | Door contact and buzzer alarm switch, left |
| $F^3$ | Door contact switch, right |
| $F^4$ | Back-up light switch |
| $F^5$ | Luggage compartment light switch |
| G | Fuel tank sending unit |
| $G^1$ | Fuel gauge |
| H | Horn button |
| $H^1$ | Horn |
| $H^5$ | Ignition key warning buzzer |
| J | Dimmer relay |
| $J^2$ | Emergency flasher relay |
| $J^{16}$ | Power supply relay for fuel injection |
| $J^{17}$ | Connection to fuel pump relay |
| $K^1$ | High beam warning light |
| $K^2$ | Generator charging warning light |
| $K^3$ | Oil pressure warning light |
| $K^4$ | Parking light warning light |
| $K^5$ | Turn signal warning light |
| $K^6$ | Emergency flasher warning light |
| $K^7$ | Dual brake circuit warning light |
| $L^1$ | Sealed-Beam unit left headlight |
| $L^2$ | Sealed-Beam unit right headlight |
| $L^6$ | Speedometer light |
| $L^8$ | Clock light |
| $L^{10}$ | Instrument panel light |

| | |
|---|---|
| $M^2$ | Tail/brake light, right |
| $M^4$ | Tail/brake light, left |
| $M^5$ | Turn signal and parking light, front, left |
| $M^6$ | Turn signal, rear, left |
| $M^7$ | Turn signal and parking light, front, right |
| $M^8$ | Turn signal, rear, right |
| $M^{11}$ | Side marker light, front |
| $M^{16}$ | Back-up light, left |
| $M^{17}$ | Back-up light, right |
| N | Ignition coil |
| O | Distributor |
| $P^1$ | Spark plug connector, No. 1 cylinder |
| $P^2$ | Spark plug connector, No. 2 cylinder |
| $P^3$ | Spark plug connector, No. 3 cylinder |
| $P^4$ | Spark plug connector, No. 4 cylinder |
| $Q^1$ | Spark plug, No. 1 cylinder |
| $Q^2$ | Spark plug No. 2 cylinder |
| $Q^3$ | Spark plug, No. 3 cylinder |
| $Q^4$ | Spark plug, No. 4 cylinder |
| S | Fuse box |
| $S^1$ | In-line fuse for back-up lights and fresh air fan motor |
| T | Cable adapter |
| $T^1$ | Cable connector, single |
| $T^2$ | Cable connector, double |
| $T^3$ | Cable connector, triple |
| V | Windshield wiper motor |
| $V^2$ | Fresh air motor front |
| W | Interior light |
| $W^3$ | Luggage compartment light |
| X | License plate light |
| Y | Clock |

| | |
|---|---|
| ① | Ground strap from battery to frame |
| ② | Ground strap from transmission to frame |
| ④ | Ground cable from horn to steering coupling |
| ⑤ | Ground cable from front axle to frame |

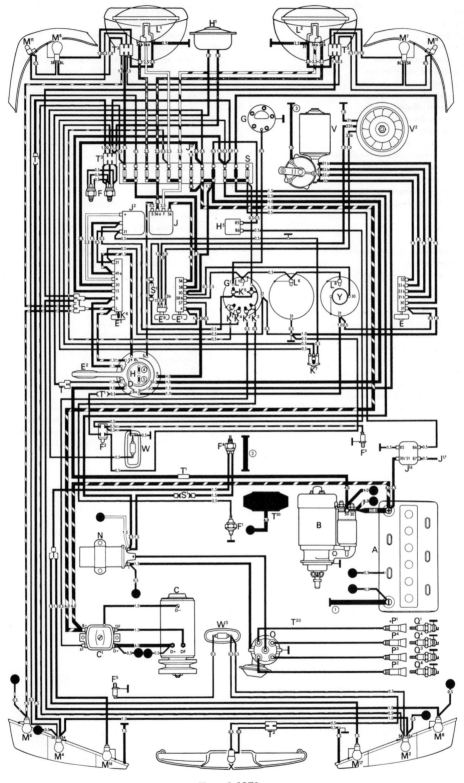

Type 3 1972

| | |
|---|---|
| A | Battery |
| B | Starter |
| C | Generator |
| $C^1$ | Regulator |
| D | Ignition/starter switch |
| E | Windshield wiper switch |
| $E^1$ | Light switch |
| $E^2$ | Turn signal and headlight dimmer switch |
| $E^3$ | Emergency flasher switch |
| $E^9$ | Fresh air fan motor switch |
| F | Brake light switch |
| $F^1$ | Oil pressure switch |
| $F^2$ | Door contact and buzzer alarm switch, left |
| $F^3$ | Door contact switch, right |
| $F^4$ | Back-up light switch |
| $F^5$ | Luggage compartment light switch |
| G | Fuel gauge sending unit |
| $G^1$ | Fuel gauge |
| H | Horn button |
| $H^1$ | Horn |
| $H^5$ | Ignition key warning buzzer |
| J | Dimmer relay |
| $J^2$ | Emergency flasher relay |
| $J^{16}$ | Power supply relay for fuel injection |
| $J^{17}$ | Connection to fuel pump relay |
| $K^1$ | High beam warning light |
| $K^2$ | Generator charging warning light |
| $K^3$ | Oil pressure warning light |
| $K^4$ | Parking light warning light |
| $K^5$ | Turn signal warning light |
| $K^6$ | Emergency flasher warning light |
| $K^7$ | Dual brake circuit warning light |
| $L^1$ | Sealed-Beam unit left headlight |
| $L^2$ | Sealed-Beam unit right headlight |
| $L^6$ | Speedometer light |
| $L^8$ | Clock light |
| $L^{10}$ | Instrument panel light |

| | |
|---|---|
| $M^2$ | Tail/brake light, right |
| $M^4$ | Tail/brake light, left |
| $M^5$ | Turn signal and parking light, front, left |
| $M^6$ | Turn signal, rear, left |
| $M^7$ | Turn signal and parking light, front, right |
| $M^8$ | Turn signal, rear, right |
| $M^{11}$ | Side marker light, front |
| $M^{16}$ | Back-up light. left |
| $M^{17}$ | Back-up light, right |
| N | Ignition coil |
| O | Distributor |
| $P^1$ | Spark plug connector, No. 1 cylinder |
| $P^2$ | Spark plug connector, No. 2 cylinder |
| $P^3$ | Spark plug connector, No. 3 cylinder |
| $P^4$ | Spark plug connector, No. 4 cylinder |
| $Q^1$ | Spark plug, No. 1 cylinder |
| $Q^2$ | Spark plug, No. 2 cylinder |
| $Q^3$ | Spark plug, No. 3 cylinder |
| $Q^4$ | Spark plug, No. 4 cylinder |
| S | Fuse box |
| $S^1$ | In-line fuse for back-up lights and fresh air fan motor |
| T | Cable adapter |
| $T^1$ | Cable connector, single |
| $T^2$ | Cable connector, double |
| $T^3$ | Cable connector, triple |
| $T^{20}$ | Test network, central plug |
| V | Windshield wiper motor |
| $V^2$ | Fresh air motor front |
| W | Interior light |
| $W^3$ | Luggage compartment light |
| X | License plate light |
| Y | Clock |
| ① | Ground strap from battery to frame |
| ② | Ground strap from transmission to frame |
| ④ | Ground cable from horn to steering coupling |
| ⑤ | Ground cable from front axle to frame |

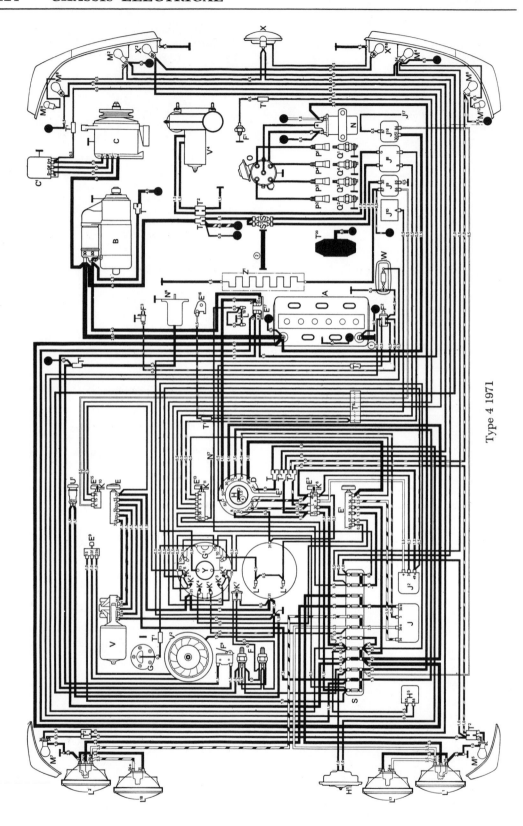

Type 4 1971

| | | | | |
|---|---|---|---|---|
| A | Battery | $L^{17}$ | Sealed-Beam unit left, high beam |
| B | Starter | $L^{18}$ | Sealed-Beam unit right, high beam |
| C | Generator | $L^{19}$ | Shift lever console light |
| $C^1$ | Regulator | $M^2$ | Tail/brake light right |
| D | Ignition/Starter switch | $M^4$ | Tail/brake light left |
| E | Windshield wiper switch | $M^5$ | Turn signal light front left |
| $E^1$ | Light switch | $M^6$ | Turn signal light rear left |
| $E^2$ | Turn signal and headlight dimmer switch | $M^7$ | Turn signal light front right |
| $E^3$ | Emergency flasher switch | $M^8$ | Turn signal light rear right |
| $E^9$ | Switch for fresh air fan motor | $M^{11}$ | Side marker light rear right |
| $E^{13}$ | Heater temperature regulating switch | $M^{12}$ | Side marker light rear left |
| $E^{15}$ | Rear window defogger switch | $M^{16}$ | Back-up light, left |
| $E^{16}$ | Heater switch | $M^{17}$ | Back-up light, right |
| $E^{17}$ | Starter cut-out switch | N | Ignition coil |
| F | Brake light switch | $N^5$ | Solenoid for kickdown switch |
| $F^1$ | Oil pressure switch | $N^7$ | Wiring for heater temperature sensor |
| $F^2$ | Door contact and buzzer alarm switch, left | O | Distributor |
| $F^3$ | Door contact switch, right | $P^1$ | Spark plug connector, No. 1 cylinder |
| $F^8$ | Kick-down switch | $P^2$ | Spark plug connector, No. 2 cylinder |
| G | Fuel gauge sending unit | $P^3$ | Spark plug connector. No. 3 cylinder |
| $G^1$ | Fuel gauge | $P^4$ | Spark plug connector, No. 4 cylinder |
| H | Horn button | $Q^1$ | Spark plug, No. 1 cylinder |
| $H^1$ | Horn | $Q^2$ | Spark plug, No. 2 cylinder |
| $H^5$ | Ignition key warning buzzer | $Q^3$ | Spark plug, No. 3 cylinder |
| J | Dimmer relay | $Q^4$ | Spark plug, No. 4 cylinder |
| $J^2$ | Emergency flasher relay | S | Fuse box |
| $J^8$ | Heater relay | $S^1$ | In-line fuse for heater |
| $J^9$ | Rear window defogger relay | $S^2$ | In-line fuse for rear window defogger |
| $J^{10}$ | Heater safety switch | T | Cable adapter |
| $J^{16}$ | Relay of electronic fuel injection | $T^1$ | Cable connector, single |
| $J^{17}$ | Cable to fuel pump relay (injection system) | $T^2$ | Cable connector, double |
| $K^1$ | High beam warning light | $T^5$ | Plug connector |
| $K^2$ | Generator charging warning light | $T^{20}$ | Test network, central plug |
| $K^3$ | Oil pressure warning light | V | Windshield wiper motor |
| $K^4$ | Parking light warning light | $V^2$ | Fresh air motor front |
| $K^5$ | Turn signal warning light | $V^4$ | Heater motor |
| $K^6$ | Emergency flasher warning light | W | Interior light |
| $K^7$ | Dual circuit brake warning light | X | License plate light |
| $K^{10}$ | Rear window defogger warning light | Y | Clock |
| $K^{11}$ | Heater warning light | $Z^1$ | Rear window defogger heating element |
| $L^1$ | Sealed-Beam unit, left head light | | |
| $L^2$ | Sealed-Beam unit, right head light | ① | Ground strap from battery to frame |
| $L^6$ | Speedometer illuminating light | ② | Ground strap from transmission to frame |
| $L^{10}$ | Instrument panel light | ④ | Ground cable for steering coupling |

# Chapter Six

# Clutch and Transaxles

## Manual Transaxle

### Removal and Installation

1. Disconnect the negative battery cable.

2. Remove the engine.

3. Remove the socket head screws which secure the drive shafts to the transmission. Remove the bolts from the transmission end first and then remove the shafts.

NOTE: *It is not necessary to remove the drive shafts entirely from the car if the car does not have to be moved while the transaxle is out.*

4. Disconnect the clutch cable from the clutch lever and remove the clutch cable and its guide tube from the transaxle. Loosen the square head bolt at the shift linkage coupling located near the rear of the transaxle. Slide the coupling off the inner shift lever. There is an access plate under the rear seat to reach the coupling on Type 1 and 3. It is necessary to work under the car to reach the coupling on Type 2 models.

5. Disconnect the starter wiring.

Socket head screws which secure the drive shafts

Shift linkage coupling

6. Disconnect the back-up light switch wiring.

7. Remove the front transaxle mounting bolts.

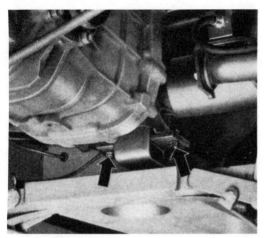

Front transaxle mounting bolts

8. Support the transaxle with a jack and remove the transmission carrier bolts.

9. Carefully lower the jack and remove the transaxle from the car.

10. To install, jack the transaxle into position and loosely install the bolts.

11. Tighten the transmission carrier bolts first, then tighten the front mounting nuts.

12. Install the drive shaft bolts with new lock washers. The lock washers should be positioned on the bolt with the convex side toward the screw head.

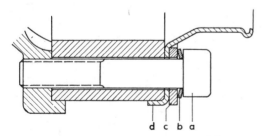

Drive axle bolts and washer position

    a. Socket head screws    c. Spacer
    b. Lock washer       d. Protective cap

13. Reconnect the wiring, the clutch cable, and the shift linkage.

NOTE: *It may be necessary to align the transmission so that the drive shaft joints do not rub the frame.*

14. Install the engine.

## Drive Shaft and
## Constant Velocity U-Joint
## Removal and Installation

1. Remove the bolts which secure the joints at each end of the shaft, tilt the shaft down, and remove the shaft.

2. Loosen the clamps which secure the rubber boot to the axle and slide the boot back on the axle.

3. Drive the stamped steel cover off of the joint with a drift.

NOTE: *After the cover is removed, do not tilt the ball hub as the balls will fall out of the hub.*

4. Remove the circlip from the end of the axle and press the axle out of the joint.

5. Reverse the above steps to install. The position of the dished washer is dependent on the type of transmission. On automatic transmissions, it is placed between the ball hub and the circlip. On manual transmissions, it is placed between the ball hub and the shoulder on the shaft. Be sure to pack the joint with grease.

NOTE: *The chamfer on the splined inside diameter of the ball hub faces the shoulder on the drive shaft.*

### Shift Linkage Adjustment

The Volkswagen shift linkage is not adjustable. When shifting becomes difficult or there is an excessive amount of play in the linkage, check the shifting mechanism for worn parts. Make sure the shift linkage coupling is tightly connected to the inner shift lever located at the rear of the transaxle under the rear seat. Worn parts may be found in the shift lever mechanism and the supports for the linkage rod sometimes wear out.

The gear shift lever can be removed after the front floor mat has been lifted. After the two retaining screws have been removed from the gear shift lever ball housing, the gear shift lever, ball housing, rubber boot, and spring are removed as a unit.

CAUTION: *Carefully mark the position of the stop plate and note the position of the turned up ramp at the side of the stop plate. Normally the ramp is turned up and on the right hand side of the hole.*

Installation is the reverse of removal.

Lubricate all moving parts with grease. Test the gear shift pattern. If there is difficulty in shifting, adjust the stop plate back and forth in its slotted holes.

# Automatic Stick Shift Transaxle

## Removal and Installation

1. Disconnect the negative battery cable.

2. Remove the engine.

3. Make a bracket to hold the torque converter in place. If a bracket is not used, the converter will slide off the transmission input shaft.

4. Detach the gearshift rod coupling.

5. Disconnect the drive shafts at the transmission end. If the driveshafts are not going to be repaired, it is not necessary to detach the wheel end.

6. Disconnect the ATF hoses from the transmission. Seal the open ends. Disconnect the temperature switch, neutral safety switch, and the back-up light switch.

7. Pull off the vacuum servo hose.

8. Disconnect the starter wiring.

9. Remove the front transaxle mounting nuts.

10. Loosen the rear transaxle mounting bolts. Support the transaxle and remove the bolts.

11. Lower the axle and remove it from the car.

12. With the torque converter bracket still in place, raise the axle into the car.

13. Tighten the nuts for the front transmission mounting. Insert the rear mounting bolts but do not tighten them at this time.

14. Replace the vacuum servo hose.

15. Connect the ATF hoses, using new washers. The washers are seals.

16. Connect the temperature switch and starter cables.

17. Install the drive shafts, using new washers. Turn the convex sides of the washers toward the screw head.

18. Align the transaxle so that the inner drive shaft joints do not rub on the frame fork and then tighten the rear mounting bolts.

19. Insert the shift rod coupling, tighten the screw, and secure it with wire.

20. Remove the torque converter bracket, and install the engine.

21. After installing the engine, bleed the ATF lines if return flow has not started after 2–3 minutes.

# Clutch

## Removal and Installation

### MANUAL TRANSMISSION

1. Remove the engine.

2. Remove the pressure plate securing bolts one turn at a time until all spring pressure is released.

3. Remove the bolts and remove the clutch assembly.

NOTE: *Notice which side of the clutch disc faces the flywheel and install the new disc in the same direction.*

4. Before installing the new clutch, check the condition of the flywheel. It should not have excessive heat cracks and the friction surface should not be scored or warped. Check the condition of the throw out bearing. If the bearing is worn, replace it.

5. Lubricate the pilot bearing in the end of the crankshaft with grease.

6. Insert a pilot shaft, used for centering the clutch disc, through the clutch disc and place the disc against the flywheel. The pilot shaft will hold the disc in place.

7. Place the pressure plate over the disc and loosely install the bolts.

NOTE: *Make sure the correct side of the clutch disc is facing outward. The disc will rub the flywheel if it is incorrectly positioned.*

8. After making sure that the pressure plate aligning dowels will fit into the pressure plate, gradually tighten the bolts.

9. Remove the pilot shaft and reinstall the engine.

10. Adjust the clutch pedal free-play.

### AUTOMATIC STICK SHIFT

1. Disconnect the negative battery cable.

2. Remove the engine.

3. Remove the transaxle.

4. Remove the torque converter by sliding it off of the input shaft. Seal off the hub opening.

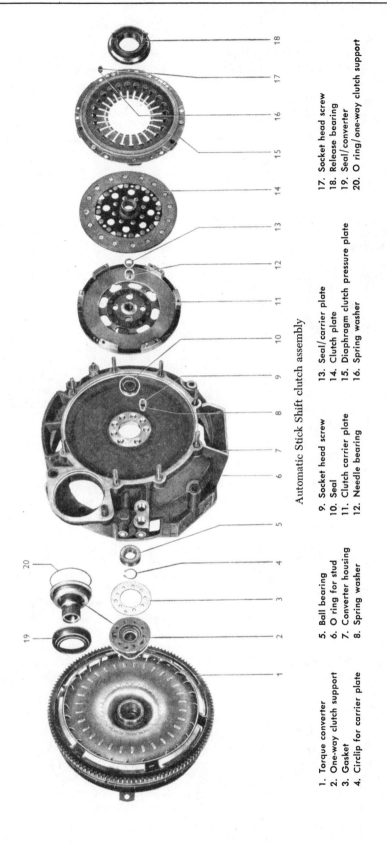

Automatic Stick Shift clutch assembly

1. Torque converter
2. One-way clutch support
3. Gasket
4. Circlip for carrier plate

5. Ball bearing
6. O ring for stud
7. Converter housing
8. Spring washer

9. Socket head screw
10. Seal
11. Clutch carrier plate
12. Needle bearing

13. Seal/carrier plate
14. Clutch plate
15. Diaphragm clutch pressure plate
16. Spring washer

17. Socket head screw
18. Release bearing
19. Seal/converter
20. O ring/one-way clutch support

5. Mount the transaxle in a repair stand or on a suitable bench.

6. Loosen the clamp screw and pull off the clutch operating lever. Remove the transmission cover.

7. Remove the hex nuts between the clutch housing and the transmission case.

NOTE: *Two nuts are located inside the differential housing.*

8. The oil need not be drained if the clutch is removed with the cover opening up and the gearshift housing breather blocked.

9. Pull the transmission from the clutch housing studs.

10. Turn the clutch lever shaft to disengage the release bearing.

11. Remove both lower engine mounting bolts.

12. Loosen the clutch retaining bolts gradually and alternately to prevent distortion. Remove the bolts, pressure plate, clutch plate, and release bearing.

13. Do not wash the release bearing. Wipe it dry only.

14. Check the clutch plate, pressure plate, and release bearing for wear and damage. Check the clutch carrier plate, needle bearing, and seat for wear. Replace the necessary parts.

15. If the clutch is wet with ATF, replace the clutch carrier plate seal and the clutch disc. If the clutch is wet with transmission oil, replace the transmission case seal and clutch disc.

16. Coat the release bearing guide on the transmission case neck and both lugs on the release bearing with grease. Insert the bearing into the clutch.

17. Grease the carrier plate needle bearing. Install the clutch disc and pressure plate using a pilot shaft to center the disc on the flywheel.

18. Tighten the pressure plate retaining bolts evenly and alternately. Make sure that the release bearing is correctly located in the diaphragm spring.

19. Insert the lower engine mounting bolts from the front. Replace the sealing rings if necessary. Some units have aluminum sealing rings and cap nuts.

20. Push the transmission onto the converter housing studs. Insert the clutch lever shaft behind the release bearing lugs. Push the release bearing onto the transmission case neck. Tighten the bolts which hold the clutch housing to the transmission case.

21. Install the clutch operating lever.

22. It is necessary to adjust the basic clutch setting. The clutch operating lever should contact the clutch housing. Tighten the lever clamp screw slightly.

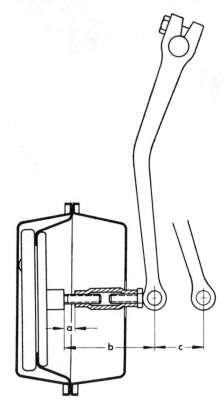

Automatic Stick Shift basic clutch adjusting dimensions

23. First adjust dimension (a) to 0.335 in. Adjust dimension (b) to 3.03 in. Finally adjust dimension (c) to 1.6 in. by repositioning the clutch lever on the clutch shaft. Tighten the lever clamp screw.

24. Push the torque converter onto the support tube. Insert it into the turbine shaft by turning the converter.

25. Check the clutch play after installing the transaxle and engine.

## Clutch Cable Adjustment

### Manual Transmission

1. Check the clutch pedal travel by measuring the distance the pedal travels toward the floor until pressure is exerted against the clutch. The distance is 3/8 to 3/4 in.

2. To adjust the clutch, jack up the rear of the car and support it on jackstands.

3. Remove the left rear wheel.

Clutch pedal travel is dimension (a)

4. Adjust the cable tension by turning the wing nut on the end of the clutch cable. Turning the wing nut counterclockwise decreases pedal free-play, turning it clockwise increases free-play.

Wing nut for clutch cable adjustment

5. When the adjustment is completed, the wings of the wing nut must be horizontal so that the lugs on the nut engage the recesses in the clutch lever.

6. Push on the clutch pedal several times and check the pedal free-play.

7. Install the wheel and lower the car.

### Automatic Stick Shift

The adjustment is made on the linkage between the clutch arm and the vacuum servo unit. To check the clutch play:

1. Disconnect the servo vacuum hose.

2. Measure the clearance between the up-

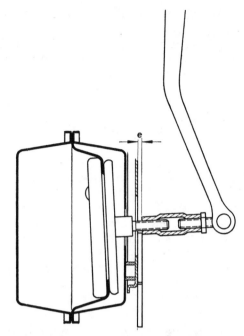

Checking clutch adjustment—Automatic Stick Shift

per edge of the servo unit mounting bracket and the lower edge of the adjusting turnbuckle. If the clearance is 0.16 in. or more, the clutch needs adjustment.

3. Reconnect the vacuum hose.

To adjust the clutch:

1. Disconnect the servo vacuum hose.

2. Loosen the turnbuckle locknut and back it off completely to the lever arm. Then turn the servo turnbuckle against the lock nut. Now back off the turnbuckle 5–5½ turns. The distance between the locknut and the turnbuckle should be 0.25 in.

Adjusting Automatic Stick Shift clutch—(d) is 0.25 in., measured between the locknut and turnbuckle

3. Tighten the lock nut against the adjusting sleeve.

4. Reconnect the vacuum hose and road test the vehicle. The clutch is properly adjusted when Reverse gear can be engaged silently and the clutch does not slip on acceleration. If the clutch arm contacts the clutch housing, there is no more adjustment possible and the clutch plate must be replaced.

The speed of engagement of the Automatic Stick Shift clutch is regulated by the vacuum operated valve rather than by the driver's foot. The adjusting screw is on top of the valve under a small protective cap. Adjust the valve as follows:

1. Remove the cap.

2. To slow the engagement, turn the adjusting screw ¼–½ turn clockwise. To speed engagement, turn the screw counterclockwise.

Speed of engagement adjustment screw

3. Replace the cap.

4. Test operation by shifting from Second to First at 44 mph without depressing the accelerator. The shift should take exactly one second to occur.

*CLUTCH CABLE*

**Removal and Installation**

1. Jack up the car and remove the left rear wheel.

2. Disconnect the cable from the clutch operating lever.

3. Remove the rubber boot from the end of the guide tube and off the end of the cable.

4. On Type 1, unbolt the pedal cluster and remove it from the car. It will also be necessary to disconnect the brake master cylinder push rod and throttle cable from the pedal cluster. On Type 2, remove the cover under the pedal cluster, then remove the pin from the clevis on the end of the clutch cable. On Type 3, remove the frame head cover and remove the pin from the clevis on the end of the clutch cable.

5. Pull the cable out of its guide tube from the pedal cluster end.

6. Installation is the reverse of the above. NOTE: *Grease the cable before installing it and readjust the clutch pedal free-play.*

## Automatic Transmission

**Removal and Installation**

NOTE: *The engine and transmission must be removed as an assembly on the Type 4 and Type 2/1700.*

1. Remove the battery ground cable.

2. On the sedan, remove the cooling air intake duct with the heating fan and hoses. Remove the cooling air intake connection and bellows, then detach the hoses to the air cleaner.

3. On the station wagons, remove the warm air hoses and air cleaner. Remove the boot between the dipstick tube and the body and the boot between the oil filler neck and the body. Disconnect the cooling air bellows at the body.

4. Disconnect the wires at the regulator and the alternator wires at the snap-connector located by the regulator. Disconnect the auxiliary air regulator and the oil pressure switch at the snap connectors located by the distributor.

5. Disconnect the fuel injection wiring. There are 12 connections and they are listed as follows:

    a. Fuel injector cylinder 2, 2-pole, protective gray cap

    b. Fuel injector cylinder 1, 2-pole, protective black cap

    c. Starter, 1-pole, white

    d. Throttle valve switch, 4-pole

    e. Distributor, 3-pole

    f. Thermo switch, 1-pole, white

    g. Cold start valve, 3-pole

h. Temperature sensor crankcase, 2-pole

i. Ground connection, 3-pole, white wires

j. Temperature sensor for the cylinder head, 1-pole

k. Fuel injector cylinder 3, 2-pole, protective black cap

l. Fuel injector cylinder 4, 2-pole, protective gray cap

6. Disconnect the accelerator cable.

7. Disconnect the right fuel return line.

8. Raise the car.

9. Disconnect the warm hoses from the heat exchangers.

10. Disconnect the starter wires and push the engine wiring harness through the engine cover plate.

11. Disconnect the fuel supply line and plug it.

12. Remove the heater booster exhaust pipe.

13. Remove the rear axles and cover the ends to protect them from dirt.

14. Remove the selector cable by unscrewing the cable sleeve.

15. Remove the wire from the kickdown switch.

16. Remove the bolts from the rubber transmission mountings, taking careful note of the position, number, and thickness of the spacers that are present.

CAUTION: *These spacers must be reinstalled exactly as they were removed. Do not detach the transmission carrier from the body.*

17. Support the engine and transmission assembly in such a way that it may be lowered and moved rearward at the same time.

18. Remove the engine carrier bolts and the engine and transmission assembly from the car.

19. Matchmark the flywheel and the torque converter and remove the three attaching bolts.

20. Remove the engine-to-transmission bolts and separate the engine and transmission.

CAUTION: *Exercise care when separating the engine and transmission as the torque converter will easily slip off the input shaft if the transmission is tilted downward.*

21. Installation is as follows. Install and tighten the engine-to-transmission bolts af-

ter aligning the match marks on the flywheel and converter.

22. Making sure the match marks are aligned, install the converter-to-flywheel bolts.

23. Make sure the rubber buffer is in place and the two securing studs do not project more than 0.7 in. from the transmission case.

24. Tie a cord to the slot in the engine compartment seal. This will make positioning the seal easier.

25. Lift the assembly far enough to allow the accelerator cable to be pushed through the front engine cover.

26. Continue lifting the assembly into place. Slide the rubber buffer into the locating tube in the rear axle carrier.

27. Insert the engine carrier bolts and raise the engine until the bolts are at the top of their elongated slots. Tighten the bolts.

Engine carrier bolts positioned at the top of their elongated slots

NOTE: *A set of three gauges must be obtained to check the alignment of the rubber buffer in its locating tube. The dimensions are given in the illustration*

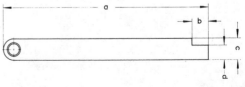

Buffer alignment gauges

| | |
|---|---|
| a. 5.095 in. | c. 0.590 in. |
| b. 0.472 in. | d. 0.393, 0.433, and 0.472 in. |

*as is the measuring technique. The rubber buffer is centered horizontally when the 11 mm gauge can be inserted on both sides. The buffer is located vertically when the 10 mm gauge can be inserted on the bottom side and the 12 mm gauge can be inserted on the top side. See Steps 28 and 29 for adjustment procedure.*

28. Install the rubber transmission mount bolts with spacers of the correct thickness. The purpose of the spacers is to center the rubber buffer vertically in its support tube. The buffer is not supposed to carry any weight; it absorbs torsional forces only.

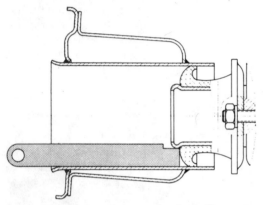

Measuring technique for centering the buffer

29. To locate the buffer horizontally in its locating tube, the engine carrier must be vertical and parallel to the fan housing. It is adjusted by moving the engine carrier bolts in elongated slots. Further travel may be obtained by moving the brackets attached to the body. It may be necessary to

Checking the position of engine carrier

adjust the two rear suspension wishbones with the center of the transmission after the rubber buffer is horizontally centered. Take the car to a dealer or alignment specialist to align the rear suspension.

30. Adjust the selector lever cable.

31. Connect the wire to the kickdown switch.

32. Install the rear axles. Make sure the lockwashers are placed with the convex side out.

33. Reconnect the fuel hoses and heat exchanger hoses. Install the pipe for the heater booster.

34. Lower the car and pull the engine compartment seal into place with the cord.

35. Reconnect the fuel injection and engine wiring. Push the starter wires through the engine cover plate and connect the wires to the starter.

36. Install the intake duct with the fan and hoses, also the cooling air intake.

### Pan Removal

1. Some models have a drain plug in the pan. Remove the plug and drain the transmission oil. On models without the plug, loosen the pan bolts 2–3 turns and lower one corner of the pan to drain the oil.

2. Remove the pan bolts and remove the pan from the transmission.

NOTE: *It may be necessary to tap the pan with a rubber hammer to loosen it.*

3. Use a new gasket and install the pan. Tighten the bolts loosely until the pan is properly in place, then tighten the bolts fully, moving in a diagonal pattern.

NOTE: *Do not overtighten the bolts.*

4. Refill the transmission with ATF.

5. At 5 minute intervals, retighten the pan bolts two or three times.

### Filter Service

The Volkswagen automatic transmission has a filter screen secured by a screw to the bottom of the valve body. Remove the pan and remove the filter screen from the valve body.

CAUTION: *Never use a cloth that will leave the slightest bit of lint in the transmission when cleaning transmission parts. The lint will expand when exposed to transmission fluid and clog the valve body and filter.*

Clean the filter screen with compressed air.

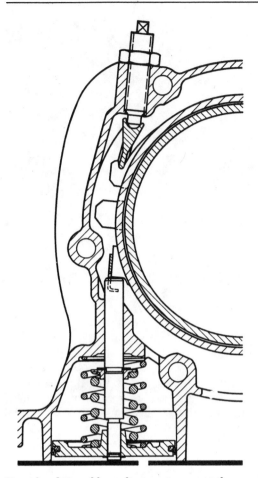

Front band assembly—adjustment screw at the top

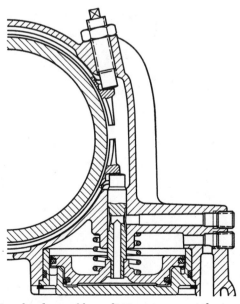

Rear band assembly—adjustment screw at the top

### Front (Second) Band Adjustment

Tighten the front band adjusting screw to 7 ft lbs. Then loosen the screw and tighten it to 3.5 ft lbs. From this position, loosen the screw exactly 1¾ to 2 turns and tighten the lock nut.

### Rear (First) Band Adjustment

Tighten the rear band adjusting screw to 7 ft lbs. Then loosen the screw and re-tighten it to 3.5 ft lbs. From this position, loosen the screw exactly 3¼ to 3½ turns and tighten the lock nut.

### Kickdown Switch Adjustment

#### TYPE 3

1. Disconnect the accelerator cable return spring.

2. Move the throttle to the fully open position. Adjust the accelerator cable to give 0.02–0.04 in. clearance between the stop and the end of the throttle valve lever.

3. When the accelerator cable is adjusted and the throttle is moved to the fully open position, the kickdown switch should click. The ignition switch must be ON for this test.

4. To adjust the switch, loosen the switch securing screws and slide the switch back and forth until the test in Step 3 is satisfied.

5. Reconnect the accelerator cable return spring.

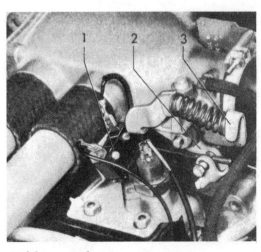

Kickdown switch

1. Kickdown switch          2. Accelerator cable lever
3. Throttle valve lever

TYPE 4

The Type 4 switch is not adjustable.

### Shift Linkage Adjustment

Make sure the shifting cable is not kinked or bent and that the linkage and cable are properly lubricated.

.1. Move the gear shift lever to the Park position.

2. Loosen the clamp which holds the front and rear halves of the shifting rod to-

Push the transmission lever rearward against its stop

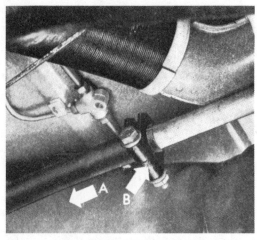

Clamp which secures the shift linkage rod halves

gether. Loosen the clamping bolts on the transmission lever.

3. Press the lever on the transmission rearward as far as possible. Spring pressure will be felt. The manual valve must be on the stop in the valve body.

4. Holding the transmission lever against its stop, tighten the clamping bolt.

5. Holding the rear shifting rod half, push the front half forward to take up any clearance and tighten the clamp bolt.

6. Test the shift pattern.

# Chapter Seven

# Suspension and Steering

## Rear Suspension

*DIAGONAL ARM AND A-ARM*

**Removal and Installation**

DIAGONAL ARM SUSPENSION—
TYPES 1, 2, AND 3

1. Remove the wheel shaft nuts.
CAUTION: *Do not raise the car to remove the nuts. They can be safely removed only if the weight on the car is on its wheels.*
2. Disconnect the drive shaft of the side to be removed.
3. Remove the lower shock absorber mount. Raise the car and remove the wheel and tire.
4. Remove the brake drum, disconnect the brake lines and emergency brake cable, and remove the backing plate.
5. Matchmark the torsion bar plate and the diagonal arm with a cold chisel.
6. Remove the four bolts and nuts which secure the plate to the diagonal arm.
7. Remove the pivot bolts for the diagonal arm and remove the arm from the car.
NOTE: *Take careful note of the washers at the pivot bolts. These washers are used to determine alignment and they must be put back in the same place.*
8. Remove the spring plate hub cover.

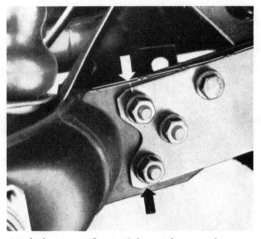

Mark the torsion bar and diagonal arm with a chisel

9. Using a steel bar, lift the spring plate off of the lower suspension stop.
10. On Type 1, remove the five bolts at the front of the fender. On all others, remove the cover in the side of the fender.
11. Remove the spring plate and pull the torsion bar out of its housing.
NOTE: *There are left and right torsion bars designated by an (L) or (R) on the end face. (Coat any rubber bushings with talcum powder upon installation. Do not use graphite, silicon, or grease.*
12. To install, insert the torsion bar, outer bushing, and spring plate. The tor-

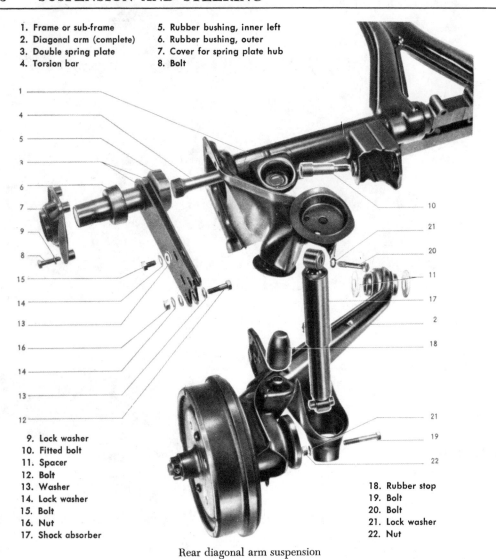

1. Frame or sub-frame
2. Diagonal arm (complete)
3. Double spring plate
4. Torsion bar
5. Rubber bushing, inner left
6. Rubber bushing, outer
7. Cover for spring plate hub
8. Bolt

9. Lock washer
10. Fitted bolt
11. Spacer
12. Bolt
13. Washer
14. Lock washer
15. Bolt
16. Nut
17. Shock absorber

18. Rubber stop
19. Bolt
20. Bolt
21. Lock washer
22. Nut

Rear diagonal arm suspension

sion bar is properly adjusted when the spring plate, with no load, is the specified number of degrees below a horizontal position.

13. Using two bolts, loosely secure the spring plate hub cover. Place a thick nut between the leaves of the spring plate.

14. Lift the spring plate up to the lower suspension stop and install the remaining bolts into the hub cover. Tighten the hub cover bolts.

15. Install the diagonal arm pivot bolt and washers and peen it with a chisel. There must always be at least one washer on the outside end of the bolt.

16. Align the chisel marks and attach the diagonal arm to the spring plate.

Diagonal arm pivot bolt—both spacer washers on the outside

17. Install the backing plate, parking brake cable, and brake lines.

18. Reconnect the shock absorber. Install the brake drum and wheel shaft nuts.

19. Reconnect the drive shaft. Bleed the brakes.

20. Install the wheel and tire.

21. Check the suspension alignment.

### A-Arm—Type 4

1. Raise the car and place it on jackstands. Securely block up the A-arm.

CAUTION: *The A-arm must be securely supported when the shock absorber is disconnected to prevent the spring tension from being released suddenly. The shock absorber is the lower stop for the suspension.*

2. Disconnect the drive shaft.

3. Disconnect the handbrake cable at the brake lever and remove it.

4. Disconnect the brake lines and the stabilizer bar if equipped.

5. With the vehicle on the ground or the A-arm securely supported, remove the lower shock absorber mounting bolt.

6. Slowly release the A-arm and remove the coil springs.

7. Mark the position of the brackets or the eccentric bolts, whichever are removed, with a chisel. Remove the nuts which secure the brackets in the rear axle carrier, or the pivot bolts in the bonded rubber bushings, and remove the A-arm.

8. Loosely install the A-arm. If the pivot bolts were removed, install them loosely. If the eccentric bolts and brackets were removed, install them, aligning the chisel marks, and then tighten them.

9. Insert the coil spring and slowly compress it into place. Install the lower shock absorber mount.

10. Reverse Steps 1–4 to complete.

## SHOCK ABSORBERS

### Removal and Installation

#### Diagonal Arm Suspension

The shock absorber is secured at the top and bottom by a through bolt. Raise the car and remove the bolts. Remove the shock absorber from the car.

#### A-Arm Suspension

The shock absorber is the lower stop for the suspension.

CAUTION: *The A-arm must be securely supported when the shock absorber is disconnected to prevent the spring tension from being released suddenly.*

Leaving the car on the ground or raising the car and securely supporting the A-arm, remove the lower shock absorber through bolt. To gain access to the upper shock mounting, remove the access panel for each shock located at the sides of the rear luggage shelf. Remove the self locking nut from the shock absorber shaft and remove the shock. Installation is the reverse of removal.

## REAR SUSPENSION ADJUSTMENTS

### Type 1, Diagonal Arm Suspension

The only adjustment is the toe-in adjustment. The adjustment is performed by varying the number of washers at the diagonal arm pivot. There must always be one washer located on the outboard side of the pivot.

### Type 2, 3, Diagonal Arm Suspension

The transmission and engine assembly position in the vehicle is adjustable. It is necessary that the assembly be correctly centered before the suspension is aligned. It may be adjusted by moving the engine and transmission brackets in their elongated slots.

The distance between the diagonal arms may be adjusted by moving the washers at the A-arm pivots. The washers may be positioned only two ways. Either both washers on the outboard side of the pivot or a single washer on each side of the pivot. To adjust the distance, position the diagonal arms and move the washers in the same manner at both pivots.

The wheel track angle may be adjusted by moving the diagonal arm flange in the elongated slot in the spring plate.

The toe-in is adjusted by positioning the washers and the diagonal arm pivot.

### Type 4, A-Arm Suspension

The toe-in is adjusted by the eccentric A-arm pivot bolts.

The rubber buffer centralization procedure is given in the "Type 4 Transaxle Removal and Installation" procedure.

The track width can be adjusted by

1. Rear axle carrier
2. A-arm (left/right)
3. Coil spring with plastic tube
4. Shock absorber
5. Bracket—inner (eccentric)
6. Bracket—outer left/right
7. Eccentric bolt
8. Eccentric washer
9. Bolt
10. Bolt
11. Damping ring, shock absorber
12. Damping washer, shock absorber
13. Spacer sleeve
14. Self-locking nut
15. Damping ring, rear axle carrier
16. Damping bushing, rear axle carrier
17. Plate
18. Plate
19. Nut
20. Lock washer
21. Cover plate
22. Bolt
23. Lock washer
24. Bolt
25. Lock washer

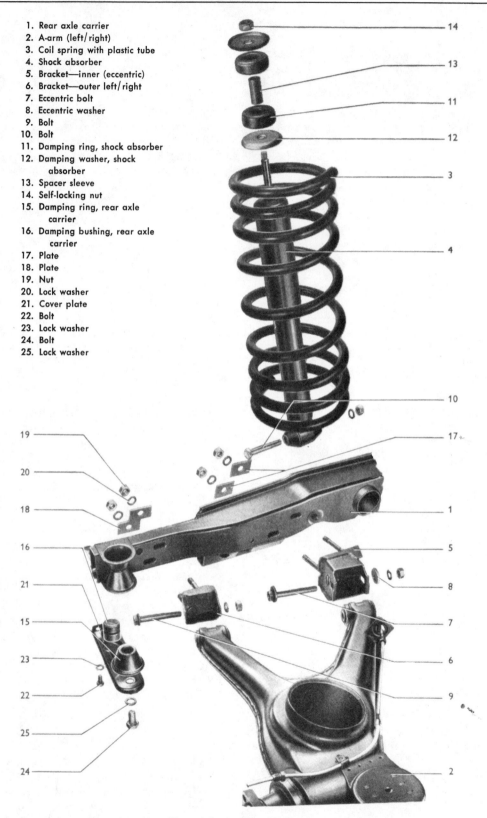

Type 4 A-arm suspension

loosening the A-arm mounting bracket bolts and moving the brackets in or out to the proper position.

# Front Suspension

## TORSION BARS, TORSION BAR SUSPENSION

### Removal and Installation

#### TYPES 1, 2, AND 3 (EXCEPT SUPER BEETLE)

1. Jack up the car and remove both wheels and brake drums.

2. Remove the ball joint nuts and remove the left and right steering knuckles. A forked ball joint removing tool is available at an auto parts store. CAUTION: *Never strike the ball joint stud.*

3. Remove those arms attached to the torsion bars on one side only. To remove the arms, loosen and remove the arm set-screw and pull the arm off the end of the torsion bar.

4. Loosen and remove the set-screw which secures the torsion bar to the torsion bar housing.

5. Pull the torsion bar out of its housing.

6. To install, carefully note the number of leaves and the position of the countersink marks for the torsion bar and the torsion arm.

7. Align the countersink mark in the center of the bar with the hole for the set-screw and insert the torsion bar into its housing. Install the set screw. Install the torsion arm.

8. Reverse Steps 1–3 to complete.

## SUSPENSION STRUT

### Removal and Installation

#### SUPER BEETLE AND TYPE 4

1. Jack up the car and remove the wheel and tire.

2. ¶If the left strut is to be removed, remove the speedometer cable from the steering knuckle.

3. Disconnect the brake line from the bracket on the strut.

4. At the base of the strut, bend down the locking tabs for the three bolts and remove the bolts.

5. Push down on the steering knuckle and pull the strut out of the knuckle.

6. Remove the three nuts which secure the top of the strut to the body. Before removing the last nut, support the strut so that it does not fall out of the car.

7. Reverse the above steps to install the strut. Always use new nuts and locking tabs during installation.

## SHOCK ABSORBERS

### Removal and Installation

#### TORSION BAR SUSPENSION (TYPES 1, 2, AND 3)

1. Remove the wheel and tire.

2. Remove the nut from the torsion arm stud and slide the lower end of the shock off of the stud.

3. Remove the nut from the shock absorber shaft at the upper mounting and remove the shock from the vehicle.

4. The shock is tested by operating it by hand. As the shock is extended and compressed, it should operate smoothly over its entire stroke with an even pressure. Its damping action should be clearly felt at the end of each stroke. If the shock is leaking slightly, the shock need not be replaced. A shock that has had an excessive loss of fluid will have flat spots in the stroke as the shock is compressed and extended. That is, the pressure will feel as though it has been suddenly released for a short distance during the stroke.

5. Installation is the reverse of Steps 1–3.

#### STRUT SUSPENSION (SUPER BEETLE AND TYPE 4)

In this type suspension system, the shock absorber is actually the supporting vertical member.

1. Remove the strut as outlined above.

2. It is necessary to disassemble the strut to replace the shock absorber. To remove the spring, it must be compressed. The proper type compressor is available at an auto parts store.

3. Remove the nut from the end of the shock absorber shaft and slowly release the spring. The strut can now be disassembled. Testing is the same as the torsion bar shock absorber.

4. Reverse the above steps to install.

## BALL JOINTS

### Removal and Installation

Vehicles with strut suspension have only one ball joint on each side located at the

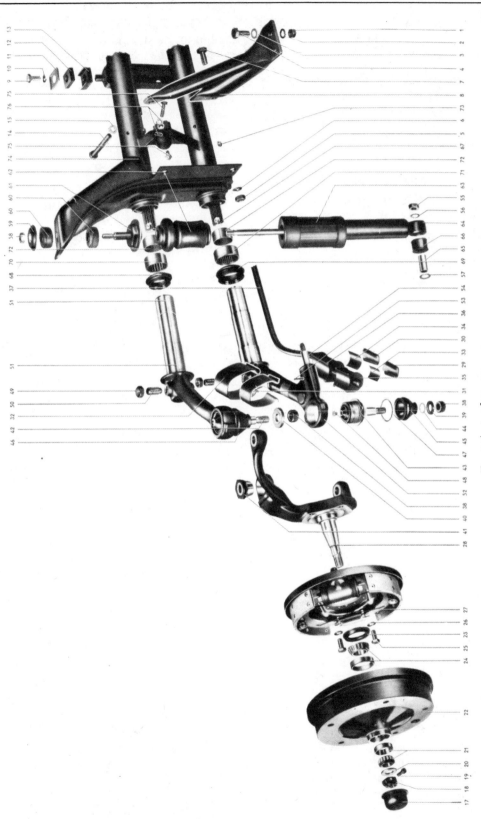

Front torsion bar suspension

Compressing the coil spring for the strut type suspension

base of the strut in the track control arm. Vehicles with torsion bar suspension have two ball joints on each side located at the end of each torsion arm.

### Torsion Bar Suspension

1. Jack up the car and remove the wheel and tire.

2. Remove the brake drum and disconnect the brake line from the backing plate.

3. Remove the nut from each ball joint stud and remove the ball joint stud from the steering knuckle. Remove the steering knuckle from the car. A ball joint removal tool is available at an auto parts store. Do not strike the ball joint stud.

4. Remove the torsion arm from the torsion bar.

5. Remove the ball joint from the torsion arm by pressing it out.

6. Press a new ball joint in, making sure that the square notch in the joint is in line with the notch in the torsion arm eye.

NOTE: *Ball joints are supplied in different sizes designated by V-notches in the*

A notched ball joint indicating that it is oversized—torsion bar suspension

| | | |
|---|---|---|
| 1. Nut | 26. Spring washer | 50. Setscrew for torsion bar |
| 2. Spring washer | 27. Front wheel brake and | 51. Torsion arm, upper |
| 3. Washer | backing plate | 52. Torsion arm, lower |
| 4. Bolt | 28. Steering knuckle | 53. Pin |
| 5. Nut | 29. Retainer, small | 54. Pin for shock absorber |
| 6. Spring washer | 30. Retainer, large | 55. Nut |
| 7. Bolt | 31. Clip, small | 56. Lock washer |
| 8. Support for axle | 32. Clip, large | 57. Lock washer |
| 9. Bolt | 33. Plate, small | 58. Nut |
| 10. Spring washer | 34. Plate, large | 59. Plate for damper bushing |
| 11. Plate | 35. Rubber mounting, small | 60. Damper bushing |
| 12. Rubber packing, upper | 36. Rubber mounting, large | 61. Pin for buffer |
| 13. Rubber packing, lower | 37. Stabilizer bar | 62. Buffer |
| 14. Bolt | 38. Self-locking nut | 63. Tube |
| 15. Spring washer | 39. Washer, small | 64. Shock absorber |
| 16. Lock washer | 40. Washer, large | 65. Sleeve for rubber bushing |
| 17. Dust cap | 41. Eccentric bushing for camber | 66. Rubber bushing |
| 18. Clamp nut for wheel bearing | adjustment | 67. Torsion bar—10 leaf |
| 19. Socket hd. screw for | 42. Upper ball joint | 68. Seal for upper torsion arm |
| clamp nut | 43. Lower ball joint | 69. Seal for lower torsion arm |
| 20. Thrust washer | 44. Ring for rubber boot | 70. Needle bearing, upper |
| 21. Outer tapered roller bearing | 45. Boot for lower joint | 71. Needle bearing, lower |
| 22. Brake drum | 46. Boot for upper joint | 72. Metal bushing for torsion arms |
| 23. Oil seal | 47. Ring for rubber boot | 73. Grease fitting |
| 24. Inner tapered roller bearing | 48. Plug | 74. Axle beam |
| 25. Bolt | 49. Locknut | 75. Bolt |

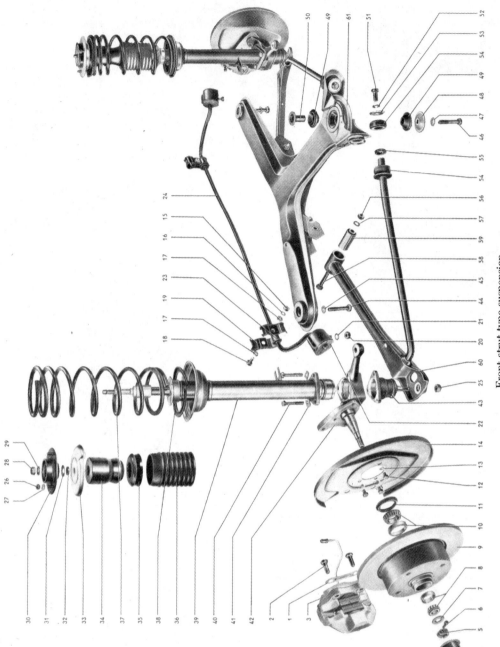

Front strut type suspension

Align the square notch in the ball joint with notch in the torsion arm upon installation

*ring around the side of the joint. When replacing a ball joint, make sure that the new part has the same number of V-notches. If it has no notches, the replacement joint should have no notches.*

7. Reverse Steps 1–4 to complete the installation.

### Strut Suspension

1. Jack up the car and remove the wheel and tire.

2. Remove the nut from the ball joint stud and remove the stud from the track control arm.

3. Bend back the locking tab and remove the three ball joint securing screws.

4. Pull the track control arm downward and remove the ball joint from the strut.

5. Reverse the above steps to install.

### Inspection

#### Torsion Bar Suspension

A quick initial inspection can be made with the vehicle on the ground. Grasp the top of the tire and vigorously pull the top of the tire in and out. Test both sides in this manner. If the ball joints are excessively worn, there will be an audible tap as the ball moves around in its socket. Excess play can sometimes be felt through the tire.

A more rigorous test may be performed by jacking the car under the lower torsion arm and inserting a lever under the tire. Lift up gently on the lever so as to pry the tire upward. If the ball joints are worn, the tire will move upward $\frac{1}{8}$–$\frac{1}{4}$ in. or more. If the tire displays excessive movement, have an assistant inspect each joint, as the tire is pryed upward, to determine which ball joint is defective.

#### Strut Suspension

Raise the car and support it under the frame. The wheel must be clear of the ground.

With a lever, apply upward pressure to the track control arm. Apply the pressure gently and slowly; it is important that only enough pressure is exerted to check the play in the ball joint and not compress the suspension.

Using a vernier caliper, measure the distance between the control arm and the

| | | |
|---|---|---|
| 1. Lockplate | 23. Rubber bushing for clamp | 43. Ball joint |
| 2. Bolt | 24. Stabilizer bar | 44. Bolt |
| 3. Caliper | 25. Self-locking nut | 45. Lock washer |
| 4. Hub cap | 26. Self-locking nut | 46. Bolt |
| 5. Wheel bearing locknut | 27. Washer | 47. Lock washer |
| 6. Allen screw for locknut | 28. Self-locking nut | 48. Seat for damping ring |
| 7. Thrust washer | 29. Washer, small | 49. Damping ring for front axle |
| 8. Outer taper roller bearing | 30. Suspension strut bearing | carrier |
| 9. Brake disc | 31. Sealing plate | 50. Spacer sleeve |
| 10. Inner taper roller bearing | 32. Spacer ring | 51. Bolt |
| 11. Oil seal | 33. Spring plate | 52. Spring washer |
| 12. Bolt | 34. Rubber stop for shock | 53. Plate for damping ring |
| 13. Spring washer | absorber | 54. Damping ring for radius rod |
| 14. Splash shield for disc | 35. Retaining ring for protective | 55. Locating ring for radius rod |
| 15. Nut | tube | 56. Nut |
| 16. Spring washer | 36. Protective tube for shock | 57. Spring washer |
| 17. Washer | absorber | 58. Bolt |
| 18. Bolt | 37. Coil spring | 59. Bushing for track control arm |
| 19. Clamp for stabilizer bar | 38. Damping ring, coil spring | 60. Track control arm |
| 20. Nut | 39. Shock absorber | 61. Front axle carrier |
| 21. Spring washer | 40. Bolt | |
| 22. Stabilizer mounting for control arm | 41. Lock washer | |
| | 42. Steering knuckle | |

lower edge of the ball joint flange. Record the reading. Release the pressure on the track control arm and again measure the distance between the control arm and the lower edge of the ball joint flange. Record the reading. Subtract the higher reading from the lower reading. If the difference is more than 0.10 in., the ball joint should be replaced.

NOTE: *Remember that even in a new joint there will be measurable play because the ball in the ball joint is spring loaded.*

### TORSION ARMS, TORSION BAR SUSPENSION

#### Removal and Installation

1. Jack up the car and remove the wheel and tire.
2. Remove the brake drum and the steering knuckle.
3. If the lower torsion arm is being removed, disconnect the stabilizer bar. To remove the stabilizer bar clamp, tap the wedge shaped keeper toward the outside of the car or in the direction the narrow end of the keeper is pointing.
4. On Type 1 and 2, back off on the set-screw locknut and remove the set-screw. On Type 3, remove the bolt and keeper from the end of the torsion bar.

5. Slide the torsion arm off the end of the torsion bar.
6. Reverse the above steps to install. Check the camber and toe-in settings.

### TRACK CONTROL ARM, STRUT SUSPENSION

#### Removal and Installation

1. Remove the ball joint stud nut and remove the stud from the control arm.
2. Disconnect the stabilizer bar from the control arm.
3. Remove the nut and eccentric bolt at the frame. This is the pivot bolt for the control arm and is used to adjust camber.
4. Pull the arm downward and remove it from the vehicle.
5. Reverse the above steps to install. Make sure the groove in the stabilizer bar bushing is horizontal.
6. Realign the front end.

### FRONT END ALIGNMENT

#### Caster Adjustment

Caster is the forward or backward tilt of the spindle. Forward tilt is negative caster and backward tilt is positive caster. Caster is not adjustable on either the torsion bar or the strut suspensions.

## Wheel Alignment

| | | FRONT AXLE | | | | | REAR AXLE | | |
| | | CASTER | | CAMBER | | | CAMBER | | |
| Year | Model | Range (deg) | Pref Setting (deg) | Range (deg) | Pref Setting (deg) | Toe-in (in.) | Range (deg) | Pref Setting (deg) | Toe-in (deg) |
|---|---|---|---|---|---|---|---|---|---|
| 1970–73 | Type 1 | ±1° | +3° 20′ | ±20′ | +30′ | +0.071– +0.213 | ±40′ | −1° 20′ | 0′±15′ |
| 1970–73 | Type 1① | ±35′ | +2° | +20′ −40′ | +1° | +0.071– +0.231 | ±40′ | −1° 20′ | 0′±15′ |
| 1970–73 | Type 2 | ±40′ | +3° | ±15′ | +40′ | 0.0– +0.136 | ±30′ | −50′ | +10′±20′ |
| 1970–73 | Type 3 | ±40′ | +4° | ±20′ | +1° 20′ | +0.118– +0.260 | ±40′ | −1° 20′ | 0′±15′② |
| 1970–73 | Type 4 | ±35′ | +1° 45′ | +25′ −30′ | +1° 10′ | +0.024– +0.165 | ±1° | −1° | +5′±5′ |

① Super Beetle
② Squareback given; Sedan 5′±15′

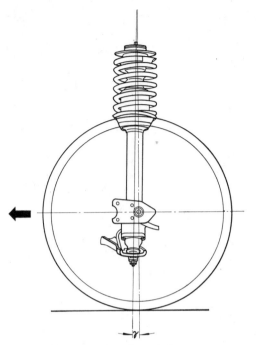

Caster—strut suspension illustrated

γ = Caster angle

## Camber Adjustment

Camber is the tilt of the top of the wheel, inward or outward, from true vertical. Outward tilt is positive, inward tilt is negative.

## Unloaded Torsion Bar Settings, Rear

| Type | Model | Transmission | Setting | Range |
|------|-------|-------------|---------|-------|
| 1 | all | all | 20° 30′ | +50′ |
| 2① | 221, 223, 226 | Manual | 21° 10′ | +50′ |
| 2② | 222 | Manual | 23° | +50′ |
| 2③ | 221, 223 | all | 20° | +50′ |
| 2④ | 222 | all | 23° | +50′ |
| 3 | 311 | Manual | 23° | +50′ |
| 3 | 311 | Automatic | 24° | +50′ |
| 3 | 361 | all | 21° 30′ | +50′ |

① From chassis 218 000 002
② From chassis 218 000 002
③ From chassis 212 2 000 001
④ From chassis 212 2 000 001

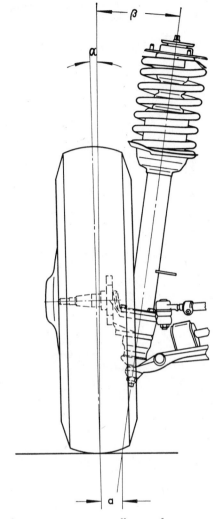

Camber—strut suspension illustrated

Angle α = camber
Angle β = steering pivot angle
a = steering roll radius

### Torsion Bar Suspension

The upper ball joint on each side is mounted in an eccentric bushing. The bushing has a hex head and it may be rotated in either direction using a wrench.

### Strut Suspension

The track control arm pivots on an eccentric bolt. Camber is adjusted by loosening the nut and rotating the bolt.

## Toe-in Adjustment

Toe-in is the adjustment made to make the front wheels point slightly into the

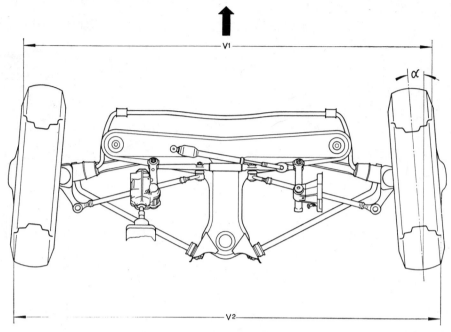

Toe-in—strut suspension illustrated

V₁—distance between the rims on the forward side of the tire
V₂—distance between the rims on the rear side of the tire
α—the angle of toe-in, measured in degrees for one wheel only
If V₂ is larger than V₁, the wheels are said to have toe-in

front. Toe-in is adjusted on both types of front suspensions by adjusting the length of the tie-rod sleeves.

## Type 4 Engine and Transmission Assembly Centering Specifications

| | |
|---|---|
| Offset between vehicle center and engine/transmission unit center | 1.0 in. |
| Center of left measuring hole to center of right measuring hole | 44.3 ±0.04 in. |
| Center of left measuring hole to center of rib on transmission | 23.1 ±0.02 in. |
| Center of right measuring hole to center of rib on transmission | 21.2 ±0.02 in. |

## Steering

### STEERING WHEEL

#### Removal and Installation

1. Disconnect the negative battery cable.
2. Remove the center emblem. This emblem will gently pry off the wheel, or is attached by screws from the back of the steering wheel.
3. Remove the nut from the steering shaft. This is a right-hand thread.
NOTE: *Mark the steering shaft and steering wheel so that the wheel may be installed in the same position on the shaft.*
4. Using a steering wheel puller, remove the wheel from the splined steering shaft. Do not strike the end of the steering shaft.
5. Reverse the above steps to install. Make sure to align the match marks made on the steering wheel and steering shaft. The gap between the turn signal switch

housing and the back of the wheel is 0.08–0.16 in.

### TURN SIGNAL SWITCH

**Removal and Installation**

1. Disconnect the negative battery cable.
2. Remove the steering wheel.
3. Remove the four turn signal switch securing screws.
4. Disconnect the turn signal switch wiring plug under the steering column.
5. Pull the switch and wiring guide rail up and out of the steering column.
6. Reverse the above steps to install. Make sure the spacers located behind the switch, if installed originally, are in position. The distance between the steering wheel and the steering column housing is 0.08–0.12 in. Install the switch with the lever in the central position.

### STEERING LINKAGE

**Removal and Installation**

All tie-rod ends are secured by a nut which holds the tapered tie-rod end stud into a matching tapered hole. There are several ways to remove the tapered stud from its hole after the nut has been removed.

First, there are several types of removal tools available from auto parts stores. These tools include directions for their use. One of the most commonly available tools is the fork shaped tool which is a

Removing a tie-rod end stud with one of the available removal tools

wedge that is forced under the tie-rod end. This tool should be used with caution because instead of removing the tie-rod end from its hole it may pull the ball out of its socket, ruining the tie-rod end.

It is also possible to remove the tie-rod end by holding a heavy hammer on one side of the tapered hole and striking the opposite side of the hole sharply with another hammer. The stud will pop out of its hole.

CAUTION: *Never strike the end of the tie-rod end stud. It is impossible to remove the tie-rod end in this manner.*

Once the tie-rod end stud has been removed, turn the tie-rod end out of the adjusting sleeve. On the pieces of the steering linkage that are not used to adjust the toe-in, the tie-rod end is welded in place and it will be necessary to replace the whole assembly.

When reassembling the steering linkage, never put lubricant in the tapered hole.

### MANUAL STEERING GEAR

**Adjustment**

There are two types of steering gear box. The first type is the roller type, identified by the square housing cover secured by four screws, one at each corner. The second type is the worm and peg type, identified by an assymetric housing cover with the adjusting screw located at one side of the housing cover.

#### ROLLER TYPE

Disconnect the steering linkage from the pitman arm and make sure the gearbox mounting bolts are tight. Have an assistant rotate the steering wheel so that the pitman arm moves alternately 10° to the left and then 10° to the right of the straight ahead position. Turn the adjusting screw in until no further play can be felt while moving the pitman arm. Tighten the adjusting screw locknut and recheck the adjustment.

#### WORM AND PEG TYPE

Have an assistant turn the steering wheel back and forth through the center position several times. The steering wheel should turn through the center position without any noticeable binding.

To adjust, turn the adjusting screw inward while the assistant is turning the steering wheel. Turn the screw in until the steering begins to tighten up. Back out the adjusting screw until the steering no longer binds while turning through the center point and tighten the adjusting screw locknut.

The adjustment is correct when there is no binding and no perceptible play.

# Chapter Eight

# Brakes

## Brake System

### ADJUSTMENT

All Volkswagens have rear drum brakes and, depending on the model, are equipped with either front drum brakes or front disc brakes.

Disc brakes are self adjusting and cannot be adjusted by hand. As the pads wear, they will automatically compensate for the wear by moving closer to the disc, maintaining the proper operating clearance.

Drum brakes, however, must be manually adjusted to take up excess clearance as the shoes wear. To adjust drum brakes, both front and rear, it is necessary to jack up the car and support it on a jackstand. The wheel must spin freely. On the backing plate there are four inspection holes with a rubber plug in each hole. Two of the holes are for checking the thickness of the brake lining and the other two are used for adjustment.

NOTE: *There is an adjustment for each brake shoe. That means that on each wheel it is necessary to make two adjustments, one for each shoe on that wheel.*

Remove the adjustment hole plugs and, using a screwdriver or brake adjusting tool, insert the tool into the hole. Turn the

Brake adjusting tool inserted into the hole in the backing plate—rear wheel illustrated

star wheel until a slight drag is noticed as the wheel is rotated by hand. Back off on the star wheel 3–4 notches so that the wheel turns freely. Perform the same adjustment on the other shoe.

NOTE: *One of the star wheels in each wheel has left-hand threads and the other star wheel has right-hand threads.*

Repeat the above procedure on each wheel with drum brakes.

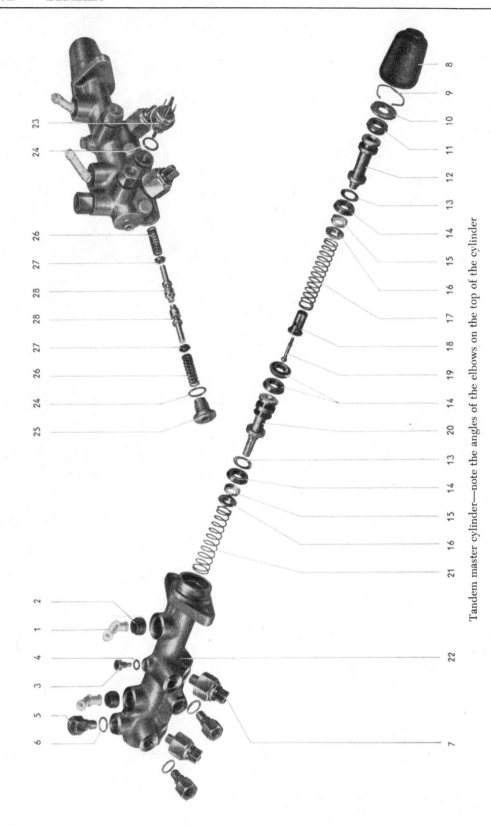

Tandem master cylinder—note the angles of the elbows on the top of the cylinder

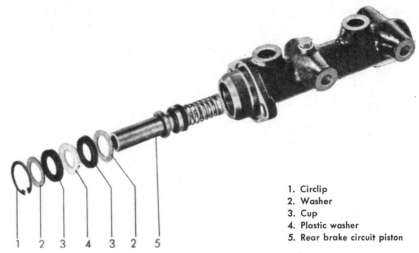

1. Circlip
2. Washer
3. Cup
4. Plastic washer
5. Rear brake circuit piston

Type 2 brake servo

## Hydraulic System

### MASTER CYLINDER

**Removal and Installation**

1. Drain the brake fluid from the master cylinder reservoir.

CAUTION: *Do not get any brake fluid on the paint, as it will dissolve the paint.*

2. On Type 3, remove the master cylinder cover plate.

3. Pull the plastic elbows out of the rubber sealing rings on the top of the master cylinder.

4. Remove the two bolts which secure the master cylinder to the frame and remove the cylinder. Note the spacers on the Type 1 between the frame and the master cylinder.

5. To install, bolt the master cylinder to the frame. Do not forget the spacers on the Type 1.

6. Lubricate the elbows with brake fluid and insert them into the rubber seals.

7. If necessary, adjust the brake pedal free travel. On Type 1, 3, and 4, adjust the length of the master cylinder pushrod so that there is 5–7 mm of brake pedal free-play before the pushrod contacts the master cylinder piston. On Type 2, the free-play is properly adjusted when the length of the pushrod, measured between the ball end and the center of the clevis pin hole, is 4.17 in.

8. Refill the master cylinder reservoir and bleed the brakes.

**Overhaul**

1. Remove the master cylinder from the car.

2. Remove the rubber sealing boot.

3. Remove the stop screw and sealing ring on the top of the unit.

4. Insert a screwdriver in the master cylinder piston, exert inward pressure, and remove the snap-ring from its groove in the end of the unit. The internal parts are spring loaded and must be kept from flying out when the snap-ring is removed.

5. Carefully remove the internal parts

| | | |
|---|---|---|
| 1. Elbow | 11. Secondary cup | 21. Front brake circuit spring |
| 2. Sealing plug | 12. Rear brake circuit piston | 22. Master cylinder housing |
| 3. Stop screw | 13. Cup washer | 23. Warning light switch |
| 4. Seal | 14. Cup | 24. Seal |
| 5. Residual pressure valve | 15. Support washer | 25. Plug |
| 6. Sealing ring | 16. Spring retainer | 26. Spring |
| 7. Brake light switch | 17. Rear brake circuit spring | 27. Cup |
| 8. Rubber boot | 18. Stop sleeve | 28. Piston |
| 9. Lock ring | 19. Stroke limiting screw | |
| 10. Stop washer | 20. Front brake circuit piston | |

of the unit and make note of their order and the orientation of the internal parts. If parts remain in the cylinder bore, they may be removed with a wire hook or very gentle application of low pressure air to the stop screw hole. Cover the end of the cylinder bore with a rag and stand away from the open end of the bore when using compressed air.

6. Use alcohol or brake fluid to clean the master cylinder and its parts.

7. It may be necessary to hone the cylinder bore, or clean it by lightly sanding it with emery cloth. Clean thoroughly after honing or sanding. Lubricate the bore with brake fluid before reassembly.

8. Holding the master cylinder with the open end downward, place the cup washer, primary cup, support washer, spring retainer, and spring onto the front brake circuit piston and insert the piston vertically into the master cylinder bore.

9. Assemble the rear brake circuit piston, cup washer, primary cup, support washer, spring retainer, stop sleeve, spring, and stroke limiting screw and insert the assembly into the master cylinder.

10. Install the stop washer and snapring.

11. Install the stop screw and seal, making sure the hole for the screw is not blocked by the piston. If the hole is blocked, it will be necessary to push the piston further in until the screw can be turned in.

NOTE: *Some Type 2 vehicles have a brake servo and the order of assembly of the additional seals is illustrated.*

12. Install the master cylinder and bleed the brakes.

## BLEEDING THE BRAKES

The hydraulic brake system must be bled any time one of the lines is disconnected or air enters the system. This may be done manually or by the pressure method.

### Pressure Bleeding

1. Clean the top of the master cylinder, remove the caps, and attach the pressure bleeding adapter.

2. Check the pressure bleeder reservoir for correct pressure and fluid level, then open the release valve.

3. Fasten a bleeder hose to the wheel cylinder bleeder nipple and submerge the free end of the hose in a transparent receptacle. The receptacle should contain enough brake fluid to cover the open end of the hose.

4. Open the wheel cylinder bleeder nipple and allow the fluid to flow until all bubbles disappear and an uncontaminated flow of fluid exists.

5. Close the nipple, remove the bleeder hose, and repeat the procedure on the other wheel cylinders or brake calipers as equipped.

### Manual Bleeding

This method requires two people: one to depress the brake pedal and the other to open the bleeder nipples.

1. Remove the reservoir caps and fill the reservoir.

2. Attach a bleeder hose and a clear container as outlined in the pressure bleeding procedure.

3. Have the assistant depress the brake pedal to the floor several times and then have him hold the pedal to the floor. With the pedal to the floor, open the bleeder nipple until the fluid flow ceases and then close the nipple. Repeat this sequence until there are no more air bubbles in the fluid.

NOTE: *As the air is gradually forced out of the system, it will no longer be possible to force the brake pedal to the floor.*

Periodically check the master cylinder for an adequate supply of fluid. Keep the master cylinder reservoir full of fluid to prevent air from entering the system. If the reservoir does run dry during bleeding, it will be necessary to rebleed the entire system.

# Front Disc Brakes

## DISC BRAKE PADS

### Removal and Installation

1. Loosen but do not remove the reservoir cover.

2. Jack up the car and remove the wheel and tire.

3. Using a punch, remove the two pins which retain the disc brake pads in the caliper.

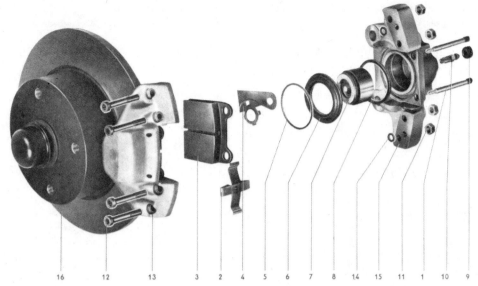

Front disc brake assembly

| | | | |
|---|---|---|---|
| 1. Friction pad retaining pin | 5. Clamp ring | 9. Dust cap | 13. Caliper outer housing |
| 2. Spreader spring | 6. Seal | 10. Bleeder valve | 14. Seal |
| 3. Friction pad | 7. Piston | 11. Nut | 15. Caliper inner housing |
| 4. Piston retaining plate | 8. Rubber seal | 12. Cheese head screw | 16. Brake disc |

NOTE: *If the pads are to be reused, mark the pads to insure that they are reinstalled in the same caliper and on the same side of the disc. Do not invert the pads. Changing pads from one location to another can cause uneven braking.*

4. If the pads are not going to be reused, force a wedge between the disc and the pad and pry the piston back into the caliper as far as possible.

5. Using compressed air, blow away the brake dust. Pull the old pad out of the caliper and insert a new one.

6. Now insert the wedge between the disc and pad on the opposite side and force that piston into the caliper. Remove the old pad and insert a new one.

7. If the old pads are to be reused, it is not necessary to push the piston into the caliper. Pull the pads from the caliper and reinstall the pads when necessary.

8. Install a new brake pad spreader spring and insert the retaining pins. Be careful not to shear the split clamping bushing from the pin. Insert the pin from the inside of the caliper and drive it to the outside.

9. Pump the brake pedal several times to take up the clearance between the pads and the disc before driving the car.

10. Install the wheel and tire and carefully road test the car. Apply the brakes gently for 500 to 1000 miles to properly break in the pads and prevent glazing them.

## DISC BRAKE CALIPERS

### Removal and Installation

1. Jack up the car and remove the wheel and tire.

2. Remove the brake pads.

3. Disconnect the brake line from the caliper.

4. Remove the two bolts which secure the caliper to the steering knuckle and remove the caliper from the vehicle.

5. Reverse the above steps to install the caliper and bleed the brakes after the caliper is installed.

### Overhaul

Clean all parts in alcohol or brake fluid.

1. Remove the caliper from the vehicle.

2. Remove the piston retaining plates.

3. Pry out the seal spring ring using a small screwdriver. Do not damage the seal beneath the ring.

4. Remove the seal with a plastic or

hard rubber rod. Do not use sharp edged or metal tools.

5. Rebuild one piston at a time. Securely clamp one piston in place so that it cannot come out of its bore. Place a block of wood between the two pistons and apply air pressure to the brake fluid port.

Clamping a piston in place and applying compressed air to the brake hose port

CAUTION: *Use extreme care with this technique because the piston can fly out of the caliper with tremendous force.*

6. Remove the rubber seal at the bottom of the piston bore using a rubber or plastic tool.

7. Check the bore and piston for wear, rust, and pitting.

8. Install a new seal in the bottom of the bore and lubricate the bore and seal with brake fluid.

9. Gently insert the piston, making sure it does not cock and jamb in the bore.

10. Install the new outer seal and new spring ring.

11. Install the piston retaining plate.

12. Repeat the above procedure on the other piston. Never rebuild only one side of a caliper.

## BRAKE DISC

### Removal and Installation

1. Jack up the car and remove the wheel and tire.

2. Remove the caliper.

3. On Type 2, remove the three socket head bolts which secure the disc to the hub and remove the disc from the hub. Sometimes the disc is rusted to the hub. Spray penetrating oil on the seam and tap the disc with a lead or brass hammer. If it still does not come off, screw three 8 mm by 40 screws into the socket head holes. Tighten the screws evenly and pull the disc from the hub.

4. On Type 1, 3, and 4, remove the wheel bearing cover. On the left side it will be necessary to remove the small clip which secures the end of the speedometer cable to the cover.

5. Unscrew the wheel bearing nut and remove the nut and outer wheel bearing.

6. Pull the disc off of the spindle.

7. To remove the wheel bearing races, see the "Wheel Bearing Removal and Installation" procedure.

8. Installation is the reverse of the above. Make sure the wheel bearing is properly adjusted.

### Inspection

Visually check the rotor for excessive scoring. Minor scores will not affect the performance; however, if the scores are over $\frac{1}{32}$ in., it is necessary to replace the disc or have it resurfaced. The disc must be 0.02 in. over the wear limit to be resurfaced. The disc must be free of surface cracks and discoloration (heat bluing). Hand spin the disc and make sure that it does not wobble from side to side.

## WHEEL BEARINGS

### Removal and Installation

1. Jack up the car and remove the wheel and tire.

2. Remove the caliper and disc.

3. To remove the inside wheel bearing, pry the dust seal out of the hub with a screwdriver. Lift out the bearing and its inner race.

4. To remove the outer race for either the inner or outer wheel bearing, insert a long punch into the hub opposite the end from which the race is to be removed. The race rests against a shoulder in the hub. The shoulder has two notches cut into it so that it is possible to place the end of the punch directly against the back side of the race and drive it out of the hub.

5. Carefully clean the hub.

6. Install new races in the hub. Drive them in with a soft faced hammer or a large piece of pipe of the proper diameter. Lubricate the races with a light coating of wheel bearing grease.

7. Force wheel bearing grease into the sides of the tapered roller bearings so that all the spaces are filled.

8. Place a small amount of grease inside the hub.

9. Place the inner wheel bearing into its race in the hub and tap a new seal into the hub. Lubricate the sealing surface of the seal with grease.

10. Install the hub on the spindle and install the outer wheel bearing.

11. Adjust the wheel bearing and install the dust cover.

### Adjustment

The bearing may adjusted by feel or by a dial indicator.

To adjust the bearing by feel, tighten the adjusting nut so that all the play is taken up in the bearing. There will be a slight amount of drag on the wheel if it is hand spun. Back off fully on the adjusting nut and retighten very lightly. There should be no drag when the wheel is hand spun and there should be no perceptible play in the bearing when the wheel is grasped and wiggled from side to side.

To use a dial indicator, remove the dust cover and mount a dial indicator against the hub. Grasp the wheel at the side and pull the wheel in and out along the axis of the spindle. Read the axial play on the dial indicator. Screw the adjusting nut in or out to obtain 0.001–0.005 in. of axial play. Secure the adjusting nut and recheck the axial play.

# Front Drum Brakes

## BRAKE DRUMS

### Removal and Installation

1. Jack up the car and remove the wheel and tire.

2. On the left side, remove the clip which secures the speedometer cable to the wheel bearing dust cover. Remove the dust cover.

3. Remove the wheel bearing adjusting nut and slide the brake drum off of the spindle. It may be necessary to back off on the brake shoe star wheels so that there is enough clearance to remove the drum.

4. Installation is the reverse of removal. Adjust the wheel bearings after installing the drum.

CAUTION: *Do not forget to readjust the brake shoes if they were disturbed during removal.*

### Inspection

If the brake drums are scored or cracked, they must be replaced or machined. If the vehicle pulls to one side or exhibits a pulsating braking action, the drum is probably out of round and should be checked at a machine shop. The drum may have a smooth even surface and still be out of round. The drum should be free of surface cracks and dark spots.

## BRAKE SHOES

### Removal and Installation

#### TYPE 1

1. Jack up the car and remove the wheel and tire.

2. Remove the brake drum.

3. Remove the small disc and spring which secure each shoe to the backing plate.

4. Remove the two long springs between the two shoes.

5. Remove the shoes from the backing plate.

To be properly installed, Type 1 brake shoes should keep the notches in the shoes on the wheel cylinder side

6. If new shoes are being installed, remove the adjusters in the end of each wheel cylinder and screw the star wheel up against the head of the adjuster. When inserting the adjusters back in the wheel cylinders, notice that the slot in the adjuster is angled and must be positioned as illustrated.

The notched adjusters must be positioned as shown above

7. Position new shoes on the backing plate. The slot in the shoes and the stronger return spring must be at the wheel cylinder end.

8. Install the disc and spring which secure the shoe to the backing plate.

9. Install the brake drum and adjust the wheel bearing.

### TYPE 2

1. Remove the brake drum.

2. Pry the rear brake shoe out of the adjuster, as illustrated, and detach the return springs. Remove the forward shoe.

3. If new shoes are to be installed, screw the star wheel up against the head of the adjuster.

4. Install the rear brake shoe.

5. Attach the return spring to the front brake shoe and then to the rear shoe.

6. Position the front brake shoe in the slot of the adjusting screw and lever it into position in the same manner as it was removed. Make sure that the return springs do not touch the brake line between the upper and lower wheel cylinders.

7. Install the brake drum and adjust the wheel bearings.

Removing Type 2 front brake shoes

### WHEEL CYLINDERS

#### Removal and Installation

1. Remove the brake shoes.

2. On Type 1, disconnect the brake line from the rear of the cylinder. On Type 2, disconnect the brake line from the rear of the cylinder and the transfer line from the front of the cylinder.

3. Remove the bolts which secure the cylinder to the backing plate and remove the cylinder from the vehicle.

4. Reverse the above steps to install and bleed the brakes.

#### Overhaul

1. Remove the wheel cylinder.

2. Remove the brake adjusters and remove the rubber boot from each end.

NOTE: *The Type 2 cylinder has only one rubber boot, piston, and cup. The rebuilding procedures are the same.*

3. On Type 1, push in on one of the pistons to force out the opposite piston and rubber cup. On Type 2, remove the piston and cup by blowing compressed air into the brake hose hole.

4. Wash the pistons and cylinder in clean brake fluid or alcohol.

5. Inspect the cylinder bore for signs of

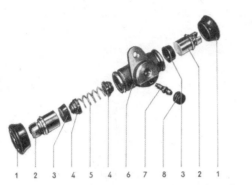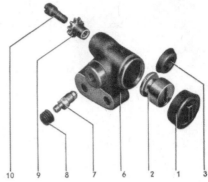

Front wheel cylinders—Type 1 on the left, Type 2 on the right

| | | | |
|---|---|---|---|
| 1. Boot | 3. Cup | 5. Spring | 7. Bleeder valve | 9. Adjusting nut |
| 2. Piston | 4. Cup expander | 6. Housing | 8. Dust cap | 10. Adjusting screw |

pitting, scoring, and excessive wear. If it is badly scored or pitted, the whole cylinder should be replaced. It is possible to remove the glaze and light scores with crocus cloth or a brake cylinder hone. Before rebuilding the cylinder, make sure the bleeder screw is free. If the bleeder is rusted shut or broken off, replace the entire cylinder.

6. Dip the new pistons and rubber cups in brake fluid. Place the spring in the bore and insert the rubber cups into the bore against the spring. The concave side of the rubber cup should face inward.

7. Place the pistons in the bore and install the rubber boot.

8. Install the cylinder and bleed the brakes after the shoes and drum are in place. Make sure that the brakes are adjusted.

### WHEEL BEARINGS

The procedures for removing and installing the wheel bearings and adjusting the wheel bearings are the same as front disc brake procedures.

## Rear Drum Brakes

### BRAKE DRUMS
#### Removal and Installation
##### TYPE 1, 2, 3

1. With the wheels still on the ground, remove the cotter pin from the slotted nut on the rear axle and remove the nut from the axle.

CAUTION: *Make sure the emergency brake is now released.*

2. Jack up the car and remove the wheel and tire.

3. The brake drum is splined to the rear axle and the drum should slip off the axle. However, the drum sometimes rusts on the splines and it is necessary to remove the drum using a puller.

4. Before installing the drum, lubricate the splines. Install the drum on the axle and tighten the nut on the axle. Line up a slot in the nut with a hole in the axle and insert a cotter pin. Never loosen the nut to align the slot and hole.

Removing the rear brake drum with a puller—Type 1, 2, 3 illustrated

### TYPE 4

The drum is held in place by the wheel lugs. Jack up the car and remove the wheel and tire. After the wheel is removed, there are two small screws that secure the drum to the hub and they must be removed before the drum will slip off the hub.

### Inspection

Inspection is the same as given in the "Front Drum Brake" section.

Rear wheel brake assembly

### *BRAKE SHOES*

### Removal and Installation

1. Remove the brake drum.
2. Remove both shoe retaining springs.
3. Disconnect the lower return spring.
4. Disconnect the hand brake cable from the lever attached to the rear shoe.
5. Remove the upper return spring and clip.
6. Remove the brake shoes and connecting link.
7. Remove the emergency brake lever from the rear shoe.
8. Lubricate the adjusting screws and the star wheel against the head of the adjusting screw.
9. Reverse Steps 1–7 to install the shoes.
10. Adjust the brakes.

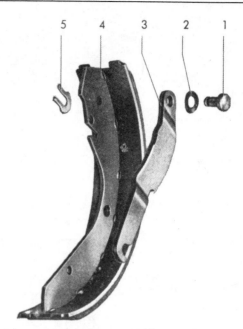

Emergency brake lever assembly

| | |
|---|---|
| 1. Pin | 4. Shoe |
| 2. Spring washer | 5. Clip |
| 3. Lever | |

### *WHEEL CYLINDERS*

### Removal and Installation

Remove the brake drum and brake shoes. Disconnect the brake line from the cylinder and remove the bolts which secure the cylinder to the backing plate. Remove the cylinder from the vehicle.

### Overhaul

Overhaul is the same as given in the "Front Drum Brake" section.

---

# Handbrake

---

### *CABLES REMOVAL AND INSTALLATION*

1. Disconnect the cables at the handbrake lever by removing the two nuts which secure the cables to the lever. Pull the cables rearward to remove that end from the lever bracket.
2. Remove the brake drum and detach the cable end from the lever attached to the rear brake shoe.

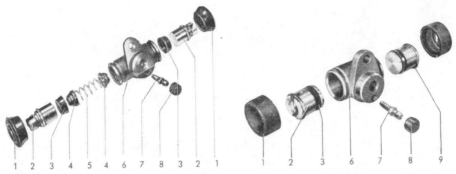

Rear wheel brake cylinder assembly—Type 1, 3, 4 on the left, Type 2 on the right.

| | | |
|---|---|---|
| 1. Boot | 4. Cup expander | 7. Bleeder valve |
| 2. Piston | 5. Spring | 8. Dust cap |
| 3. Cup | 6. Housing | 9. Circlip |

3. Remove the brake cable bracket from the backing plate and remove the cable from the vehicle.

4. Reverse the above steps to install and adjust the cable.

*ADJUSTMENT*

Brake cable adjustment is performed at the handbrake lever in the passenger compartment. There is a cable for each rear wheel and there are two adjusting nuts at the lever.

Brake cable adjusting nuts

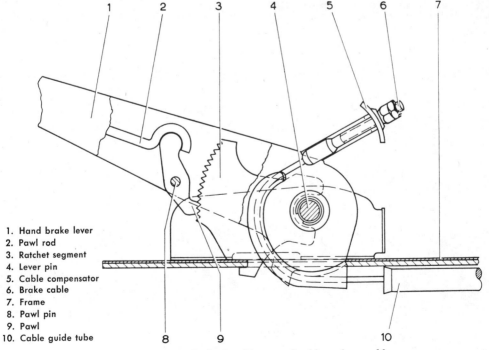

1. Hand brake lever
2. Pawl rod
3. Ratchet segment
4. Lever pin
5. Cable compensator
6. Brake cable
7. Frame
8. Pawl pin
9. Pawl
10. Cable guide tube

Emergency brake hand lever and cable end assembly

To adjust the cable, loosen the lock nut. Jack up the rear wheel to be adjusted so that it can be hand spun. Turn the adjusting nut until a very slight drag is felt as the wheel is spun. Then back off on the adjusting nut until the lever can be pulled up three notches.

CAUTION: *Never pull up on the handbrake lever with the cables disconnected.*

## Brake Specifications

(All measurements are given in in.)

| Year | Model | Master Cylinder Bore | Wheel Cylinder Bore | | | Drum Diameter | | Brake Disc | |
|---|---|---|---|---|---|---|---|---|---|
| | | | Front | | Rear | Front | Rear | Thickness | Thickness after Machining (minimum) |
| | | | Disc | Drum | | | | | |
| 1970–73 | Type 1 | 0.750 | 1.575 ③ | 0.936 | 0.687 | 9.768 ④ +0.008 | 9.055 +0.008 | 0.372– 0.374 | 0.335 |
| 1970 | Type 2 | 0.875 | 1.00 | —— | 0.875 | 9.843 +0.008 | 9.843 +0.008 | —— | —— |
| 1971–73 | Type 2 | 0.938 | 2.126 | —— | 0.874 | —— | 9.920 +0.008 | 0.511 | 0.472 |
| 1970–73 | Type 3 | 0.750 | 1.654 | —— | 0.874 | —— | 9.768 +0.008 | 0.372– 0.374① | 0.335② |
| 1970–73 | Type 4 | 0.750 | 1.654 | —— | 0.874 | —— | 9.768 +0.008 | 0.433 | 0.393 |

① 1972–73—thickness 0.433
② 1972–73—thickness after machining 0.393
③ Karmann Ghia—1971–73
④ Disc—10.9

*Chapter Nine*

# Body

## Doors

### Removal and Installation

1. Remove the pin which secures the door check strap to the door jamb and remove the strap.

2. Scribe a line around the edge of the hinge so that the door may be installed in the same position.

3. Remove the screws which secure the upper and lower hinges and remove the door from the vehicle.

4. To install, position the hinges on the previously scribed marks and hand-tighten the screws.

5. Check for proper door closing and adjust the hinge positioning to obtain proper operation of the door.

6. Tighten the hinge screws and adjust the door latch striker plate.

### *DOOR PANELS*

### Removal and Installation

1. Remove the screw in the center of the window crank arm and remove the crank.

2. Pry the plastic insert out of the door latch cover plate. Remove the screw which secures the cover plate and remove the plate.

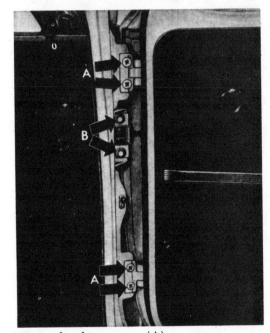

Remove door hinge screws (A)

3. The arm rest on some models is secured by two screws. Remove the screws and remove the arm rest. On other models, the arm rest is permanently attached to the door panel and is removed with the panel. Behind the arm rest, on these models, are two metal tongues. After the clips which secure the panel to the door have been

163

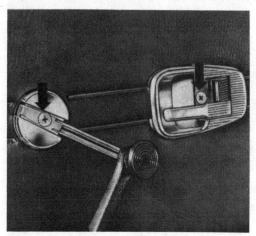

Remove the screws from the door handle and door handle cover plate

pulled out of their nylon keepers in the door, lift up on the panel to disengage the metal tongues.

4. After the clips which secure the panel to the door have been pulled out, remove the panel from the vehicle.

5. Reverse the above steps to install.

### *WINDOWS*

#### Adjustment

Window position in the door frame is adjusted by moving the window attaching screws in elongated slots in the window lift bracket.

Some models may have window channels that are adjusted by loosening the screws which secure the channel to the door and moving the channels in elongated slots.

## Hood

#### Alignment

Install the hood on its hinges and move the hood back and forth in its elongated holes until the gap around the hood is uniform all around the edge of the hood. Tighten the bolts.

Align the hood with the adjoining panels by screwing the adjustable buffers in or out.

Open and close the hood several times and adjust the position of the upper lock to obtain proper operation of the hood latch.

## Trunk Lid

#### Alignment

The trunk lid screws are mounted in elongated holes and the trunk lid is aligned in the same manner as the hood.

The trunk lid is aligned with the surrounding body panels by raising or lowering the rubber bumpers in the same manner as the hood.

## Fuel Tank

#### Removal and Installation

##### TYPE 1, 2, AND 3

1. Disconnect the line from the fuel tank to the frame head and drain the tank.

2. Remove the luggage compartment fiberboard.

3. Disconnect the wire at the fuel gauge sending unit.

4. Disconnect the fuel tank breather hose and remove it.

5. Loosen the connecting hose clamp at the fuel tank and disconnect the hose.

6. Remove the four fuel tank securing screws and remove the tank from the vehicle.

7. Reverse the above steps to install.

##### TYPE 4

1. Drain the fuel from the tank.

2. Remove the luggage compartment lining and remove the tank access covers.

3. Disconnect the wire from the fuel gauge sending unit.

4. Loosen the clamp which secures the tank connecting hose to the tank filler neck.

5. Remove the filler neck after removing the boot for the filler neck and the mounting bolt.

6. Remove the front axle carrier complete with the track control arms, tie-rods, steering box, and bracket for the steering idler arm. Also, detach the stabilizer from the track control arms.

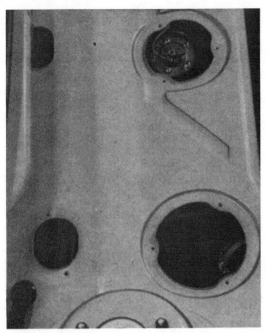

Type 4 gas tank access panels removed

7. Disconnect the outlet hose from the tank and plug it.

8. Remove the two tank retainers and nuts and remove the tank downward.

9. Reverse the above steps to install.

## Sunroof

### Adjustment

#### Adjusting Cables

1. Remove the trim panel and push it to the rear. Close the sunroof.

2. Remove the crank and cover plate.

3. Loosen the screws which hold the drive gear by about six turns.

4. Pull the drive gear down until the gear no longer engages the cables.

5. Check the position of the sliding roof in the roof opening and correct it if necessary. This brings the cables into a parallel and free of tension position.

6. Place the lifters of the rear guides in a vertical position and adjust the height.

7. Turn the drive gear shaft to the right as far as it will go then turn it back half a turn.

8. Press the drive gear up again and

tighten the screws. Make sure that the gear properly engages in both cables.

9. Install the crank and cover plate.

10. Check the cable adjustment and crank position by opening and closing the roof a few times. Repeat the adjustment if necessary. Then pull the trim panel forward and attach it to the sunroof.

#### Height of Sunroof At the Front

1. Open the roof slightly and remove the trim panel. Close the sunroof.

2. Loosen the two screws in both front guides.

3. Adjust the height of the panel by turning the adjusting screw on each side.

4. Tighten the guide securing screws.

5. Reinstall the trim panel.

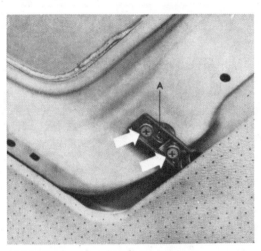

(A) is the front height adjusting screw

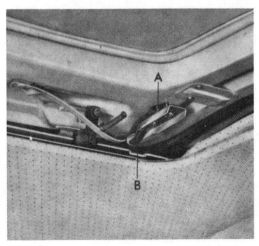

(A) is the rear height adjusting screw, (B) is the recess in the runner

HEIGHT OF SUNROOF AT THE REAR

1. Open the roof slightly, unhook the leaf spring, and swing it to the side.

2. Loosen the nut and screw at the latch.

3. Correct the height by moving the lifter pin in its elongated hole in the latch.

4. Turn the screw above the rear guide on each side to adjust the height of the rear guide so that it fits in the recess in the runner when the roof is opening and closing. This adjustment will also keep the sunroof from rattling.

5. Tighten the rear guide securing screws. Reinstall the leaf spring.

6. Check the roof to make sure that it runs parallel.

7. Install the trim panel.

# Fenders

**Removal and Installation**

### FRONT

The following is a general procedure for removing the front fender. The location and number of screws are the major differences between the types. Never exert a lot of force when trying to remove the fender. When all the screws are out, the fender is easily removed.

1. Disconnect the turn signal wire and the wire for the side light if so equipped.

2. On the right fender, remove the clamping ring on the fuel tank filler neck rubber boot and push the boot through the hole in the fender. Remove the fuel tank filler flap lock.

3. Cut the PVC underseal between the fender and the hinge pillar.

4. Remove the screws which secure the fender to the vehicle. Check the luggage compartment, hinge pillar, rocker panels near the front bumper, and in the fender well, for screws.

5. Remove the fender.

NOTE: *It may be necessary to push the fender forward slightly to remove it from the vehicle.*

6. Reverse the above steps to install.

### REAR

1. Disconnect the side light and tail light wiring.

2. Remove the screws which attach the fender to the vehicle. Look for screws in the fender well, near the bumper mounting, inside the passenger compartment, under the luggage compartment lining and headlining, beneath the rear seat and backrest and quarter panel lining, and inside the engine compartment.

3. Reverse the above steps to install.

## General Conversion Table

| Multiply by | To convert | To | |
|---|---|---|---|
| 2.54 | Inches | Centimeters | .3937 |
| 30.48 | Feet | Centimeters | .0328 |
| .914 | Yards | Meters | 1.094 |
| 1.609 | Miles | Kilometers | .621 |
| .645 | Square inches | Square cm. | .155 |
| .836 | Square yards | Square meters | 1.196 |
| 16.39 | Cubic inches | Cubic cm. | .061 |
| 28.3 | Cubic feet | Liters | .0353 |
| .4536 | Pounds | Kilograms | 2.2045 |
| 4.546 | Gallons | Liters | .22 |
| .068 | Lbs./sq. in. (psi) | Atmospheres | 14.7 |
| .138 | Foot pounds | Kg. m. | 7.23 |
| 1.014 | H.P. (DIN) | H.P. (SAE) | .9861 |
| ——— | To obtain | From | Multiply by |

*Note:* 1 cm. equals 10 mm.; 1 mm. equals .0394″.

## Conversion—Common Fractions to Decimals and Millimeters

| INCHES | | | INCHES | | | INCHES | | |
|---|---|---|---|---|---|---|---|---|
| Common Fractions | Decimal Fractions | Millimeters (approx.) | Common Fractions | Decimal Fractions | Millimeters (approx.) | Common Fractions | Decimal Fractions | Millimeters (approx.) |
| 1/128 | .008 | 0.20 | 11/32 | .344 | 8.73 | 43/64 | .672 | 17.07 |
| 1/64 | .016 | 0.40 | 23/64 | .359 | 9.13 | 11/16 | .688 | 17.46 |
| 1/32 | .031 | 0.79 | 3/8 | .375 | 9.53 | 45/64 | .703 | 17.86 |
| 3/64 | .047 | 1.19 | 25/64 | .391 | 9.92 | 23/32 | .719 | 18.26 |
| 1/16 | .063 | 1.59 | 13/32 | .406 | 10.32 | 47/64 | .734 | 18.65 |
| 5/64 | .078 | 1.98 | 27/64 | .422 | 10.72 | 3/4 | .750 | 19.05 |
| 3/32 | .094 | 2.38 | 7/16 | .438 | 11.11 | 49/64 | .766 | 19.45 |
| 7/64 | .109 | 2.78 | 29/64 | .453 | 11.51 | 25/32 | .781 | 19.84 |
| 1/8 | .125 | 3.18 | 15/32 | .469 | 11.91 | 51/64 | .797 | 20.24 |
| 9/64 | .141 | 3.57 | 31/64 | .484 | 12.30 | 13/16 | .813 | 20.64 |
| 5/32 | .156 | 3.97 | 1/2 | .500 | 12.70 | 53/64 | .828 | 21.03 |
| 11/64 | .172 | 4.37 | 33/64 | .516 | 13.10 | 27/32 | .844 | 21.43 |
| 3/16 | .188 | 4.76 | 17/32 | .531 | 13.49 | 55/64 | .859 | 21.83 |
| 13/64 | .203 | 5.16 | 35/64 | .547 | 13.89 | 7/8 | .875 | 22.23 |
| 7/32 | .219 | 5.56 | 9/16 | .563 | 14.29 | 57/64 | .891 | 22.62 |
| 15/64 | .234 | 5.95 | 37/64 | .578 | 14.68 | 29/32 | .906 | 23.02 |
| 1/4 | .250 | 6.35 | 19/32 | .594 | 15.08 | 59/64 | .922 | 23.42 |
| 17/64 | .266 | 6.75 | 39/64 | .609 | 15.48 | 15/16 | .938 | 23.81 |
| 9/32 | .281 | 7.14 | 5/8 | .625 | 15.88 | 61/64 | .953 | 24.21 |
| 19/64 | .297 | 7.54 | 41/64 | .641 | 16.27 | 31/32 | .969 | 24.61 |
| 5/16 | .313 | 7.94 | 21/32 | .656 | 16.67 | 63/64 | .984 | 25.00 |
| 21/64 | .328 | 8.33 | | | | | | |

## Conversion—Millimeters to Decimal Inches

| mm | inches | mm | inches | mm | inches | mm | inches | mm | inches |
|----|--------|----|--------|----|--------|----|--------|----|--------|
| 1 | .039 370 | 31 | 1.220 470 | 61 | 2.401 570 | 91 | 3.582 670 | 210 | 8.267 700 |
| 2 | .078 740 | 32 | 1.259 840 | 62 | 2.440 940 | 92 | 3.622 040 | 220 | 8.661 400 |
| 3 | .118 110 | 33 | 1.299 210 | 63 | 2.480 310 | 93 | 3.661 410 | 230 | 9.055 100 |
| 4 | .157 480 | 34 | 1.338 580 | 64 | 2.519 680 | 94 | 3.700 780 | 240 | 9.448 800 |
| 5 | .196 850 | 35 | 1.377 949 | 65 | 2.559 050 | 95 | 3.740 150 | 250 | 9.842 500 |
| 6 | .236 220 | 36 | 1.417 319 | 66 | 2.598 420 | 96 | 3.779 520 | 260 | 10.236 200 |
| 7 | .275 590 | 37 | 1.456 689 | 67 | 2.637 790 | 97 | 3.818 890 | 270 | 10.629 900 |
| 8 | .314 960 | 38 | 1.496 050 | 68 | 2.677 160 | 98 | 3.858 260 | 280 | 11.032 600 |
| 9 | .354 330 | 39 | 1.535 430 | 69 | 2.716 530 | 99 | 3.897 630 | 290 | 11.417 300 |
| 10 | .393 700 | 40 | 1.574 800 | 70 | 2.755 900 | 100 | 3.937 000 | 300 | 11.811 000 |
| 11 | .433 070 | 41 | 1.614 170 | 71 | 2.795 270 | 105 | 4.133 848 | 310 | 12.204 700 |
| 12 | .472 440 | 42 | 1.653 540 | 72 | 2.834 640 | 110 | 4.330 700 | 320 | 12.598 400 |
| 13 | .511 810 | 43 | 1.692 910 | 73 | 2.874 010 | 115 | 4.527 550 | 330 | 12.992 100 |
| 14 | .551 180 | 44 | 1.732 280 | 74 | 2.913 380 | 120 | 4.724 400 | 340 | 13.385 800 |
| 15 | .590 550 | 45 | 1.771 650 | 75 | 2.952 750 | 125 | 4.921 250 | 350 | 13.779 500 |
| 16 | .629 920 | 46 | 1.811 020 | 76 | 2.992 120 | 130 | 5.118 100 | 360 | 14.173 200 |
| 17 | .669 290 | 47 | 1.850 390 | 77 | 3.031 490 | 135 | 5.314 950 | 370 | 14.566 900 |
| 18 | .708 660 | 48 | 1.889 760 | 78 | 3.070 860 | 140 | 5.511 800 | 380 | 14.960 600 |
| 19 | .748 030 | 49 | 1.929 130 | 79 | 3.110 230 | 145 | 5.708 650 | 390 | 15.354 300 |
| 20 | .787 400 | 50 | 1.968 500 | 80 | 3.149 600 | 150 | 5.905 500 | 400 | 15.748 000 |
| 21 | .826 770 | 51 | 2.007 870 | 81 | 3.188 970 | 155 | 6.102 350 | 500 | 19.685 000 |
| 22 | .866 140 | 52 | 2.047 240 | 82 | 3.228 340 | 160 | 6.299 200 | 600 | 23.622 000 |
| 23 | .905 510 | 53 | 2.086 610 | 83 | 3.267 710 | 165 | 6.496 050 | 700 | 27.559 000 |
| 24 | .944 880 | 54 | 2.125 980 | 84 | 3.307 080 | 170 | 6.692 900 | 800 | 31.496 000 |
| 25 | .984 250 | 55 | 2.165 350 | 85 | 3.346 450 | 175 | 6.889 750 | 900 | 35.433 000 |
| 26 | 1.023 620 | 56 | 2.204 720 | 86 | 3.385 820 | 180 | 7.086 600 | 1000 | 39.370 000 |
| 27 | 1.062 990 | 57 | 2.244 090 | 87 | 3.425 190 | 185 | 7.283 450 | 2000 | 78.740 000 |
| 28 | 1.102 360 | 58 | 2.283 460 | 88 | 3.464 560 | 190 | 7.480 300 | 3000 | 118.110 000 |
| 29 | 1.141 730 | 59 | 2.322 830 | 89 | 3.503 903 | 195 | 7.677 150 | 4000 | 157.480 000 |
| 30 | 1.181 100 | 60 | 2.362 200 | 90 | 3.543 300 | 200 | 7.874 000 | 5000 | 196.850 000 |

To change decimal millimeters to decimal inches, position the decimal point where desired on either side of the millimeter measurement shown and reset the inches decimal by the same number of digits in the same direction. For example, to convert .001 mm into decimal inches, reset the decimal behind the 1 mm (shown on the chart) to .001; change the decimal inch equivalent (.039″ shown) to .00039″).

## Tap Drill Sizes

| National Fine or S.A.E. | | |
|---|---|---|
| Screw & Tap Size | Threads Per Inch | Use Drill Number |
| No.  5. | 44 | 37 |
| No.  6. | 40 | 33 |
| No.  8. | 36 | 29 |
| No. 10. | 32 | 21 |
| No. 12. | 28 | 15 |
| $\frac{1}{4}$ | 28 | 3 |
| $\frac{5}{16}$ | 24 | 1 |
| $\frac{3}{8}$ | 24 | Q |
| $\frac{7}{16}$ | 20 | W |
| $\frac{1}{2}$ | 20 | $\frac{29}{64}$ |
| $\frac{9}{16}$ | 18 | $\frac{33}{64}$ |
| $\frac{5}{8}$ | 18 | $\frac{37}{64}$ |
| $\frac{3}{4}$ | 16 | $\frac{11}{16}$ |
| $\frac{7}{8}$ | 14 | $\frac{13}{16}$ |
| $1\frac{1}{8}$ | 12 | $1\frac{3}{64}$ |
| $1\frac{1}{4}$ | 12 | $1\frac{11}{64}$ |
| $1\frac{1}{2}$ | 12 | $1\frac{27}{64}$ |

| National Coarse or U.S.S. | | |
|---|---|---|
| Screw & Tap Size | Threads Per Inch | Use Drill Number |
| No.  5. | 40 | 39 |
| No.  6. | 32 | 36 |
| No.  8. | 32 | 29 |
| No. 10. | 24 | 25 |
| No. 12. | 24 | 17 |
| $\frac{1}{4}$ | 20 | 8 |
| $\frac{5}{16}$ | 18 | F |
| $\frac{3}{8}$ | 16 | $\frac{5}{16}$ |
| $\frac{7}{16}$ | 14 | U |
| $\frac{1}{2}$ | 13 | $\frac{27}{64}$ |
| $\frac{9}{16}$ | 12 | $\frac{31}{64}$ |
| $\frac{5}{8}$ | 11 | $\frac{17}{32}$ |
| $\frac{3}{4}$ | 10 | $\frac{21}{32}$ |
| $\frac{7}{8}$ | 9 | $\frac{49}{64}$ |
| 1. | 8 | $\frac{7}{8}$ |
| $1\frac{1}{8}$ | 7 | $\frac{63}{64}$ |
| $1\frac{1}{4}$ | 7 | $1\frac{7}{64}$ |
| $1\frac{1}{2}$ | 6 | $1\frac{11}{32}$ |

## Decimal Equivalent Size of the Number Drills

| Drill No. | Decimal Equivalent | Drill No. | Decimal Equivalent | Drill No. | Decimal Equivalent |
|---|---|---|---|---|---|
| 80 | .0135 | 53 | .0595 | 26 | .1470 |
| 79 | .0145 | 52 | .0635 | 25 | .1495 |
| 78 | .0160 | 51 | .0670 | 24 | .1520 |
| 77 | .0180 | 50 | .0700 | 23 | .1540 |
| 76 | .0200 | 49 | .0730 | 22 | .1570 |
| 75 | .0210 | 48 | .0760 | 21 | .1590 |
| 74 | .0225 | 47 | .0785 | 20 | .1610 |
| 73 | .0240 | 46 | .0810 | 19 | .1660 |
| 72 | .0250 | 45 | .0820 | 18 | .1695 |
| 71 | .0260 | 44 | .0860 | 17 | .1730 |
| 70 | .0280 | 43 | .0890 | 16 | .1770 |
| 69 | .0292 | 42 | .0935 | 15 | .1800 |
| 68 | .0310 | 41 | .0960 | 14 | .1820 |
| 67 | .0320 | 40 | .0980 | 13 | .1850 |
| 66 | .0330 | 39 | .0995 | 12 | .1890 |
| 65 | .0350 | 38 | .1015 | 11 | .1910 |
| 64 | .0360 | 37 | .1040 | 10 | .1935 |
| 63 | .0370 | 36 | .1065 | 9 | .1960 |
| 62 | .0380 | 35 | .1100 | 8 | .1990 |
| 61 | .0390 | 34 | .1110 | 7 | .2010 |
| 60 | .0400 | 33 | .1130 | 6 | .2040 |
| 59 | .0410 | 32 | .1160 | 5 | .2055 |
| 58 | .0420 | 31 | .1200 | 4 | .2090 |
| 57 | .0430 | 30 | .1285 | 3 | .2130 |
| 56 | .0465 | 29 | .1360 | 2 | .2210 |
| 55 | .0520 | 28 | .1405 | 1 | .2280 |
| 54 | .0550 | 27 | .1440 | | |

## Decimal Equivalent Size of the Letter Drills

| Letter Drill | Decimal Equivalent | Letter Drill | Decimal Equivalent | Letter Drill | Decimal Equivalent |
|---|---|---|---|---|---|
| A | .234 | J | .277 | S | .348 |
| B | .238 | K | .281 | T | .358 |
| C | .242 | L | .290 | U | .368 |
| D | .246 | M | .295 | V | .377 |
| E | .250 | N | .302 | W | .386 |
| F | .257 | O | .316 | X | .397 |
| G | .261 | P | .323 | Y | .404 |
| H | .266 | Q | .332 | Z | .413 |
| I | .272 | R | .339 | | |

# ANTI-FREEZE INFORMATION

## Freezing and Boiling Points of Solutions
## According to Percentage of Alcohol or Ethylene Glycol

| Freezing Point of Solution | Alcohol Volume % | Alcohol Solution Boils at | Ethylene Glycol Volume % | Ethylene Glycol Solution Boils at |
|---|---|---|---|---|
| 20°F. | 12 | 196°F. | 16 | 216°F. |
| 10°F. | 20 | 189°F. | 25 | 218°F. |
| 0°F. | 27 | 184°F. | 33 | 220°F. |
| −10°F. | 32 | 181°F. | 39 | 222°F. |
| −20°F. | 38 | 178°F. | 44 | 224°F. |
| −30°F. | 42 | 176°F. | 48 | 225°F. |

Note: above boiling points are at sea level. For every 1,000 feet of altitude, boiling points are approximately 2°F. lower than those shown. For every pound of pressure exerted by the pressure cap, the boiling points are approximately 3°F. higher than those shown.

## To Increase the Freezing Protection of Anti-Freeze Solutions Already Installed

| Cooling System Capacity Quarts | Number of Quarts of **ALCOHOL** Anti-Freeze Required to Increase Protection | | | | | | | | | | | | | |
|---|---|---|---|---|---|---|---|---|---|---|---|---|---|---|
| | From +20°F. to | | | | | From +10°F. to | | | | | From 0°F. to | | | |
| | 0° | −10° | −20° | −30° | −40° | 0° | −10° | −20° | −30° | −40° | −10° | −20° | −30° | −40° |
| 10 | 2 | 2¾ | 3½ | 4 | 4½ | 1 | 2 | 2⅓ | 3¼ | 3¾ | 1 | 1¾ | 2½ | 3 |
| 12 | 2½ | 3¼ | 4 | 4¾ | 5¼ | 1¼ | 2¼ | 3 | 3¾ | 4½ | 1¼ | 2 | 2¾ | 3½ |
| 14 | 3 | 4 | 4¾ | 5½ | 6 | 1½ | 2½ | 3½ | 4½ | 5 | 1¼ | 2½ | 3¼ | 4 |
| 16 | 3¼ | 4½ | 5½ | 6¼ | 7 | 1¾ | 3 | 4 | 5 | 5¾ | 1½ | 2¾ | 3¾ | 4¾ |
| 18 | 3¾ | 5 | 6 | 7 | 7¾ | 2 | 3¼ | 4½ | 5¾ | 6½ | 1¾ | 3 | 4¼ | 5¼ |
| 20 | 4 | 5½ | 6¾ | 7¾ | 8¾ | 2 | 3¼ | 5 | 6¼ | 7¼ | 1¾ | 3½ | 4¾ | 5¾ |
| 22 | 4½ | 6 | 7½ | 8½ | 9½ | 2¼ | 4 | 5½ | 6¾ | 8 | 2 | 3¾ | 5¼ | 6½ |
| 24 | 5 | 6¾ | 8 | 9¼ | 10½ | 2½ | 4½ | 6 | 7½ | 8¾ | 2¼ | 4 | 5½ | 7 |
| 26 | 5¼ | 7¼ | 8¾ | 10 | 11¼ | 2¾ | 4¾ | 6½ | 8 | 9½ | 2½ | 4½ | 6 | 7½ |
| 28 | 5¾ | 7¾ | 9½ | 11 | 12 | 3 | 5¼ | 7 | 8¾ | 10¼ | 2½ | 4¾ | 6½ | 8 |
| 30 | 6 | 8¼ | 10 | 11¾ | 13 | 3 | 5½ | 7½ | 9¼ | 10¾ | 2¾ | 5 | 7 | 8¾ |

Test radiator solution with proper tester. Determine from the table the number of quarts of solution to be drawn off from a full cooling system and replace with concentrated anti-freeze, to give the desired increased protection. For example, to increase protection of a 22-quart cooling system containing Alcohol anti-freeze, from +10°F. to −20°F. will require the replacement of 5½ quarts of solution with concentrated anti-freeze.

| Cooling System Capacity Quarts | Number of Quarts of **ETHYLENE GLYCOL** Anti-Freeze Required to Increase Protection | | | | | | | | | | | | | |
|---|---|---|---|---|---|---|---|---|---|---|---|---|---|---|
| | From +20°F. to | | | | | From +10°F. to | | | | | From 0°F. to | | | |
| | 0° | −10° | −20° | −30° | −40° | 0° | −10° | −20° | −30° | −40° | −10° | −20° | −30° | −40° |
| 10 | 1¾ | 2¼ | 3 | 3½ | 3¾ | ¾ | 1½ | 2¼ | 2¾ | 3¼ | ¾ | 1½ | 2 | 2½ |
| 12 | 2 | 2¾ | 3½ | 4 | 4½ | 1 | 1¾ | 2½ | 3¼ | 3¾ | 1 | 1¾ | 2½ | 3¼ |
| 14 | 2¼ | 3¼ | 4 | 4¾ | 5½ | 1¼ | 2 | 3 | 3¾ | 4½ | 1 | 2 | 3 | 3½ |
| 16 | 2½ | 3½ | 4½ | 5¼ | 6 | 1¼ | 2½ | 3½ | 4¼ | 5¼ | 1¼ | 2¼ | 3¼ | 4 |
| 18 | 3 | 4 | 5 | 6 | 7 | 1½ | 2¾ | 4 | 5 | 5¾ | 1½ | 2½ | 3¾ | 4¾ |
| 20 | 3¼ | 4½ | 5¾ | 6¾ | 7½ | 1¾ | 3 | 4¼ | 5½ | 6½ | 1½ | 2¾ | 4¼ | 5¼ |
| 22 | 3½ | 5 | 6¼ | 7¼ | 8¼ | 1¾ | 3¼ | 4¾ | 6 | 7¼ | 1¾ | 3¼ | 4½ | 5½ |
| 24 | 4 | 5½ | 7 | 8 | 9 | 2 | 3½ | 5 | 6½ | 7½ | 1¾ | 3½ | 5 | 6 |
| 26 | 4¼ | 6 | 7½ | 8¾ | 10 | 2 | 4 | 5½ | 7 | 8¼ | 2 | 3¾ | 5½ | 6¾ |
| 28 | 4½ | 6¼ | 8 | 9½ | 10½ | 2¼ | 4¼ | 6 | 7½ | 9 | 2 | 4 | 5¾ | 7¼ |
| 30 | 5 | 6¾ | 8½ | 10 | 11½ | 2½ | 4½ | 6½ | 8 | 9½ | 2¼ | 4¼ | 6¼ | 7¾ |

Test radiator solution with proper hydrometer. Determine from the table the number of quarts of solution to be drawn off from a full cooling system and replace with undiluted anti-freeze, to give the desired increased protection. For example, to increase protection of a 22-quart cooling system containing Ethylene Glycol (permanent type) anti-freeze, from +20°F. to −20°F. will require the replacement of 6¼ quarts of solution with undiluted anti-freeze.

# ANTI-FREEZE CHART

### Temperatures Shown in Degrees Fahrenheit
### +32 is Freezing

**Quarts of ALCOHOL Needed for Protection to Temperatures Shown Below**

| Cooling System Capacity Quarts | 1 | 2 | 3 | 4 | 5 | 6 | 7 | 8 | 9 | 10 | 11 | 12 | 13 |
|---|---|---|---|---|---|---|---|---|---|---|---|---|---|
| 10 | +23° | +11° | −5° | −27° | | | | | | | | | |
| 11 | +25 | +13 | 0 | −18 | −40° | | | | | | | | |
| 12 | | +15 | +3 | −12 | −31 | | | | | | | | |
| 13 | | +17 | +7 | −7 | −23 | | | | | | | | |
| 14 | | +19 | +9 | −3 | −17 | −34° | | | | | | | |
| 15 | | +20 | +11 | +1 | −12 | −27 | | | | | | | |
| 16 | | +21 | +13 | +3 | −8 | −21 | −36° | | | | | | |
| 17 | | +22 | +16 | +6 | −4 | −16 | −29 | | | | | | |
| 18 | | +23 | +17 | +8 | −1 | −12 | −25 | −38° | | | | | |
| 19 | | +24 | +17 | +9 | +2 | −8 | −21 | −32 | | | | | |
| 20 | | | +18 | +11 | +4 | −5 | −16 | −27 | −39° | | | | |
| 21 | | | +19 | +12 | +5 | −3 | −12 | −22 | −34 | | | | |
| 22 | | | +20 | +14 | +7 | 0 | −9 | −18 | −29 | −40° | | | |
| 23 | | | +21 | +15 | +8 | +2 | −7 | −15 | −25 | −36° | | | |
| 24 | | | +21 | +16 | +10 | +4 | −4 | −12 | −21 | −31 | | | |
| 25 | | | +22 | +17 | +11 | +6 | −2 | −9 | −18 | −27 | −37° | | |
| 26 | | | +22 | +17 | +12 | +7 | +1 | −7 | −14 | −23 | −32 | | |
| 27 | | | +23 | +18 | +13 | +8 | +3 | −5 | −12 | −20 | −28 | −39° | |
| 28 | | | +23 | +19 | +14 | +9 | +4 | −3 | −9 | −17 | −25 | −34 | |
| 29 | | | +24 | +19 | +15 | +10 | +6 | −1 | −7 | −15 | −22 | −30 | −39° |
| 30 | | | +24 | +20 | +16 | +11 | +7 | +1 | −5 | −12 | −19 | −27 | −35 |

+ Figures are above Zero, but below Freezing.

− Figures are below Zero. Also below Freezing.

**Quarts of ETHYLENE GLYCOL Needed for Protection to Temperatures Shown Below**

| Cooling System Capacity Quarts | 1 | 2 | 3 | 4 | 5 | 6 | 7 | 8 | 9 | 10 | 11 | 12 | 13 | 14 |
|---|---|---|---|---|---|---|---|---|---|---|---|---|---|---|
| 10 | +24° | +16° | +4° | −12° | −34° | −62° | | | | | | | | |
| 11 | +25 | +18 | +8 | −6 | −23 | −47 | | | | | | | | |
| 12 | +26 | +19 | +10 | 0 | −15 | −34 | −57° | | | | | | | |
| 13 | +27 | +21 | +13 | +3 | −9 | −25 | −45 | | | | | | | |
| 14 | | | +15 | +6 | −5 | −18 | −34 | | | | | | | |
| 15 | | | +16 | +8 | 0 | −12 | −26 | | | | | | | |
| 16 | | | +17 | +10 | +2 | −8 | −19 | −34 | −52° | | | | | |
| 17 | | | +18 | +12 | +5 | −4 | −14 | −27 | −42 | | | | | |
| 18 | | | +19 | +14 | +7 | 0 | −10 | −21 | −34 | −50° | | | | |
| 19 | | | +20 | +15 | +9 | +2 | −7 | −16 | −28 | −42 | | | | |
| 20 | | | | +16 | +10 | +4 | −3 | −12 | −22 | −34 | −48° | | | |
| 21 | | | | +17 | +12 | +6 | 0 | −9 | −17 | −28 | −41 | | | |
| 22 | | | | +18 | +13 | +8 | +2 | −6 | −14 | −23 | −34 | −47° | | |
| 23 | | | | +19 | +14 | +9 | +4 | −3 | −10 | −19 | −29 | −40 | | |
| 24 | | | | +19 | +15 | +10 | +5 | 0 | −8 | −15 | −23 | −34 | −46° | |
| 25 | | | | +20 | +16 | +12 | +7 | +1 | −5 | −12 | −20 | −29 | −40 | −50° |
| 26 | | | | | +17 | +13 | +8 | +3 | −3 | −9 | −16 | −25 | −34 | −44 |
| 27 | | | | | +18 | +14 | +9 | +5 | −1 | −7 | −13 | −21 | −29 | −39 |
| 28 | | | | | +18 | +15 | +10 | +6 | +1 | −5 | −11 | −18 | −25 | −34 |
| 29 | | | | | +19 | +16 | +12 | +7 | +2 | −3 | −8 | −15 | −22 | −29 |
| 30 | | | | | +20 | +17 | +13 | +8 | +4 | −1 | −6 | −12 | −18 | −25 |

For capacities over 30 quarts divide true capacity by 3. Find quarts Anti-Freeze for the ⅓ and multiply by 3 for quarts to add.

For capacities under 10 quarts multiply true capacity by 3. Find quarts Anti-Freeze for the tripled volume and divide by 3 for quarts to add.